VISUAL QUICKSTART GUIDE

Excel 98

FOR MACINTOSH

Maria Langer

Peachpit Press

Visual QuickStart Guide
Excel 98 for Macintosh
Maria Langer

Peachpit Press
1249 Eighth Street
Berkeley, CA 94710
510/524-2178
510/524-2221 (fax)

Find us on the World Wide Web at: http://www.peachpit.com/

Peachpit Press is a division of Addison Wesley Longman

Editor: Nancy Davis, Becky Morgan
Indexer: Emily Glossbrenner
Cover Design: The Visual Group
Production: Maria Langer, Mimi Heft

Notice of Rights

Notice of Liability

Trademarks

ISBN 0-201-35360-1

9 8 7 6 5 4 3 2 1

Printed and bound in the United States of America.

 Printed on recycled paper.

Dedication

To Nancy Davis,
with thanks and best wishes

Thanks!

To Nancy Davis and Becky Morgan for their guidance and gentle editing. Nancy is one of the few people I know who comes to work earlier than I do—even when she's two weeks away from giving birth! Becky, who took over when the baby finally arrived, did a great job of nagging me without really nagging me.

To Mimi Heft for her layout and production assistance and advice. Mimi slaps my hand via e-mail (so it hurts less) when I don't name files properly or include crop marks when I should. I'll be a good girl next time.

To everyone at Peachpit Press for putting up with author burn-out and slipping deadlines.

To Danielle Tiedt and Deanna Meyer at Microsoft Corporation, for helping me get the material I needed to write this book. And to the folks on the Microsoft Office 98 for Macintosh development team, for putting together an excellent program!

And to Mike, for driving 2,600 miles in four days in a 1988 Jeep Wrangler with me this summer. It wasn't *that* bad without air conditioning, was it?

http://www.gilesrd.com/mlanger/

TABLE OF CONTENTS

Table of Contents

Table of Contents

Table of Contents

INTRODUCTION TO EXCEL 98

Introduction

Excel 98, a component of Microsoft Office, is a powerful spreadsheet software package. With it, you can create picture-perfect worksheets, charts, and lists based on just about any data you can enter into a Macintosh.

This Visual QuickStart Guide will help you take control of Excel's feature-rich work environment by providing step-by-step instructions and plenty of illustrations. A generous helping of tips show you how you can be more productive and avoid the "traps" that new Excel users may encounter. On these pages, you'll find everything you need to know to get up and running quickly with Excel 98—and more!

This book was designed for page flipping. Use the thumb tabs, index, or table of contents to find the topics for which you need help. If you're brand new to Excel or spreadsheets, however, I recommend that you begin by reading at least the first two chapters. **Chapter 1** provides basic information about Excel's interface. **Chapter 2** introduces spreadsheet concepts and explains exactly how they work in Excel.

If you've used other versions of Excel and are interested in information about new Excel 98 features, be sure to browse through this **Introduction**. It'll give you a good idea of the new things Excel has in store for you.

One last word of advice before you start: don't let Excel intimidate you! Sure, it's big, and yes, it has lots of commands. But as you work with Excel, you'll quickly learn the techniques you need to get your work done. That's when you'll be on your way to harnessing the real power of Excel.

Start Here

New & Improved Features in Excel 98

Excel 98 includes many brand new features, as well as major improvements to some existing features. Here's a list.

✔ Tip

■ This book covers most—but not all—of these features.

Worksheet creation

■ You can now create worksheets with up to 256 columns and 65,535 rows and enter up to 32,000 characters into each cell.

■ Multiple levels of undo enable you to undo or redo more than one action.

■ Formula AutoCorrect can automatically correct 15 of the most common formula errors (**Figure 1**).

■ Natural language formulas make it possible to write formulas using the names of column and row headings rather than cell addresses (**Figure 2**).

■ Range Finder uses colored frames to indicate the cells referenced by a formula. You can adjust the size of a frame to change the corresponding formula reference (**Figure 3**).

■ Data validation enables you to set up rules for cell entries, as well as messages and dialog boxes to help users comply with the rules (**Figure 4**).

Figure 1. *Formula AutoCorrect helps you correct errors in your formulas.*

	A	B	C	D
1		Jan	Feb	Mar
2	John	1536	1542	2415
3	Jean	2014	1548	2147
4	Joe	1158	1235	1489
5	Joan	1999	2587	2048
6	Total	=SUM(Jan)		

Figure 2. *With natural language formulas, you can write a formula using column or row headings rather than cell references.*

Range Finder frames   Formula

	A	B	C	D	E	F
1		Jan	Feb	Mar		Commission
2	John	1536	1542	2415		=SUM(B2:D2)*B8
3	Jean	2014	1548	2147		
4	Joe	1158	1235	1489		
5	Joan	1999	2587	2048		
6	Total	6707	6912	8099		
7						
8	Commission Rate	15%				

Figure 3. *The Range Finder feature uses color-coded frames to identify formula references.*

	A	B	C	D	E	F
1		Jan	Feb	Mar		Commiss
2	John	1536	1542	2415		823
3	Jean	2014	1548	2147		856
4	Joe	1158	**Enter the Commission Rate**			2
5	Joan	1999	Enter the commission rate for this			5
6	Total	6707	division. The value you enter must			7
7			be between 5% and 25%.			
8	Commission Rate		15%			
9						

Figure 4. *Data validation makes it easy to prompt users for correct entries.*

Figure 5. *The Conditional Formatting dialog box enables you to specify formatting based on the contents of a cell.*

Figure 6. *This example illustrates both rotated text and the conditional formatting set in* **Figure 5**.

Figure 7. *The Chart Options dialog box offers access to a variety of chart settings.*

Figure 8. *Pointing to a chart element displays a ChartTip with information about that element.*

Formatting

- Conditional formatting automatically applies special formatting to cells based on the value of their contents (**Figure 5**).

- Custom Cells enables you to rotate text (**Figure 6**), indent text, and merge cells. The AutoSize Text feature automatically shrinks the font size of a cell's contents to fit within the cell.

Charts

- The Chart Wizard is now easier to use. In addition, chart options now appear in a single dialog box (**Figure 7**).

- ChartTips identify chart elements and values when you point to them (**Figure 8**).

- There are new chart types, including cylinder, pyramid, cone, bubble, pie-of-pie, and bar-of-pie charts.

- Chart Data Tables enable you to display data in tabular format, right on a chart.

- There are additional graphic effects that can be applied to chart elements, including picture, texture, and gradient fills.

New & Improved Features in Excel 98

Printing

- Visual Printing makes it easier to determine the exact layout of a printed page by offering two new features (**Figure 9**):

  ▲ Page Break Preview view offers a fully editable view of the spreadsheet with page breaks and page numbers.

  ▲ Draggable Page Breaks enable you to change a page break by simply dragging it to a new position.

Collaboration

- Shared workbooks (**Figure 10**) makes it possible for multiple users to simultaneously access the same spreadsheet over a network connection.

- Track Changes indicates the changes made by various document editors, as well as the name of the editor and the date the change was made.

- Comments have been improved to allow multiple comments per cell. The comments can now be viewed in place by simply pointing to the cell (**Figure 11**).

- Merge Workbooks makes it possible to merge different versions of the same document together to create a final version.

Figure 9. *Draggable Page Breaks enable you to drag page breaks to change them.*

Figure 10. *You can use the Share Workbook dialog box to set up a workbook file for sharing over a network.*

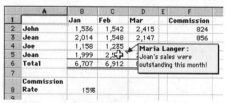

Figure 11. *When you point to a cell containing a comment, the comment appears.*

Figure 12. *The Internet Assistant Wizard makes it easy to publish worksheets and charts on the Web.*

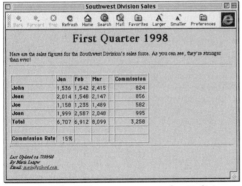

Figure 13. *This Web page was created entirely in Excel 98.*

Figure 14. *The Office Assistant introduces itself when you first launch Excel.*

Web connectivity

- The Internet Assistant Wizard (**Figure 12**) enables you to create HTML documents based on Excel worksheets and charts (**Figure 13**).

- Microsoft Excel HTML tags make it possible to create HTML tables that include Excel functionality. When viewed with an incompatible browser, the data appears in normal HTML tables.

- Web Queries enable you to import dynamic, tabular data (such as stock quotes) into a spreadsheet for analysis and charting.

Help

- The Office Assistant (**Figure 14**) monitors your work and offers tips to help you be more productive.

- The Office Assistant can answer questions that you ask in your own words (**Figure 15**).

Figure 15. *Enter a question and the Office Assistant lists help topics that could answer it.*

THE EXCEL WORKPLACE

Meet Microsoft Excel

Microsoft Excel is a full-featured spreadsheet application that you can use to create worksheets, charts, lists, and even Web pages.

Excel's interface combines common Mac OS screen elements with buttons, commands, and controls that are specific to Excel. To use Excel effectively, you must have at least a basic understanding of these elements.

This chapter introduces the Excel workplace by illustrating and describing the following elements:

- The Excel screen, including window elements.
- Menus, shortcut keys, toolbars, and dialog boxes.
- Document scrolling techniques.
- Excel's Help feature, including the Office Assistant.

✔ Tips

- If you're brand new to the Mac OS, don't skip this chapter. Many of the interface elements discussed in this chapter apply to all Mac OS programs, not just Excel.
- If you've used previous versions of Excel, browse through this chapter to learn about some of the interface elements that are new to this version of Excel.

The Excel Screen

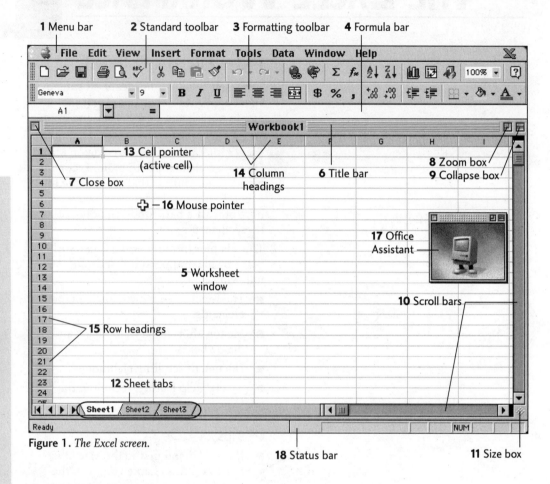

1 Menu bar   **2** Standard toolbar   **3** Formatting toolbar   **4** Formula bar

13 Cell pointer (active cell)

7 Close box

14 Column headings

6 Title bar

8 Zoom box

9 Collapse box

16 Mouse pointer

17 Office Assistant

5 Worksheet window

10 Scroll bars

15 Row headings

12 Sheet tabs

Figure 1. *The Excel screen.*

18 Status bar

11 Size box

Key to the Excel Screen

1 *Menu bar*

The menu bar appears at the top of the screen and offers access to Excel's commands, as well as the Apple menu and other open applications.

2 *Standard toolbar*

The Standard toolbar offers buttons for many basic Excel commands. This toolbar is similar in other Microsoft Office 98 applications.

3 *Formatting toolbar*

The Formatting toolbar offers buttons for formatting commands.

4 *Formula bar*

The formula bar displays the contents of the active cell, as well as that cell's address or reference.

5 *Worksheet window*

The worksheet window is where you'll do most of your work with Excel. This window has columns and rows which intersect at cells. You enter data and formulas in the cells to build your spreadsheet.

6 *Title bar*

The title bar displays the document's title. You can drag the title bar to move the window. (If your computer has Mac OS 8 or later installed, you can also move a window by dragging any of its edges.)

7 *Close box*

The close box offers one way to close the window. To use the close box, just click it.

8 *Zoom box*

The zoom box enables you to toggle the window's size from full size (**Figure 1**) to a custom size that you create with the size box. To use the zoom box, just click it.

9 *Collapse box*

The collapse box enables you to collapse or expand the window. When collapsed, only the title bar appears. To use the collapse box, just click it. (The collapse box only appears on computers with Mac OS 8 or later installed.)

10 *Scroll bars*

Scroll bars enable you to shift the window's contents to view different parts of the document. To use a scroll bar, click an arrow at one end, click in the gray area between the arrows, or drag the scroll box.

11 *Size box*

The size box enables you to resize the window to a custom size. To use the size box, drag it to move the right and bottom sides of the window. When you release the mouse button, the window changes its size.

12 *Sheet tabs*

Each Excel document has one or more sheets combined together in a Workbook. The sheet tabs let you move from one sheet to another within the workbook. To use the sheet tabs, just click on the tab for the sheet that you want to view.

13 *Cell pointer (active cell)*

The cell pointer is a heavy or colored border surrounding the active cell. The active cell is the cell in which text and numbers appear when you type.

14 *Column headings*

Column headings are the alphabetical labels that appear at the top of each column.

15 *Row headings*

Row headings are the numbered labels that appear on the left side of each row.

16 *Mouse pointer*

When positioned within the worksheet window, the mouse pointer appears as a hollow plus sign. You can use the mouse pointer to select cells, enter data, choose menu commands, and click buttons.

17 *Office Assistant*

The Office Assistant provides help and tips as you work.

18 *Status bar*

The status bar displays information about the document.

The Excel Screen

The Mouse

As with most Mac OS programs, you use the mouse to select text, activate buttons, and choose menu commands.

Mouse pointer appearance

The appearance of the mouse pointer varies depending on its location and the item to which it is pointing. Here are some examples:

- In the document window, the mouse pointer usually looks like a hollow plus sign **(Figure 1)**.

- On a menu name **(Figure 2)** or selection border **(Figure 3)**, the mouse pointer appears as an arrow pointing up and to the left.

- In the formula bar **(Figure 4)** or when positioned over a cell being edited **(Figure 5)**, the mouse pointer appears as an I-beam pointer.

To use the mouse

There are four basic mouse techniques:

- **Pointing** means to position the mouse pointer so that its tip is on the item to which you are pointing **(Figures 2** and **3)**.

- **Clicking** means to press the mouse button once and release it. You click to make a cell active, position the insertion point, or choose a toolbar button.

- **Double-clicking** means to press the mouse button twice in rapid succession. You double-click to open an item or to select a word for editing.

- **Dragging** means to press the mouse button down and hold it while moving the mouse. You drag to resize or reposition a window, select multiple cells, or choose menu commands.

Figure 2. *The mouse pointer looks like an arrow when pointing to a menu command...*

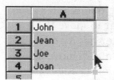

Figure 3. *...or selection border.*

Figure 4. *The mouse pointer looks like an I-beam pointer when positioned over the formula bar...*

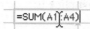

Figure 5. *...or the contents of a cell being edited.*

The Mouse

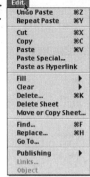

Figure 6.
The Edit menu.

Figure 7.
*The Toolbars
submenu under
the View menu.*

Menus

All of Excel's commands are accessible through its menus. Excel has two types of menus:

- Standard menus appear on the menu bar at the top of the screen. **Figures 6** and **7** show examples of standard Excel menus.

- Shortcut menus appear at the mouse pointer. **Figure 10** on the next page shows an example of a shortcut menu.

Here are some rules to keep in mind when working with menus:

- A menu command that appears in gray cannot be selected.

- A menu command followed by an ellipsis (…) displays a dialog box.

- A menu command followed by a triangle has a submenu. The submenu displays additional commands when the main command is highlighted.

- A menu command followed by the Command or Option key symbol and a letter or number can be chosen with a shortcut key.

- A menu command preceded by a check mark has been "turned on." To toggle the command from on to off or off to on, choose it from the menu.

✔ Tips

- The above menu rules apply to the menus of most Mac OS applications, not just Excel.

- I discuss dialog boxes and shortcut keys later in this chapter.

To choose a menu command

1. Point to the menu from which you want to choose the command.

2. Press the mouse button down and hold it to display the menu (**Figure 6**).

3. Drag the mouse pointer down the menu until the command you want is highlighted (**Figure 8**). If the command is on a submenu, display the submenu (**Figure 7**) and then drag the mouse pointer to the right and down until the submenu command is highlighted (**Figure 9**).

4. Release the mouse button. The command may blink before the menu disappears, confirming that it has been successfully selected.

✔ Tip

■ If your computer has Mac OS 8.0 or later installed, you don't have to hold the mouse button down and drag to choose a command. Instead, just click on the name of the menu to display the menu, then click on the name of the command to choose the command.

To use a shortcut menu

1. Point to the item on which you want to use the shortcut menu.

2. Hold down [Control] and press the mouse button down. The shortcut menu appears (**Figure 10**).

3. Choose the command that you want.

✔ Tips

■ The shortcut menu only displays the commands that can be applied to the item to which you are pointing.

■ Shortcut menus are often referred to as *contextual menus.*

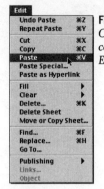

Figure 8.
Choosing the Paste command from the Edit menu.

Figure 9. *Choosing the Formatting command from the Toolbars submenu.*

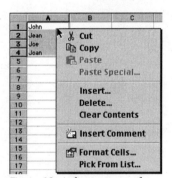

Figure 10. *A shortcut menu for selected cells.*

Using Menus

Shortcut Keys

Shortcut keys are combinations of keyboard keys that, when pressed, choose a menu command without displaying the menu. For example, the shortcut key for the Paste command under the Edit menu (**Figure 8**) is ⌘V. Pressing this key combination chooses the command.

✔ Tips

- All shortcut keys use at least one of the following modifier keys:

Key Name	Keyboard Key
Command	⌘
Option	Option
Shift	Shift
Control	Control

- A menu command's shortcut key is displayed to its right on the menu (**Figure 8**).

- Many shortcut keys are standardized from one application to another. The Save, Print, and Quit commands are three good examples; they're usually ⌘S, ⌘P, and ⌘Q.

- Appendix A includes a complete list of shortcut keys.

To use a shortcut key

1. Hold down the modifier key for the shortcut (normally ⌘).

2. Press the letter or number key for the shortcut.

For example, to choose the Paste command, hold down the Command key and press the V key.

Toolbars

Excel includes a number of toolbars for various purposes. Each toolbar includes buttons or menus that activate menu commands or set options.

By default, Excel automatically displays two toolbars when you launch it:

- The Standard toolbar (**Figure 11**) offers buttons for a wide range of commonly used commands.

- The Formatting toolbar (**Figure 12**) offers buttons for formatting selected items.

✔ Tips

- Other toolbars may appear automatically depending on the task you are performing with Excel.

- You can identify a toolbar button by its ToolTip (**Figure 13**).

- Toolbar buttons that are gray (for example, Paste and Redo in **Figure 11**) cannot be selected.

- Toolbar buttons that appear in a dark gray box (**Figure 14**) are "turned on."

- A toolbar button that includes a triangle (for example, Borders in **Figure 12**) displays a menu (**Figure 15**).

- A toolbar can be *docked* or *floating*. A docked toolbar (**Figure 20**) is positioned against any edge of the screen. A floating toolbar (**Figure 21**) can be moved anywhere within the screen.

Figure 11. *The Standard toolbar.*

Figure 12. *The Formatting toolbar.*

Figure 13. *A ToolTip appears when you point to a button.*

Figure 14. *The Center button, turned on.*

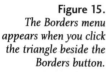

Figure 15. *The Borders menu appears when you click the triangle beside the Borders button.*

Figure 16. *Drag the menu away from the toolbar.*

Figure 17. *The menu appears as a floating menu or palette.*

Figure 18. *Select the contents of the edit box.*

Figure 19. *Enter a new value and press* Return.

To view ToolTips

Point to a toolbar button. A tiny yellow box containing the name of the button appears (**Figure 13**).

To use a toolbar button

1. Point to the button for the command or option that you want (**Figure 13**).
2. Click once on the toolbar button to activate the command or select the option.

✔ Tip

■ Some toolbar buttons, such as the alignment buttons on the Formatting toolbar, are "turned on" when you click them (**Figure 14**).

To use a toolbar menu

1. Point to the triangle to the right of the the button.
2. Press the mouse button down to display the menu (**Figure 15**).
3. Choose an option from the menu.

✔ Tips

■ Toolbar menus that display a dotted move handle along the top edge (**Figure 15**) can be "torn off" and used as floating menus or palettes. Just display the menu, then drag the dotted move handle to move the menu away from the toolbar. When the outline of the palette appears (**Figure 16**), release the mouse button. The menu is displayed as a floating menu with a title bar that displays its name (**Figure 17**).

■ Toolbar menus that display edit boxes (**Figure 18**) can be changed by typing a new value into the edit box. Just click the contents of the edit box to select it, then type in the new value and press Return (**Figure 19**).

Using Toolbars

To float a docked toolbar

Double-click or drag the toolbar's move handle (**Figure 20**). The toolbar appears as a floating toolbar (**Figure 21**).

To dock a floating toolbar

1. Drag the toolbar's title bar to the edge of the screen.
2. When the shape of the toolbar's outline changes to match the edge of the screen (**Figure 22**), release the mouse button to anchor the toolbar there (**Figure 23**).

✔ Tip

■ You can dock a toolbar against the top (**Figure 20**), either side (**Figure 23**), or the bottom of the screen. Buttons may change appearance when the toolbar is docked on the side of the screen.

To move a toolbar

1. If the toolbar is docked, double-click its move handle (**Figure 20**) to turn it into a floating toolbar (**Figure 21**).
2. Drag the floating toolbar's title bar to reposition it on screen.

To display or hide a toolbar

Choose the name of the toolbar that you want to display or hide from the Toolbars submenu under the View menu (**Figure 7**).

If the toolbar name has a check mark to its left, it is currently displayed and will be hidden.

or

If the toolbar name does not have a check mark to its left, it is currently hidden and will be displayed.

✔ Tip

■ If a toolbar is floating, you can click its close box to hide it.

Move handles

Figure 20. *By default, the Standard and Formatting toolbars are docked.*

Figure 21. *A floating toolbar.*

Figures 22 & 23. *Drag the toolbar to the edge of the window (left). When you release the mouse button, the toolbar is docked (right).*

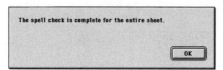

Figure 24. *The dialog box that appears at the end of a spelling check simply displays information.*

Figure 25. *The Font tab of the Format Cells dialog box.*

Dialog Boxes

Like most other Mac OS applications, Excel uses dialog boxes to communicate with you.

Excel can display many different dialog boxes, each with its own purpose. There are two basic types of dialog boxes:

■ Dialog boxes that simply provide information (**Figure 24**).

■ Dialog boxes that offer options to select (**Figure 25**) before Excel completes the execution of a command.

✔ Tip

■ Often, when a dialog box appears, you must dismiss it by clicking OK or Cancel before you can continue working with Excel.

Anatomy of an Excel dialog box

Here are the components of many Excel dialog boxes, along with information about how they work.

■ **Tabs (Figure 25)**, which appear at the top of some dialog boxes, let you move from one group of dialog box options to another. To switch to another group of options, click its tab.

■ **Edit boxes (Figures 25** and **27)** let you enter information from the keyboard. You can press (Tab) to move from one edit box to the next or click in an edit box to position the insertion point within it. Then enter a new value.

■ **Scrolling lists (Figure 25)** offer a number of options to choose from. Use the scroll bar to view options that don't fit in the list window. Click an option to select it; it becomes highlighted and appears in the edit box.

continued on next page...

Dialog Boxes

continued from previous page

Dialog Boxes

- **Check boxes (Figure 25)** let you turn options on or off. Click in a check box to toggle it. When a check mark or X appears in the check box, its option is turned on.

- **Radio buttons (Figure 26)** let you select only one option from a group. Click on an option to select it; the option that was selected before you clicked is deselected.

- **Pop-up menus (Figure 25)** also let you select one option from a group. Display a pop-up menu as you would any other menu **(Figure 27)**, then choose the option that you want.

- **Preview areas (Figure 25)**, when available, illustrate the effects of your changes before you finalize them by clicking the OK button.

- **Push buttons (Figures 24, 25, and 26)** let you access other dialog boxes, accept the changes and close the dialog box (OK), or close the dialog box without making changes (Cancel). To choose a button, click it once.

Radio buttons

Figure 26.
The Insert dialog box.

Figure 27.
Displaying a pop-up menu.

✔ Tips

- When the contents of an edit box are selected, whatever you type will replace the selection.

- Excel often uses edit boxes and scrolling lists together **(Figure 25)**. You can use either one to make a selection.

- If a pair of tiny triangles appear to the right of an edit box, you can click a triangle to increase or decrease the value in the edit box.

- In some scrolling lists, double-clicking an option selects it and dismisses the dialog box.

- You can turn on any number of check boxes in a group, but you can select only one radio button in a group.

- The Excel 98 documentation and help system sometimes refers to pop-up menus as *drop-down lists*.

- A push button with an extra border around it is the default button; you can "click" it by pressing [Enter].

- You can usually "click" the Cancel button by pressing [Esc] or [⌘ .].

Scroll arrow

Scroll bar

Scroll box

Figure 28. *The vertical scroll bar shifts the window's contents up or down. The horizontal scroll bar has the same parts, but shifts the window's contents left and right.*

Scroll arrow

Figures 29 & 30. *When you drag the scroll box, a yellow box with the row heading number (left) or the column heading letter (right) appears.*

Scrolling Window Contents

You can use Excel's scroll bars to shift the contents of a document window so you can see items that don't fit in the window.

✔ Tip

- I tell you more about working with document windows in **Chapter 4**.

To scroll the contents of the document window

Click the scroll arrow (**Figure 28**) for the direction that you want to view. For example, to scroll down to view the end of a document, click the down arrow.

or

Drag the scroll box (**Figure 28**) in the direction that you want to view. As you drag, a yellow box with a row or column heading appears on screen. It indicates the topmost row (**Figure 29**) or leftmost column (**Figure 30**) that will appear on screen when you release the mouse button. Release the mouse button to view the indicated part of the document.

or

Click in the scroll bar above or below the scroll box (**Figure 28**). This shifts the window contents one screenful at a time.

✔ Tips

- Having trouble remembering which scroll arrow to click? Just remember this: click up to see up, click down to see down, click left to see left, and click right to see right.

- Although some keyboard keys change the portion of the document being viewed, they also move the cell pointer. I tell you about these keys in **Chapter 2**.

The Office Assistant

The Office Assistant displays an animated character (**Figure 31**) that can provide tips and assistance while you work.

To close the Office Assistant

Click the close box in the Office Assistant window (**Figure 31**). The Office Assistant waves goodbye before disappearing.

To open the Office Assistant

Click the Office Assistant button on the Standard toolbar. The Office Assistant appears.

To get tips

1. Click the light bulb that appears in the Office Assistant window (**Figure 31**) when the Office Assistant has a tip for you. The tip appears in a balloon beside the Office Assistant (**Figure 32**).

2. When you are finished reading the tip, click the Close button.

✔ Tip

■ A light bulb appears on the Office Assistant button when a tip is available.

To ask a question

1. Click the Office Assistant to get its attention. A balloon with instructions appears (**Figure 33**).

2. Type your question into the edit box (**Figure 34**) and click the Search button. A list of possible topics appears in another balloon (**Figure 35**).

3. Click a topic that interests you until the MS Excel Help window appears (**Figure 36**).

4. When you are finished reading help information, click the MS Excel Help window's close box.

Figure 31.
The Office Assistant, waiting to share a tip with you.

Figure 32. *An Office Assistant tip.*

Figure 33.
Get the Office Assistant's attention,...

Figure 34.
...then type in your question.

Figure 35.
A list of possible topics appears in a balloon beside the Office Assistant.

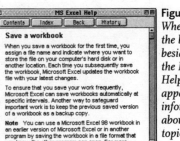
Figure 36.
When you click the button beside a topic, the MS Excel Help window appears with information about that topic.

Figure 37.
Excel's Help menu.

Figure 38.
The Help Table of Contents.

Figure 39.
Clicking a Table of Contents entry displays subtopics.

Figure 40.
Clicking a subtopic displays the specific help topics available.

Figure 41. *You can choose Print Topic from the File menu to print displayed help topic information.*

Excel Help

Excel has an extensive online help feature that provides information about using Excel to complete specific tasks. You access Excel Help via the Office Assistant (as discussed on the previous page) or commands under the Help menu (**Figure 37**).

✔ Tip

■ The Help menu in **Figure 37** appears if Mac OS 8.1 is installed on your computer; this menu may appear differently if another version of the operating system is installed.

To browse Excel Help

1. Choose Contents and Index from the Help menu (**Figure 37**). The MS Excel Help window appears, displaying the Help Table of Contents (**Figure 38**).

2. Click a topic that interests you. A list of subtopics appears beneath it (**Figure 39**).

3. Click a subtopic that interests you. A list of specific help topics appears (**Figure 40**).

4. Click a specific topic to display information about it (**Figure 36**).

✔ Tips

■ You can click the Back or History buttons in the Help window to browse topics you browsed earlier in the help session.

■ You can print information about a topic by choosing Print Topic from the File menu (**Figure 41**) while the topic is displayed.

To use the Help Index

1. Choose Contents and Index from the Help menu (**Figure 37**). The MS Excel Help window appears, displaying the Help Table of Contents (**Figure 38**).

2. Click the Index button. An alphabetical listing of references appears (**Figure 42**).

3. Scroll through the list to find a reference that interests you.

   or

   Type a reference into the edit box at the top of the dialog box. The view of the list shifts to match what you type (**Figure 43**).

4. Select the reference that interests you and click the Show Topics button. A list of topics appears in the bottom of the dialog box (**Figure 44**).

5. Select the topic that interests you and click the Go To button. Information about that topic appears in a window line the one in **Figure 36**.

Figure 42. *The Help Index dialog box.*

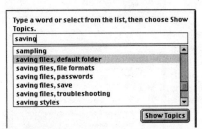

Figure 43. *Type a reference to move quickly to that reference in the list.*

Figure 44. *When you select a reference that interests you and click the Show Topics button, a list of topics appears at the bottom of the dialog box.*

WORKSHEET BASICS 2

Numeric values

Text values   Formula: =B1-B2

	A	B
1	Sales	$ 1,000.00
2	Cost	400.00
3	Profit	$ 600.00

Figure 1. *This very simple worksheet illustrates how a spreadsheet program like Excel works with values and formulas.*

	A	B
1	Sales	$ 1,150.00
2	Cost	400.00
3	Profit	$ 750.00

Figure 2. *When the value for Sales changes from $1,000 to $1,150, the Profit result changes automatically.*

How Worksheets Work

Excel is most commonly used to create *worksheets*. A worksheet is a collection of information laid out in columns and rows. As illustrated in **Figure 1**, each worksheet cell can contain one of two kinds of input:

- A *value* is a piece of information that does not change. Values can be text, numbers, dates, or times. A cell containing a value usually displays the value.

- A *formula* is a collection of values, cell references, operators, and predefined functions that, when evaluated by Excel, produces a result. A cell containing a formula usually displays the results of the formula.

Although any information can be presented in a worksheet, spreadsheet programs like Excel are usually used to organize and calculate numerical or financial information. Why? Well, when properly prepared, a worksheet acts like a super calculator. You enter values and formulas and it calculates and displays the results. If you change one of the values, no problem. Excel recalculates the results almost instantaneously without any additional effort on your part (**Figure 2**).

How does this work? By using cell *references* rather than actual numbers in formulas, Excel knows that it should use the contents of those cells in its calculations. Thus, changing one or more values affects the results of calculations that include references to the changed cells. As you can imagine, this makes worksheets powerful business planning and analysis tools!

Understanding Worksheets

17

Launching Excel

To use Excel, you must open the Excel application. This loads Excel into RAM (Random Access Memory), so your computer can work with it.

To launch Excel by opening its application icon

1. In the Finder, locate the Microsoft Excel application icon (**Figure 3**). It should be in the Microsoft Office or Microsoft Excel folder on your hard disk.

2. Click the icon once to select it, then choose Open from the Finder's File menu or press ⌘O.

   or

   Double-click the icon.

   The Excel splash screen appears briefly (**Figure 4**), then an empty document window named *Workbook1* appears (**Figure 5**).

To launch Excel by opening an Excel document icon

1. In the Finder, locate the icon for the document that you want to open (**Figure 6**).

2. Click the icon once to select it, then choose Open from the Finder's File menu or press ⌘O.

   or

   Double-click the icon.

   The Excel splash screen appears briefly (**Figure 4**), then a document window containing the document that you opened appears (**Figure 7**).

Figure 3.
The Microsoft Excel application icon.

Microsoft Excel

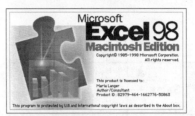

Figure 4. *The Excel 98 splash screen.*

Figure 5. *When you launch Excel by opening its icon, it displays an empty document window.*

Figure 6.
An Excel document icon.

SW Division Sales

Figure 7. *When you launch Excel by opening an Excel document icon, it displays the document that you opened.*

Figure 8.
Excel's File menu.

Figure 9. *A dialog box like this appears when a document with unsaved changes is open when you quit Word.*

Quitting Excel

When you're finished using Excel, you should use the Quit command to close the application. This completely clears Excel out of RAM, freeing up RAM for other applications.

✔ Tips

■ Closing all document windows is not the same as quitting. The only way to remove Excel from RAM is to quit. I tell you about closing document windows in **Chapter 1**.

■ Quitting Excel also instructs Excel to save preference settings.

To quit Excel

Choose Quit from the File menu (**Figure 8**) or press ⌘Q. Here's what happens:

■ If any documents are open, they close.

■ If an open document contains unsaved changes, a dialog box appears (**Figure 9**) so you can save the changes. I explain how to save documents later in this chapter.

■ The Excel application closes.

✔ Tip

■ As you've probably guessed, Excel automatically quits when you restart or shut down your computer.

Quitting Excel

Creating a New Workbook

By default, the documents you create using Excel are Excel *workbook* files. Excel enables you to create two kinds of workbook files:

- A blank workbook file is an empty workbook file with Excel's default settings.

- A workbook file based on a *template* contains the values, formulas, formatting, custom toolbars, and macros included in a template file.

Figure 10. *The General tab of the New dialog box.*

✔ Tips

- I tell you more about Excel workbook files in **Chapter 4**.

- Basing a workbook on a template can save a lot of time if you often need to create a standard document—such as a monthly report or invoice—repeatedly. I explain how to create templates in **Chapter 4**.

To create a blank workbook file

1. Choose New from the File menu (**Figure 8**).

2. If necessary, click the General tab in the New dialog box that appears to display its options (**Figure 10**).

3. Click to select the Workbook icon.

4. Click OK.

   A new, empty workbook window appears (**Figure 5**).

or

Click the New button on the Standard toolbar or press ⌘N.

Figure 11. *The Spreadsheet Solutions tab of the New dialog box offers two templates that are installed with Excel.*

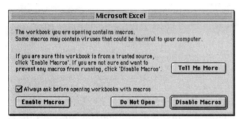

Figure 12. *Excel's macro virus protection feature allows you to disable macros in a template file.*

Figure 13. *A new workbook file based on the Invoice template that comes with Excel. Note the custom Invoice toolbar.*

To create a workbook file based on a template

1. Choose New from the File menu (**Figure 8**).

2. If necessary, click the Spreadsheet Solutions tab in the New dialog box that appears to display its options (**Figure 11**).

3. Click to select the icon for the template on which you want to base the new workbook file.

4. Click OK.

5. If macro virus protection is turned on, a dialog box (**Figure 12**) or Office Assistant balloon may warn you that the template contains macros.

   ▲ If you know the template is from a reliable source, click the Enable Macros button.

   ▲ If you are not sure about the reliability of the template's source, click the Disable Macros button.

   A new workbook based on the template that you selected appears (**Figure 13**).

✔ Tips

■ Excel comes with two sample templates (**Figure 11**) that you can experiment with.

■ If you click the Disable Macros button in step 5, the template's macros will not be available for you to use.

■ I tell you more about macros in **Chapter 11** and about macro virus protection in **Chapter 13**.

Creating a Workbook from a Template

Activating & Selecting Cells

Worksheet information is entered into *cells*. A cell is the intersection of a column and a row. Each little "box" in the worksheet window is a cell.

Each cell has a unique *address* or *reference*. The reference uses the letter(s) of the column and the number of the row. Thus, cell *B6* would be at the intersection of column *B* and row *6*. The reference for the active cell appears in the Name Box at the far left end of the formula bar (**Figure 14**).

To enter information in a cell, you must make that cell *active*. A cell is active when there is a dark or colored border called the *cell pointer* around it. When a cell is active, anything you type is entered into it.

To use Excel commands on a cell or its contents, you must *select* the cell. The active cell is also a selected cell. If desired, however, you can select multiple cells or a *range* of cells. This enables you to use commands on all selected cells at once. A range (**Figure 15**) is a rectangular selection of cells defined by the top left and bottom right cell references.

✔ Tips

- Although the active cell is always part of a selection of multiple cells, it is never highlighted like the rest of the selection. You should, however, see a dark or colored border (the cell pointer) around it (**Figure 15**).

- Although you can select multiple cells, only one cell—the one referenced in the Name Box (**Figure 15**)—is active.

- The column and row headings for selected cells appear bold (**Figures 14** and **15**).

- Using the scroll bars does not change the active or selected cell(s). It merely changes your view of the worksheet's contents.

Cell reference in Name Box of formula bar

Figure 14.
The reference for an active cell appears in the formula bar.

Active cell

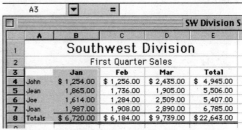

Figure 15. *In this illustration, the range A3:B8 is selected.*

Activating & Selecting Cells

Key	Movement
↑	Up one cell
↓	Down one cell
→	Right one cell
←	Left one cell
Tab	Right one cell
Home	First cell in row
Page Up	Up one window
Page Down	Down one window
⌘ Home or Control Home	Cell A1
⌘ End or Control End	Cell at intersection of last column and last row containing data

Table 1. *Keys for moving the cell pointer.*

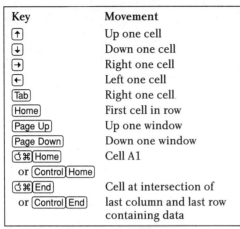

Figure 16. *To select cells, begin in one corner of the range,...*

Figure 17. *...press the mouse button down, and drag to the opposite corner of the range.*

Figure 18. *The Go To dialog box lets you move to any cell quickly.*

To activate a cell

Use the mouse pointer to click in the cell you want to make active.

or

Press the appropriate keystroke (see **Table 1**) to move the cell pointer to the cell you want to make active.

To select a range of cells with the mouse

1. Position the mouse pointer in the first cell you want to select (**Figure 16**).
2. Press the mouse button down and drag to highlight all the cells in the selection (**Figure 17**).

or

1. Click in the first cell of the range you want to select.
2. Hold down Shift and click in the last cell of the range. Everything between the first and second clicks is selected. This technique is known as "Shift-Click."

To go to a cell or range of cells

1. Choose Go To from the Edit menu or press F5 to display the Go To dialog box (see **Figure 18**).
2. Enter the reference for the cell you want to activate or the range that you want to select in the Reference edit box.
3. Click OK.

   If you entered a single cell reference, the cell is activated. If you entered a range reference, the range is selected.

✔ Tip

■ To specify a reference for a range, enter the addresses of the first and last cells of the range, separated with a colon (:). For example, **Figure 15** shows *A3:B8* selected and **Figure 17** shows *A4:E7* selected.

Activating & Selecting Cells

To select an entire column

Click on the column heading of the column you want to select (**Figure 19**).

or

Press Control Spacebar when the cell pointer is in any cell of the column you want to select.

To select an entire row

Click on the row heading of the row you want to select (**Figure 20**).

or

Press Shift Spacebar when the cell pointer is in any cell of the row you want to select.

To select multiple columns or rows

1. Position the mouse pointer on the first column or row heading.

2. Press the mouse button down, and drag along the headings until all the desired columns or rows are selected.

✔ Tip

■ When selecting multiple columns or rows, be careful to position the mouse pointer on the heading and not between two headings! If you drag the border of two columns, you will change a column's width rather than make a selection.

To select the entire worksheet

Click the Select All button at the upper-left corner of the worksheet window (**Figure 21**).

or

Press ⌃⌘A.

or

Press Control Spacebar and then Shift Spacebar.

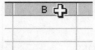

Figure 19. *Click a column heading to select that column.*

Figure 20. *Click a row heading to select that row.*

Figure 21. *The Select All button is in the corner of the worksheet where column and row headings meet.*

Selecting Columns & Rows

	A	B	C	D	E
1		**Southwest Division**			
2		First Quarter Sales			
3		Jan	Feb	Mar	Total
4	John	$ 1,254.00	$ 1,256.00	$ 2,435.00	$ 4,945.00
5	Jean	1,865.00	1,736.00	1,905.00	5,506.00
6	Joe	1,614.00	1,284.00	2,509.00	5,407.00
7	Joan	1,987.00	1,908.00	2,890.00	6,785.00
8	Total	$ 6,720.00	$ 6,184.00	$ 9,739.00	$22,643.00

Figure 22. *To select two ranges of cells, start by selecting the first range,…*

	A	B	C	D	E
1		**Southwest Division**			
2		First Quarter Sales			
3		Jan	Feb	Mar	Total
4	John	$ 1,254.00	$ 1,256.00	$ 2,435.00	$ 4,945.00
5	Jean	1,865.00	1,736.00	1,905.00	5,506.00
6	Joe	1,614.00	1,284.00	2,509.00	5,407.00
7	Joan	1,987.00	1,908.00	2,890.00	6,785.00
8	Totals	$ 6,720.00	$ 6,184.00	$ 9,739.00	$22,643.00

Figure 23. *…then hold down ⌘ and select the second range.*

To select multiple ranges

1. Use any selection technique to select the first cell or range of cells (**Figure 22**).
2. Hold down ⌘ and drag to select the second cell or range of cells (**Figure 23**).
3. Repeat step 2 until all desired ranges are selected.

✔ Tips

■ Selecting multiple ranges can be tricky. It takes practice. Don't be frustrated if you can't do it on the first few tries!

■ To add ranges that are not visible in the worksheet window, be sure to use the scroll bars to view them. Using the keyboard to move to other cells while selecting multiple ranges will remove the selections you've made so far or add undesired selections.

■ Do not click in the worksheet window or use the movement keys while multiple ranges are selected unless you are finished working with them. Doing so will deselect all the cells.

To deselect cells

Click anywhere in the worksheet.

or

Press any of the keys in **Table 1**.

✔ Tip

■ Remember, at least one cell must be selected at all times—that's the active cell.

Selecting Multiple Ranges, Deselecting

Entering Values & Formulas

To enter a value or formula into a cell, you begin by making the cell active. As you type or click to enter information, the information appears in both the cell and in the formula bar just above the window's title bar. You complete the entry by pressing (Return) or (Enter) or clicking the Enter button on the formula bar.

While you are entering information into a cell, the formula bar is *active*. You can tell that it's active because the Name Box on the far left end of the formula bar turns into a Functions list and two additional buttons appear between it and the cell contents area (**Figure 24**).

There are two important things to remember when the formula bar is active:

- Anything you type or click on may be included in the active cell.

- Many Excel options and menu commands are unavailable (**Figures 25 and 26**).

You deactivate the formula bar by accepting or cancelling the current entry.

✔ Tips

- Pressing (Return) to complete a formula entry accepts the entry and moves the cell pointer one cell down. Pressing (Enter) or clicking the Enter button accepts the entry without moving the cell pointer.

- To cancel an entry before it has been completed, press (Esc), press (⌘ .), or click the Cancel button on the formula bar. This restores the cell to the way it was before you began.

- If you include formatting notation like dollar signs, commas, and percent symbols when you enter numbers, you may apply formatting styles. I tell you more about formatting the contents of cells in **Chapter 6**.

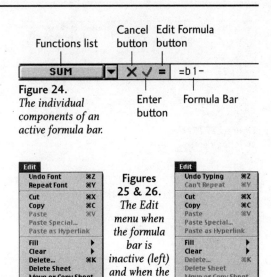

Functions list · Cancel button · Edit Formula button

Figure 24.
The individual components of an active formula bar.

Enter button · Formula Bar

Figures 25 & 26.
The Edit menu when the formula bar is inactive (left) and when the formula bar is active (right).

26

Figure 27. *As data is entered into a cell, it appears in the cell and the formula bar.*

Figure 28. *A completed entry. The insertion point and Cancel and Enter buttons are gone.*

Values

As discussed at the beginning of this chapter, a value is any text, number, date, or time you enter into a cell. Values are constant—they don't change unless you change them.

To enter a value

1. Activate the cell in which you want to enter the value.

2. Type in the value. As you type, the information appears in two places: the active cell and the formula bar, which becomes active (**Figure 27**).

3. To complete and accept the entry (**Figure 28**), press Return or Enter or click the Enter button on the formula bar.

✔ Tips

- Although you can often use the arrow keys or other movement keys in **Table 1** to complete an entry by moving to another cell, it's a bad habit because it won't always work.

- Excel aligns text against the left side of the cell and aligns numbers against the right side of the cell. I explain how to change alignment in **Chapter 6**.

- Don't worry if the data you put into a cell doesn't seem to fit. You can always change the column width or use the AutoSize Text feature to make it fit. I tell you how in **Chapter 6**.

Entering Values

Formula Basics

Excel makes calculations based on formulas you enter into cells. When you complete the entry of a formula, Excel displays the results of the formula rather than the formula you entered.

Here are some important things to keep in mind when writing formulas:

- If a formula uses cell references to refer to other cells and the contents of one or more of those cells changes, the result of the formula changes, too.

- All formulas begin with an equal (=) sign. This is how Excel knows that a cell entry is a formula and not a value.

- Formulas can contain any combination of values, references, operators (**Table 2**), and functions. I tell you about using operators in formulas in this chapter and about using functions in **Chapter 5**.

- Formulas are not case sensitive. This means that *=A1+B10* is the same as *=a1+b10*. Excel automatically converts characters in cell references and functions to uppercase.

When calculating the results of expressions with a variety of operators, Excel makes calculations in the following order:

1. Negation
2. Expressions in parentheses
3. Percentages
4. Exponentials
5. Multiplication or division
6. Addition or subtraction

Table 3 shows some examples of formulas and their results to illustrate this. As you can see, the inclusion of parentheses can really make a difference when you write a formula!

Operator	Use	Example
+	Addition	=A1+B10
-	Subtraction	=A1-B10
-	Negation	=-A1
*	Multiplication	=A1*B10
/	Division	=A1/B10
^	Exponential	=A1^3
%	Percentage	=20%

Table 2. *Mathematical operators understood by Excel. Comparison and text operators are discussed in* **Chapter 5**.

Assumptions
    A1=5
    B10=7
    C3=4

Formula	Evaluation	Result
=A1+B10*C3	=5+7*4	33
=C3*B10+A1	=4*7+5	33
=(A1+B10)*C3	=(5+7)*4	48
=A1+10%	=5+10%	5.1
=(A1+10)%	=(5+10)%	0.15
=A1^2-B10/C3	=5^2-7/4	23.25
=(A1^2-B10)/C3	=(5^2-7)/4	4.5
=A1^(2-B10)/C3	=5^(2-7)/4	0.00008

Table 3. *Excel evaluates expressions based on operators, no matter what order the expressions appear in the formula. Adding parentheses can change the order of evaluation and the results.*

	A	B
1	Sales	1000
2	Cost	400
3	Profit	600 ——— =*1000-400*
4		
5	Commission	90 ——— =*600*15%*
6		

Figure 29. *If any of the values change, the formulas will need to be rewritten!*

	A	B
1	Sales	1000
2	Cost	400
3	Profit	600 ——— =*B1-B2*
4		
5	Rate	15%
6		
7	Commission	90 ——— =*B3*B5*
8		

Figure 30. *But if the formulas reference cells containing the values, when the values change the formulas will not need to be rewritten to show correct results.*

The formula you typed contains an error.

- For information about fixing common formula problems, click Help.
- To get assistance in entering a function, click OK, then click Function on the Insert menu.
- If you are not trying to enter a formula, avoid using an equal sign (=) or minus sign (-), or precede it with a single quotation mark (').

Help   OK

Figure 31. *Excel tells you when a formula has a syntax error and provides information on where you can get help.*

Microsoft Excel

Microsoft Excel found an error in the formula you entered. Do you want to accept the correction proposed below?

=B1-b2

- To accept the correction, click Yes.
- To close this message and correct the formula yourself, click No.

Yes   No

Figure 32. *If the syntax error is one of 15 common formula errors, Excel offers to fix it for you.*

✔ Tips

- Do not use the arrow keys or other movement keys to complete an entry by moving to another cell. Doing so may add cells to the formula!

- Whenever possible, use references rather than values in formulas. This way, you won't have to rewrite formulas when values change. **Figures 29** and **30** illustrate this.

- A reference can be a cell reference, a range reference, or a cell or range name. I tell you about name references a little later in this chapter and in **Chapter 11**.

- To add a range of cells to a formula, type the first cell in the range followed by a colon (:) and then the last cell in the range. For example: *B1:B10* references the cells from *B1* straight down through *B10*.

- If you make a syntax error in a formula, a dialog box (**Figure 31**) or Office Assistant balloon (**Figure 32**) appears to tell you. If the error is one of the 15 common errors programmed into Excel's Formula AutoCorrect feature, Excel offers to correct the formula for you (**Figure 32**). Otherwise, you will have to troubleshoot the formula and correct it yourself.

- I tell you how to edit formulas in **Chapter 3** and how to include functions in formulas in **Chapter 5**.

Formula Basics

To enter a formula by typing

1. Activate the cell in which you want to enter the formula.

2. Type in the formula. As you type, the formula appears in two places: the active cell and the formula bar, which becomes active (**Figure 33**).

3. To complete the entry (**Figure 34**), press ⌷Return⌷ or ⌷Enter⌷ or click the Enter button on the formula bar.

To enter a formula by clicking

1. Activate the cell in which you want to enter the formula.

2. Type an equal (=) sign to begin the formula (**Figure 35**).

3. To enter a constant value or operator, type it in (**Figure 37**).

   or

   To enter a cell reference, click on the cell you want to reference (**Figures 36** and **38**).

4. Repeat step 3 until the entire formula appears in the formula bar.

5. To complete the entry (**Figure 39**), press ⌷Return⌷ or ⌷Enter⌷ or click the Enter button on the formula bar.

✔ Tips

- If you click a cell reference without typing an operator, Excel assumes you want to add that reference to the formula.

- Be careful where you click when writing a formula! Each click adds a reference to the formula. If you add an incorrect reference, press ⌷Delete⌷ until it has been deleted or click the Cancel button to start the entry from scratch. I tell you more about editing a cell's contents in **Chapter 3**.

- You can add a range of cells to a formula by dragging over the cells.

Figure 33. *To enter a formula, simply type it into the cell.*

Figure 34. *A completed formula entry.*

Figure 35. *To enter the formula =B1-B2, type = to begin the formula,...*

Figure 36. *...click cell B1 to add its reference to the formula,...*

Figure 37. *...type - to tell Excel to subtract,...*

Figure 38. *...click cell B2 to add its reference to the formula,...*

Figure 39. *...and finally, press* ⌷Enter⌷ *to complete the formula.*

Entering a Formula

Figure 40. *The Formula AutoCorrect feature can even help you fix incorrectly entered name references.*

Figure 41. *If a name reference in a formula is not correct, a #NAME? error appears in the cell.*

Figure 42. *To use the Natural Language Formulas simply type the formula using cell references based on adjacent cells.*

Figure 43. *When you complete the formula, the result appears in the cell.*

Natural Language Formulas

Excel's Natural Language Formulas feature enables you to write formulas using references automatically derived from the column or row headings for cells.

For example, the formula in **Figures 34** and **39** reference the cells immediately to the right of the cells containing the text *Sales* and *Cost*. Excel can recognize the text as labels or *names* for the cells beside them, thus allowing it to understand the formula *=Sales-Cost*.

✔ Tips

■ The names feature has been part of Excel for years. It is only in Excel 98, however, that Excel can automatically recognize names without you manually defining or creating them. I tell you more about names in **Chapter 11**.

■ If you enter an incorrect name reference in a formula, one of two things happens:

▲ Excel's Formula AutoCorrect feature offers to fix it (**Figure 40**)—if Excel can guess what name you meant to type.

▲ A *#NAME?* error appears in the cell (**Figure 41**).

To enter a formula using Natural Language Formulas

1. Activate the cell in which you want to enter the formula.

2. Type in the formula, using the text labels above or beside cells to identify them (**Figure 42**).

3. To complete the entry (**Figure 43**), press Return or Enter or click the Enter button on the formula bar. ✓

EDITING WORKSHEETS

Editing Worksheets

Excel offers a number of features and techniques that you can use to modify your worksheets.

- Use standard editing techniques and the Clear command to change or clear the contents of cells.

- Use Insert and Edit menu commands to insert or delete cells, columns, and rows.

- Use Edit menu commands, the fill handle, and drag-and-drop editing to copy cells from one location to another, including cells containing formulas.

- Use the fill handle and Fill submenu commands to copy cell contents to multiple cells or create a series.

- Modify formulas so they are properly updated by Excel when copied.

- Use Edit menu commands and drag-and-drop editing to move cells from one location to another.

- Undo, redo, and repeat multiple actions.

This chapter covers all of these techniques.

Editing Cell Contents

You can use standard editing techniques to edit the contents of cells either as you enter values or formulas or after you have completed an entry. You can also clear a cell's contents, leaving the cell empty.

To edit as you enter

1. If necessary, click to position the blinking insertion point cursor in the cell (**Figure 1**) or formula bar (**Figure 2**).

2. Press Delete to delete the character to the left of the insertion point.

   or

   Type the characters that you want to insert at the insertion point.

To edit a completed entry

1. Double-click the cell containing the incorrect entry to activate it for editing.

2. If the cell contains a value, follow the instructions in the previous section to insert or delete characters as desired.

   or

   If the cell contains a formula, color-coded Range Finder frames appear, to graphically identify cell references (**Figures 3** and **5**). You have three options for editing cell references:

   ▲ Edit the reference as discussed in the previous section.

   ▲ Drag a frame border to move the frame over another cell (**Figure 4**).

   ▲ Drag a frame handle to expand or contract it so the frame includes more (**Figure 6**) or fewer cells.

Figure 1. *To edit a cell's contents while entering information, click to reposition the insertion point in the cell…*

Figure 2. *…or in the formula bar and make changes as desired.*

	A	B
1	Sales	1000
2	Cost	400
3	Profit	=A1-B2

Figure 3. *The Range Finder frames clearly indicate the problem with this formula.*

	A	B
1	Sales	1000
2	Cost	400
3	Profit	=B1-B2

Figure 4. *You can drag a Range Finder frame to correct the cell reference.*

	A	B	C
1		Jan	Fel
2	John	1254	1:
3	Jean	1865	1
4	Joe	1614	1:
5	Joan	1987	1!
6	Totals	=SUM(B2:B4)	

Figure 5. *In this example, the Range Finder indicates that the range of cells in the formula excludes a cell.*

	A	B	C
1		Jan	Fe
2	John	1254	1:
3	Jean	1865	1
4	Joe	1614	1:
5	Joan	1987	1
6	Totals	=SUM(B2:B5)	

Figure 6. *You can drag a Range Finder frame handle to expand the range and correct the reference in the formula.*

Figure 7. *The Edit menu's Clear submenu offers four options for clearing selected cell(s).*

To clear cell contents

1. Select the cell(s) you want to clear.
2. Choose Contents from the Clear submenu under the Edit menu (**Figure 7**).

   or

   Press (⌘ B) or (Del).

✔ Tips

- Another way to clear the contents of just one cell is to select the cell, press (Delete), and then press (Return) or (Enter).

- Do not press (Spacebar) to clear a cell's contents! Doing so inserts a space character into the cell. Although the contents seem to disappear, they are just replaced by an invisible character.

- Clearing a cell is very different from deleting a cell. When you clear a cell, the cell remains in the worksheet—only its contents are removed. When you delete a cell, the entire cell is removed from the worksheet and other cells shift to fill the gap. I tell you about inserting and deleting cells next.

- The Contents command clears only the values or formulas entered into a cell. The other Clear submenu commands (**Figure 7**) work as follows:
  - ▲ **All** clears everything, including formatting and comments.
  - ▲ **Formats** clears only cell formatting.
  - ▲ **Comments** clears only cell comments.

  I tell you about formatting cells and adding cell comments in **Chapter 6**.

Inserting & Deleting Cells

Excel offers an Insert command and a Delete command to insert and delete columns, rows, or cells.

■ When you use the Insert command, Excel shifts cells down or to the right to make room for the new cells.

■ When you use the Delete command, Excel shifts cells up or to the left to fill the gap left by the missing cells.

Figures 8, 11, and **14** show examples of how inserting a column or deleting a row affects the addresses or references of the cells in a worksheet. Fortunately, Excel is smart enough to know how to adjust cell references in formulas so that the formulas you write remain correct.

To insert a column or row

1. Select a column or row (**Figure 9**).
2. Choose Columns or Rows from the Insert menu (**Figure 10**).

   or

   Choose Cells from the Insert menu (**Figure 10**) or press ⌃⌘Ⅰ.

   The column (**Figure 11**) or row is inserted.

✔ Tips

■ To insert multiple columns or rows, in step 1, select the number of columns or rows you want to insert. For example, if you want to insert three columns before column *B*, select columns *B*, *C*, and *D*.

■ If a complete column or row is not selected when you choose the Cells command or press ⌃⌘Ⅰ in step 2, the Insert dialog box appears (**Figure 17**). Select the appropriate radio button (Entire row or Entire column) for what you want to insert, then click OK. I tell you about inserting cells a little later in this chapter.

	A	B	C	D
1		Jan	Feb	Mar
2	John	1254	1256	2435
3	Jean	1865	1736	1905
4	Joe	1614	1284	2509
5	Joan	1987	1908	2890

Figure 8. *A simple worksheet.*

	A	B	C	D
1		Jan	Feb	Mar
2	John	1254	1256	2435
3	Jean	1865	1736	1905
4	Joe	1614	1284	2509
5	Joan	1987	1908	2890

Figure 9. *Selecting a column.*

Figure 10.
The Insert menu.

	A	B	C	D	E
1			Jan	Feb	Mar
2	John		1254	1256	2435
3	Jean		1865	1736	1905
4	Joe		1614	1284	2509
5	Joan		1987	1908	2890

Figure 11. *An inserted column.*

Inserting Columns & Rows

Figure 12. *Selecting a row.*

Figure 13.
The Edit menu.

	A	B	C	D
1		Jan	Feb	Mar
2	John	1254	1256	2435
3	Jean	1865	1736	1905
4	Joan	1987	1908	2890

Figure 14. *The row selected in* **Figure 12** *is deleted.*

	A	B
1	Sales	1000
2	Cost	400
3	Profit	600
4		
5	Commissions	#REF!

Figure 15. *In this example, I deleted a row containing a value referenced in the formula in B5. Because Excel can't find one of the references it needs, it displays a #REF! error.*

To delete a column or row

1. Select a column or row (**Figure 12**).

2. Choose Delete from the Edit menu (**Figure 13**) or press ⌃⌘K.

   The column or row (**Figure 14**)—along with all of its contents—disappears.

✔ Tips

- To delete more than one column or row at a time, in step 1, select all of the columns or rows you want to delete.

- If a complete column or row is not selected when you choose the Delete command or press ⌃⌘K in step 2, the Delete dialog box appears (**Figure 19**). Select the appropriate radio button (Entire row or Entire column) for what you want to delete, then click OK.

- If you delete a column or row that contains referenced cells, the formulas that reference the cells may display a #REF! error message (**Figure 15**). This means that Excel can't find a referenced cell. If this happens, you'll have to rewrite any formulas in cells displaying the error.

Deleting Columns & Rows

To insert cells

1. Select a cell or range of cells (**Figure 16**).

2. Choose Cells from the Insert menu (**Figure 10**) or press ⌃⌘I.

3. In the Insert dialog box that appears (**Figure 17**), select the appropriate radio button to tell Excel how to shift the selected cells to make room for new cells—Shift cells right or Shift cells down.

4. Click OK.

   The cell(s) are inserted (**Figure 118**).

✔ Tip

■ Excel always inserts the number of cells that is selected when you use the Insert command (**Figures 16** and **18**).

To delete cells

1. Select a cell or range of cells to delete (**Figure 16**).

2. Choose Delete from the Edit menu (**Figure 13**) or press ⌃⌘K.

3. In the Delete dialog box that appears (**Figure 19**), select the appropriate radio button to tell Excel how to shift the other cells when the selected cells are deleted—Shift cells left or Shift cells up.

4. Click OK.

   The cell(s) are deleted (**Figure 20**).

✔ Tip

■ If you delete a cell that contains referenced cells, the formulas that reference the cells may display a #REF! error message (**Figure 15**). If this happens, you'll have to rewrite any formulas in cells displaying the error.

	A	B	C	D
1		Jan	Feb	Mar
2	John	1254	1256	2435
3	Jean	1865	1736	1905
4	Joe	1614	1284	2509
5	Joan	1987	1908	2890

Figure 16. *Selecting a range of cells.*

Figure 17. *The Insert dialog box.*

	A	B	C	D
1		Jan	Feb	Mar
2	John	1254	1256	2435
3	Jean	1865	1736	1905
4	Joe			
5	Joan	1614	1284	2509
6		1987	1908	2890

Figure 18. *Here's what happens when you insert cells as selected in* **Figure 16**, *using the Shift cells down option.*

Figure 19. *The Delete dialog box.*

	A	B	C	D
1		Jan	Feb	Mar
2	John	1254	1256	2435
3	Jean	1865	1736	1905
4	Joe	1987	1908	2890
5	Joan			

Figure 20. *Here's what happens when you delete the cells selected in* **Figure 16**, *using the Shift cells up option.*

Figure 21.
The Copy and Paste commands can make an exact copy.

Figure 22.
Using the fill handle on a cell containing the word Monday *generates a list of the days of the week.*

	Monday
	Tuesday
	Wednesday
	Thursday
	Friday
	Saturday
	Sunday

	A	B	C	D
1		Jan	Feb	Mar
2	John	1254	1256	2435
3	Jean	1865	1736	1905
4	Joe	1614	1284	2509
5	Joan	1987	1908	2890
6		6720	6184	9739
7				

Figure 23. *Copying a formula that totals a column automatically writes correctly referenced formulas to total similar columns.*

Copying Cells

Excel offers several ways to copy the contents of one cell to another: the Copy and Paste commands, the fill handle, and the Fill command.

How Excel copies depends not only on the method used, but on the contents of the cell(s) being copied.

- When you use the Copy and Paste commands to copy a cell containing a value, Excel makes an exact copy of the cell, including any formatting (**Figure 21**). I tell you about formatting cells in **Chapter 6**.

- When you use the fill handle or Fill command to copy a cell containing a value, Excel either makes an exact copy of the cell, including any formatting, or creates a series based on the original cell's contents (**Figure 22**).

- When you copy a cell containing a formula, Excel copies the formula, changing any relative references in the formula so they're relative to the destination cell(s) (**Figure 23**).

✔ Tip

- Copy cells that contain formulas whenever possible to save time and ensure consistency.

Copying Cells

Copying with Copy & Paste

The Copy and Paste commands in Excel work very much the same way they do in other applications. Begin by selecting the source cells and copying them to the Clipboard. Then select the destination cells and paste the Clipboard contents in.

To copy with Copy and Paste

1. Select the cell(s) you want to copy (**Figure 24**).

2. Choose Copy from the Edit menu (**Figure 13**) or press ⌃⌘C.

   or

   Click the Copy button on the Standard toolbar.

   An animated marquee appears around the selection (**Figure 25**).

3. Select the cell(s) in which you want to paste the selection (**Figure 26**). If more than one cell has been copied, you can select either the first cell of the destination range or the entire range.

4. Choose Paste from the Edit menu (**Figure 27**) or press ⌃⌘V or Enter.

   or

   Click the Paste button on the Standard toolbar.

   The originally selected cells are copied to the new location (**Figure 28**).

✔ Tips

- If the destination cells contain information, Excel may overwrite them without warning you.

- If you choose the Paste command, press ⌃⌘V, or click the Paste button, the marquee remains around the copied range, indicating that it is still in the Clipboard and may be pasted elsewhere. The marquee disappears automatically as you work, but if you want to remove it manually, press Esc.

Figure 24.
Begin by selecting the cell(s) that you want to copy.

Figure 25. *A marquee appears around the selection when it has been copied to the Clipboard.*

Figure 26. *Select the destination cell(s).*

Figure 27.
The Edit menu with the Paste command available. The Paste command is only available when something has been cut or copied to the Clipboard.

Figure 28.
The contents of the copied cells appear in the destination cells.

- The Edit menu's Paste Special command (**Figure 27**) offers additional options over the regular Paste command. For example, you can use it to paste only the formatting of a copied selection, convert formulas in the selection into values, or add the contents of the source cells to the destination cells.

Copying with Copy & Paste

Figure 29.
The fill handle on a single cell.

b	Mar
5	2435
5	1905
4	2509

Fill handle

Figure 30.
The fill handle on a range of cells.

b	Mar
5	2435
5	1905
4	2509
3	2890
1	9739

Fill handle

Figure 31.
When the mouse pointer is over the fill handle, it turns into a thick crosshairs pointer.

b	Mar
5	2435
5	1905
4	2509
3	2890
1	9739

Figure 32.
As you drag the fill handle, a dark border indicates the destination cell.

5	Mar	
5	2435	
5	1905	
4	2509	
3	2890	
1	9739	

2435

Figure 33.
The destination cells fill with the contents of the source cells.

5	Mar	
5	2435	2435
5	1905	1905
4	2509	2509
3	2890	2890
1	9739	

The Fill Handle

The *fill handle* is a small black or colored box in the lower-right corner of the cell pointer (**Figure 29**) or selection (**Figure 30**). You can use the fill handle to copy the contents of one or more cells to adjacent cells.

To copy with the fill handle

1. Select the cell(s) containing the information you want to copy (**Figure 30**).

2. Position the mouse pointer on the fill handle. The mouse pointer turns into a crosshairs (**Figure 31**).

3. Press the mouse button down and drag to the adjacent cells. A dark border surrounds the destination cells (**Figure 32**).

4. When all the destination cells are surrounded by the dark border, release the mouse button. The cells are filled (**Figure 33**).

✔ Tips

- You can use the fill handle to copy any number of cells. The destination cells, however, must be adjacent to the original cells.

- When using the fill handle, you can only copy in one direction (up, down, left, or right) at a time.

- If the destination cells contain information, Excel will overwrite them without warning you.

The Fill Command

The Fill command works a lot like the fill handle in that it copies information to adjacent cells. But rather than dragging to copy, you select the source and destination cells at the same time and then use the Fill command to complete the copy. The Fill submenu offers several options for copying to adjacent selected cells:

■ **Down** copies the contents of the top cell(s) in the selection to the selected cells beneath it.

■ **Right** copies the contents of the left cell(s) in the selection to the selected cells to the right of it.

■ **Up** copies the contents of the bottom cell(s) in the selection to the selected cells above it.

■ **Left** copies the contents of the right cell(s) in the selection to the selected cells to the left of it.

To copy with the Fill command

1. Select the cell(s) you want to copy along with the adjacent destination cell(s) **(Figure 34)**.

2. Choose the appropriate command from the Fill submenu under the Edit menu **(Figure 35)**: Down, Right, Up, Left.

    The cells are filled as specified **(Figure 33)**.

✔ Tip

■ You must select both the source and destination cells when using the Fill command. If you select just the destination cells, Excel won't copy the correct cells.

Figure 34.
To use the Fill command, begin by selecting the source and destination cells.

Figure 35. *The Fill submenu under the Edit menu.*

Figure 36. *To create an AutoFill series, start by entering the first item in a cell.*

Figure 37. *Drag the fill handle to include all cells that will be part of the series.*

Figure 38. *Excel creates the series automatically.*

Figure 39. *To use the Fill command, select the source and destination cells.*

Figure 40. *Select the AutoFill radio button in the Series dialog box.*

Figures 41 & 42. *Enter the first two values in the series, then drag the fill handle (left) to complete the series (right).*

Series & AutoFill

A *series* is a sequence of cells that forms a logical progression. Excel's AutoFill feature can generate a series of numbers, months, days, dates, and quarters.

To create a series with the fill handle

1. Enter the first item of the series in a cell (**Figure 36**). Be sure to complete the entry by pressing Return or Enter.

2. Position your mouse pointer on the fill handle and drag. All the cells that will be part of the series are surrounded by a dark border and a yellow box indicates the value that will be in the last cell in the range (**Figure 37**).

3. Release the mouse button to complete the series (**Figure 38**).

To create a series with the Series command

1. Enter the first item in the series in a cell (**Figure 36**).

2. Select all cells that will be part of the series, including the first cell (**Figure 39**).

3. Choose Series from the Fill submenu under the Edit menu (**Figure 35**).

4. In the Series dialog box that appears (**Figure 40**), select the AutoFill radio button.

5. Click OK to complete the series (**Figure 38**).

✔ Tips

- To generate a series that skips values, enter the first two values of the series in adjoining cells, then use the fill handle or Fill command to create the series, including both cells as part of the source (**Figures 41** and **42**).

Creating an AutoFill Series

Copying Formulas

You copy a cell containing a formula the same way you copy any other cell in Excel: with the Copy and Paste commands, with the fill handle, or with the Fill command. These methods are discussed earlier in this chapter.

Generally speaking, Excel does not make an exact copy of a formula. Instead, it copies the formula based on the kinds of references used within it. If relative references are used, Excel changes them based on the location of the destination cell in relation to the source cell. You can see an example of this in **Figures 43** and **44**.

✔ Tips

- You'll find it much quicker to copy formulas rather than to write each and every formula from scratch.

- Not all formulas can be copied with accurate results. For example, you can't copy a formula that sums up a column of numbers to a cell that should represent a sum of cells in a row **(Figure 45)**.

- I explain the various types of cell references—relative, absolute, and mixed—beginning on the next page.

Figure 43. *Here's a formula to calculate markup percentage. If the company has 763 products, would you want to write the same basic formula 762 more times? Of course not!*

Figure 44. *Copying formulas can save time. If the original formula is properly written, the results of the copied formula should also be correct.*

=(B2-C2)/C2
=(B3-C3)/C3
=(B4-C4)/C4
=(B5-C5)/C5

=SUM(C7:C10)   =SUM(F3:F6)

Figure 45. *In this illustration, the formula in cell C11 was copied to cell F7. This doesn't work because the two cells don't add up similar ranges. The formula in cell F7 would have to be rewritten from scratch. It could then be copied to F8 through F10. (I tell you about the SUM function in **Chapter 5**.)*

Figure 46. *This formula correctly calculates a partner's share of profit.*

Figure 47. *But when the formula is copied for the other partners, the relative reference to the cell B3 is changed, causing incorrect results and an error message!*

Figure 48. *Rewrite the original formula so it includes an absolute reference to cell B3, which all the formulas must reference.*

Figure 49. *When the formula is copied for the other partners, only the relative reference (to the percentages) changes. The results are correct.*

Relative vs. Absolute Cell References

There are two primary types of cell references:

- A *relative cell reference* is the address of a cell relative to the cell the reference is in. For example, a reference to cell *B1* in cell *B3*, tells Excel to look at the cell two cells above *B3*. Most of the references you use in Excel are relative references.

- An *absolute cell reference* is the exact location of a cell. To indicate an absolute reference, enter a dollar sign ($) in front of the column letter(s) and row number of the reference. An absolute reference to cell *B1*, for example, would be written *$B$1*.

As **Figures 46** and **47** illustrate, relative cell references change when you copy them to other cells. Although in many cases, you might want the references to change, sometimes you don't. That's when you use absolute references (**Figures 48** and **49**).

✔ Tips

- Here's a trick for remembering the meaning of the notation for absolute cell references: in your mind, replace the dollar sign with the word *always*. Then you'll read *$B$1* as *always B always 1—always B1*!

- If you're having trouble understanding how these two kinds of references work and differ, don't worry. This is one of the most difficult spreadsheet concepts you'll encounter. Try creating a worksheet like the one illustrated on this page and working your way through the figures one at a time. Pay close attention to how Excel copies the formulas you write!

To include an absolute cell reference in a formula

1. Enter the formula by typing or clicking as discussed in **Chapter 2**.

2. Insert a dollar sign before the column and row references for the cell reference you want to make absolute (**Figure 50**).

   or

   With the insertion point on the cell reference that you want to make absolute, press ⌘T to have Excel insert the dollar signs automatically.

3. Complete the entry by pressing Return or Enter.

✔ Tips

- You can edit an existing formula to include absolute references by inserting dollar signs where needed or using the ⌘T shortcut on a selected reference. I tell you how to edit cell contents earlier in this chapter.

- Do not use a dollar sign in a formula to indicate currency formatting. I tell you how to apply formatting to cell contents, including currency format, in **Chapter 6**.

About Mixed References

Once you've mastered the concept of relative vs. absolute cell references, consider the third type of reference: a *mixed cell reference*.

In a mixed cell reference, either the column or row reference is absolute while the other reference remains relative. Thus, you can use cell references like *A$1* or *$A1*. Use this when a column reference must remain constant but a row reference changes or vice versa. **Figure 51** shows a good example.

Figure 50. *Either include the dollar signs as you type or press* ⌘T *when the insertion point is in a cell reference.*

	A	B	C	D	E
1			January	February	March
2		Sales	1000	1250	1485
3		Cost	400	395	412
4		Profit	600	855	1073
5					
6	Onwer	Percent	Jan Share	Feb Share	Mar Share
7	John	50%	300		
8	Jean	20%			
9	Joe	15%	=C$4*$B6		
10	Joan	15%			

Figure 51. *The formula in cell C7 includes two different kinds of mixed references. It can be copied to cells C8 through C10 and C7 through E10 for correct results in all cells. Try it for yourself and see!*

Figure 52.
Note the formula in cell C6.

	A	B	C
1	Sales	1000	
2	Cost	400	
3	Profit	600	
4			
5	**Owner**	**Percent**	**Share**
6	John	50%	300
7	Jean	20%	120
8	Joe	15%	90
9	Joan	15%	90

=$B$3*B6

Figure 53.
See how it changes when one of the cells it references is moved?

	A	B	C
1		Sales	1000
2		Cost	400
3		Profit	600
4			
5	**Owner**	**Percent**	**Share**
6	John	50%	300
7	Jean	20%	120
8	Joe	15%	90
9	Joan	15%	90

=$C$3*B6

Figure 54.
Select the cell(s) you want to move.

	A
1	
2	John
3	Jean
4	Joe
5	Joan

Figure 55. *When you use the Cut command, a marquee appears around the selection but the selected cells do not disappear.*

	A
1	
2	John
3	Jean
4	Joe
5	Joan

	A
1	
2	John
3	Jean
4	Joe
5	Joan
6	
7	
8	⊕
9	

Figure 56.
Select the destination cell(s).

	A
1	
2	
3	
4	
5	
6	
7	
8	
9	
10	
11	

Figure 57.
When you use the Paste command, the selection moves.

	A
1	
2	
3	
4	
5	
6	
7	
8	John
9	Jean
10	Joe
11	Joan

Moving Cells

Excel offers two ways to move the contents of one cell to another: the Cut and Paste commands and dragging the border of a selection. Either way, Excel moves the contents of the cell.

✔ Tip

■ When you move a cell, Excel searches the worksheet for any cells that contain references to it and changes the references to reflect the cell's new location (**Figures 52** and **53**).

To move with Cut & Paste

1. Select the cell(s) you want to move (**Figure 54**).
2. Choose Cut from the Edit menu (**Figure 13**) or press ⌘X.

   or

   Click the Cut button on the Standard toolbar.

   An animated marquee appears around the selection (**Figure 55**).
3. Select the cell(s) to which you want to paste the selection (**Figure 56**).
4. Choose Paste from the Edit menu (**Figure 27**) or press ⌘V or Enter.

   or

   Click the Paste button on the Standard toolbar.

   The cell contents are moved to the new location (**Figure 57**).

✔ Tip

■ Consult the tips at the bottom of **page 40** for Paste command warnings and tips.

Moving with Cut & Paste

To move with drag & drop

1. Select the cell(s) you want to move (**Figure 54**).

2. Position the mouse pointer on the border of the selection. It turns into an arrow pointing up and to the left (**Figure 58**).

3. Press the mouse button down and drag toward the new location. As you move the mouse, a dark border the same shape as the selection moves along with it and a yellow box indicates the range where the cells will move (**Figure 59**).

4. Release the mouse button. The selection moves to its new location (**Figure 57**).

✔ Tips

- If you try to drag a selection to cells already containing information, Excel warns you with a dialog box or Office Assistant balloon (**Figure 60**). If you click OK to complete the move, the destination cells will be overwritten with the contents of the cells you are moving.

- To copy using drag and drop, hold down [Option] as you press the mouse button down. The mouse pointer turns into an arrow with a tiny plus sign (+) beside it (**Figure 61**). When you release the mouse button, the selection is copied.

- To insert cells using drag and drop, hold down [Shift] as you press the mouse button down. As you drag, a dark bar moves along with the mouse pointer and a yellow box indicates where the cells will be inserted (**Figure 62**). When you release the mouse button, the cells are inserted (**Figure 63**).

Figure 58. *When you position the mouse pointer on the border of a selection, it turns into an arrow.*

Figure 59. *As you drag, a dark border moves along with the mouse pointer.*

Figure 60. *Excel warns you when you will overwrite cells with a selection you drag.*

Figure 61. *Hold down* [Option] *to copy a selection by dragging it. A plus sign appears beside the mouse pointer.*

Figure 62. *Hold down* [Shift] *to insert a selection between other cells. A bar indicates where the cells will be inserted.*

Figure 63. *This makes it possible to rearrange the cells in a worksheet.*

Undoing, Redoing, & Repeating Actions

Excel's Edit menu offers a trio of commands that enable you to undo, redo, or repeat the last thing you did.

- **Undo (Figures 13** and **27)** reverses your last action. Excel supports multiple levels of undo, enabling you to reverse more than just the very last action.

- **Redo (Figure 27)** reverses the Undo command. This command is only available if the last thing you did was use the Undo command.

- **Repeat (Figure 13)** performs your last action again. This command is only available when you performed any action other than use the Undo or Redo command.

✔ Tips

- The exact wording of these commands on the Edit menu **(Figures 13** and **27)** varies depending on the last action performed. The Undo command is always the first command under the Edit menu; the Redo or Repeat command (whichever appears on the menu) is always the second command under the Edit menu.

- The Redo and Repeat commands are never both available at the same time.

- Think of the Undo command as the Oops command—anytime you say "Oops," you'll probably want to use it.

To undo the last action

Choose the Undo command from the Edit menu (**Figures 13** or **27**) or press ⌃⌘Z.

or

Click the Undo button on the Standard toolbar.

To undo multiple actions

Choose the Undo command from the Edit menu (**Figures 13** or **27**) or press ⌃⌘Z repeatedly.

or

Click the triangle beside the Undo button on the standard toolbar to display a pop-up menu of recent actions. Drag down to select all the actions that you want to undo (**Figure 64**). Release the mouse button to undo all selected actions.

To reverse the last undo

Choose the Redo command from the Edit menu (**Figure 27**) or press ⌃⌘Y.

or

Click the Redo button on the Standard toolbar.

To reverse multiple undos

Choose the Redo command from the Edit menu (**Figure 27**) or press ⌃⌘Y repeatedly.

or

Click the triangle beside the Redo button on the standard toolbar to display a pop-up menu of recently undone actions. Drag down to select all the actions that you want to redo (**Figure 65**). Release the mouse button to reverse all selected undos.

To repeat the last action

Choose the Repeat command from the Edit menu (**Figure 13**) or press ⌃⌘Y.

Figure 64.
You can use the Undo button's menu to select multiple actions to undo.

Figure 65.
You can also use the Redo button's menu to select multiple actions to redo.

WORKING WITH FILES

Figure 1. *Here's a worksheet.*

Figure 2. *And here's a chart sheet in the same workbook file.*

Excel Files

Excel 98 document files are called *workbooks*.

- Each workbook file consists of multiple sheets.

- Workbook files appear in a document window.

- Workbook files can be saved on disk and reopened for editing and printing.

In this chapter, I tell you how to perform a variety of tasks with workbook sheets, windows, and files.

Workbook Sheets

Excel workbook files can include up to 255 individual *sheets*, which are like pages in the workbook. Each workbook, by default, includes three sheets named *Sheet1* through *Sheet3*.

In Excel 98, there are two kinds of sheets:

- A *worksheet* (**Figure 1**) is for entering information and performing calculations. You can also embed charts in a worksheet.

- A *chart sheet* (**Figure 2**) is for creating charts that aren't embedded in a worksheet.

✔ Tips

- Use the multiple sheet capabilities of workbook files to keep sheets for the same project together. This is an excellent way to organize related work.

- I tell you about worksheets throughout this book and about charts and chart sheets in **Chapter 8**.

To switch between sheets

Click the sheet tab at the bottom of the workbook window (**Figure 3**) for the sheet you want.

or

Press (Option)(←) or (Option)(→) to scroll through all the sheets in a workbook, one at a time.

✔ Tips

■ If the sheet tab for the sheet you want is not displayed, use the tab scrolling buttons (**Figure 4**) to scroll through the sheet tabs.

■ To display more or fewer sheet tabs, drag the tab split box (**Figure 5**) to increase or decrease the size of the sheet tab area. As you change the size of the sheet tab area, you'll also change the size of the bottom scroll bar for the workbook window.

To select multiple sheets

1. Click the sheet tab for the first sheet you want to select.

2. Hold down (⌘) and click the sheet tab(s) for the other sheet(s) you want to select. The sheet tabs for each sheet you include in the selection turn white (**Figure 6**).

✔ Tips

■ To select multiple adjacent sheets, click the sheet tab for the first sheet, then hold down (Shift) and click on the sheet tab for the last sheet you want to select. All sheet tabs in between also become selected.

■ Selecting multiple sheets makes it quick and easy to print, delete, edit, format, or perform other tasks with more than one sheet at a time.

Figure 3. *Sheet tabs let you move from sheet to sheet within a workbook.*

Figure 4. *Use the tab scrolling buttons to view sheet tabs that are not displayed.*

Figure 5. *Drag the tab split box to change the size of the sheet tab area and display more or fewer sheet tabs.*

Figure 6. *To select multiple sheets, hold down (⌘) while clicking each sheet tab.*

Figure 7. *Begin by selecting the sheet you want the new sheet to be inserted before.*

Figure 8.
The Insert menu.

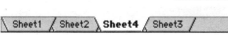

Figure 9. *An inserted worksheet.*

Figure 10. *The first step of the Chart Wizard.*

Figure 11. *The last step of the Chart Wizard enables you to insert the chart as a new sheet.*

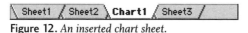

Figure 12. *An inserted chart sheet.*

To insert a worksheet

1. Click the tab for the sheet you want to insert a new sheet before (**Figure 7**).

2. Choose Worksheet from the Insert menu (**Figure 8**)

   or

   Press Shift F11 .

   A new worksheet is inserted before the one you originally selected (**Figure 9**).

✔ Tip

- By default, the new worksheet is named with the word *Sheet* followed by a number. I tell you how to rename sheets on the next page.

To insert a chart sheet

1. Click the tab for the sheet you want to insert a new sheet before (**Figure 7**).

2. Choose Chart from the Insert menu (**Figure 8**).

3. The Chart Wizard - Step 1 of 4 dialog box appears (**Figure 10**). Follow the steps in the Chart Wizard (as discussed in **Chapter 8**) to create a chart.

4. In the Chart Wizard - Step 4 of 4 dialog box (**Figure 11**), select the As new sheet radio button and enter a name for the sheet beside it. Then click Finish.

   A new chart sheet is inserted before the worksheet you originally selected (**Figure 12**).

Inserting Sheets

To delete a sheet

1. Click on the sheet tab for the sheet you want to delete to select it.

2. Choose Delete Sheet from the Edit menu (**Figure 13**).

3. A warning dialog box (**Figure 14**) or Office Assistant balloon appears. Click OK to confirm that you want to delete the sheet.

✔ Tips

■ As the dialog box warns, sheets are permanently deleted. That means even the Undo command won't get a deleted sheet back.

■ If another cell in the workbook contains a reference to a cell on the sheet you've deleted, that cell will display a #REF! error message. The formula in that cell will have to be rewritten.

To rename a sheet

1. Click on the sheet tab for the sheet you want to rename to make it active.

2. Choose Rename from the Sheet submenu under the Format menu (**Figure 15**).

   or

   Double-click the sheet tab.

3. The sheet tab becomes highlighted (**Figure 16**). Enter a new name for the sheet (**Figure 17**) and press Return or Enter to save it.

   The sheet tab displays the new name you gave it (**Figure 18**).

✔ Tips

■ The appearance of the Format menu (**Figure 15**) varies depending on the type of sheet.

■ Sheet names can be up to 31 characters long and can contain any character you can type from your keyboard.

Figure 13. *The Edit menu.*

Figure 14. *When you delete a sheet, Excel warns you that it will be permanently deleted.*

Figure 15. *The Sheet submenu under the Format menu.*

Figure 16. *Double-click the sheet tab to select its name.*

Figure 17. *Enter a new name for the sheet.*

Figure 18. *When you press Return, the new name is saved.*

Deleting & Renaming Sheets

Figure 19. *When you hide a sheet, its tab disappears.*

Figure 20. *When a sheet is hidden, the Unhide command is available on the Sheet submenu.*

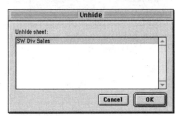

Figure 21. *The Unhide dialog box lists all hidden sheets.*

To hide a sheet

1. Select the sheet(s) you want to hide (**Figure 18**).

2. Choose Hide from the Sheet submenu under the Format menu (**Figure 15**).

   The sheet and its sheet tab disappear (**Figure 19**), just as if the sheet were deleted! But don't worry—the sheet still exists in the workbook file.

✔ Tips

- You cannot hide a sheet if it is the only sheet in a workbook.

- Don't confuse this command with the Hide command under the Window menu. These commands do two different things! I tell you about the Window menu's Hide command later in this chapter.

To unhide a sheet

1. Choose Unhide from the Sheet submenu under the Format menu (**Figure 20**).

2. In the Unhide dialog box that appears (**Figure 21**), select the sheet you want to unhide.

3. Click OK.

   The sheet and its sheet tab reappear.

✔ Tips

- You can only unhide one sheet at a time.

- If the Unhide command is gray (**Figure 15**), no sheets are hidden.

- Don't confuse this command with the Unhide command under the Window menu. I tell you about the Window menu's Unhide command later in this chapter.

Hiding & Unhiding Sheets

To move or copy a sheet

1. Select the tabs for the sheet(s) you want to move or copy.

2. Choose Move or Copy Sheet from the Edit menu (**Figure 13**). The Move or Copy dialog box appears (**Figure 22**).

3. Use the To book pop-up menu (**Figure 23**) to choose the workbook you want to move or copy the sheet(s) to.

4. Use the Before sheet scrolling list to choose the sheet you want the sheet(s) to be copied before.

5. If you want to copy or duplicate the sheet rather than move it, turn on the Create a copy check box.

6. Click OK.

✔ Tips

■ To move or copy sheets to another workbook, make sure that workbook is open (but not active) before you choose the Move or Copy Sheet command. Otherwise, it will not be listed in the To book pop-up menu (**Figure 23**).

■ If you choose (new book) from the To book pop-up menu (**Figure 23**) Excel creates a brand new, empty workbook file and places the selected sheet(s) into it.

■ You can use the Move or Copy Sheet command to change the order of sheets in a workbook. Just make sure the current workbook is selected in the To book pop-up menu (**Figure 23**). Then select the appropriate sheet from the Before sheet scrolling list or select (move to end).

■ You can also move or copy a sheet within a workbook by dragging. To move the sheet, simply drag the sheet tab to the new position (**Figure 24**). To copy the sheet, hold down (Option) while dragging the sheet tab (**Figure 25**).

Figure 22.
Use the Move or Copy dialog box to pick a destination for the selected sheet(s) and tell Excel to copy them rather than move them.

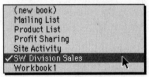

Figure 23. *The To book pop-up menu lists all the workbooks that are currently open.*

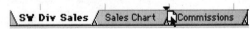

Figure 24. *You can also drag a sheet tab to move it...*

Figure 25. *...or hold down* (Option) *while dragging a sheet tab to copy it.*

Moving & Copying Sheets

Figure 26.
*The Window menu
offers commands for
working with—you
guessed it—windows.*

Figure 27. *When you open more than one window for
a file, the window number appears in the title bar…*

Figure 28.
*…and both
windows are
listed on the
Window menu.*

Workbook Windows

Like most Macintosh programs, Excel lets
you have more than one document open at
a time. But Excel goes a step further by
enabling you to open multiple windows for
the same workbook. Then, by arranging the
windows on screen, you can see and work
with more than one sheet in the same
workbook.

✔ Tip

■ I tell you how to create a new workbook
in **Chapter 2** and how to open an
existing workbook later in this chapter.

To activate another window

Choose the name of the window you want
to make active from the list of open windows at the bottom of the Window menu
(**Figure 26**).

or

Press ⌘M to go to the next window.

or

Press ⌘ Shift M to go to the previous
window.

To create a new window

1. Activate the workbook for which you
   want to create another window.

2. Choose New Window from the Window
   menu (**Figure 26**).

   A new window for that workbook appears (**Figure 27**) and the new window's
   name appears at the bottom of the
   Window menu (**Figure 28**).

✔ Tip

■ If more than one window is open for a
workbook and you close one of them,
the workbook does not close—just that
window. I tell you about closing windows on page 59.

Activating & Creating Windows

To arrange windows

1. Choose Arrange from the Window menu (**Figure 26**).

2. In the Arrange Windows dialog box that appears (**Figure 29**), select an Arrange option. **Figures 30** through **33** illustrate all of them.

3. To arrange only the windows of the active workbook, turn on the Windows of active workbook check box.

4. Click OK.

✔ Tips

- To work with one of the arranged windows, click in it to make it active.

- The window with the striped title bar is the active window.

- To make one of the arranged windows full size again, click on it to make it active and then click the window's zoom box. The window fills the screen while the other windows remain arranged behind it. Click the zoom box again to shrink it back down to its arranged size.

Figure 29.
The Arrange Windows dialog box.

Figure 30. *Tiled windows.*

Figure 31. *Horizontally arranged windows.*

Figure 32. *Vertically arranged windows.*

Figure 33. *Cascading windows.*

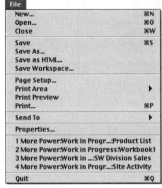

Figure 34. *The File menu.*

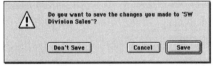

Figure 35. *Excel warns you when you attempt to close an unsaved document and gives you an opportunity to save it.*

Figure 36. *Hold down* (Shift) *to display the Close All command.*

Figure 37. *When a window is hidden, the Unhide command is available on the Window menu.*

Figure 38. *Use the Unhide dialog box to select the window you want to unhide.*

To close a window

Click the window's close box.

or

Choose Close from the File menu (**Figure 34**) or press ⌃⌘W.

✔ Tips

- If the file you are closing has unsaved changes, Excel warns you with a dialog box (**Figure 35**) or Office Assistant balloon. Click Save to save changes. I tell you about saving files later in this chapter.

- To close all open windows, hold down (Shift), pull down the File menu, and choose Close All (**Figure 36**).

To hide a window

1. Activate the window you want to hide.
2. Choose Hide from the Window menu (**Figure 26**).

✔ Tips

- Hiding a window is not the same as closing it. A hidden window remains open, even though it is not listed at the bottom of the Window menu.

- Hiding a window is not the same as hiding a sheet in a workbook. I tell you about hiding sheets earlier in this chapter.

To unhide a window

1. Choose Unhide from the Window menu (**Figure 37**).
2. In the Unhide dialog box that appears (**Figure 38**), choose the window you want to unhide.
3. Click OK.

✔ Tip

- If the Unhide command is gray (**Figures 26 and 28**), no windows are hidden.

Closing, Hiding, & Unhiding Windows

To change a window's magnification

1. Choose Zoom from the View menu (**Figure 39**).

2. In the Zoom dialog box that appears (**Figure 40**), select the radio button for the magnification you want.

3. Click OK.

or

1. Click the arrow beside the Zoom control on the Standard toolbar to display a menu of magnifications (**Figure 41**).

2. Choose the magnification you want from the menu.

✔ Tips

- To zoom selected cells so they fill the window, select the Fit selection radio button in the Zoom dialog box (**Figure 40**) or choose the Selection command on the Zoom button's menu (**Figure 41**).

- You can enter a custom magnification in the Zoom dialog box (**Figure 40**) by selecting the Custom radio button and entering a value of your choice.

- You can enter a custom magnification in the Zoom control on the Standard toolbar by clicking the value in the box to select it, typing in a new value (**Figure 42**), and pressing Return or Enter.

- Custom zoom percentages must be between 10% and 400%.

- Zooming the window using techniques discussed here does not affect the way a worksheet will print.

- A "zoomed" window's sheet works just like any other worksheet.

- When you save a workbook, the magnification settings of its sheets are saved. When you reopen the workbook, the sheets appear with the last used zoom magnification.

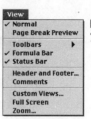

Figure 39. *The View menu.*

Figure 40. *Use the Zoom dialog box to set the window's magnification.*

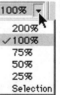

Figure 41. *You can also choose a magnification option from the Zoom menu on the Standard toolbar.*

Figure 42. *You can enter a custom zoom percentage in the Zoom box on the Standard toolbar.*

Figure 43. *Position the cell pointer where you want the split to occur.*

Figure 44. *The window splits.*

Changing a Window's Magnification

Figure 45. Position the mouse pointer on the split bar at the end of the scroll bar.

			Total	
			3735	
			1207	

Figure 46. *Drag the split bar into the window.*

[spreadsheet figure: Profit Sharing]

Figure 47. *When you release the mouse button, the window splits.*

Figure 48. *You can use the Remove Split command to remove a window split.*

Window
New Window
Arrange...
Hide
Unhide...
Remove Split
Freeze Panes
1 SW Division Sales
2 Site Activity
✓ 3 Profit Sharing
4 Mailing List

To split a window

1. Position the cell pointer in the cell immediately below and to the right of where you want the split(s) to occur (**Figure 43**).

2. Choose Split from the Window menu (**Figure 26**).

   The window splits at the location you specified (**Figure 44**).

or

1. Position the mouse pointer on the black split bar at the top of the vertical scroll bar or right end of the horizontal scroll bar. The mouse pointer turns into a double line with arrows coming out of it (**Figure 45**).

2. Press the mouse button down and drag. A dark split bar moves along with the mouse pointer (**Figure 46**).

3. Release the mouse button.

   The window splits at the bar (**Figure 47**).

✔ Tip

- Splitting a window enables you to see and work with two or more parts of a sheet at a time.

To adjust the size of panes

1. Position the mouse pointer on a split bar.

2. Press the mouse button down and drag until the split bar is in the desired position.

3. Release the mouse button.

   The window split moves.

To remove a window split

Choose Remove Split from the Window menu (**Figure 48**).

or

Double-click a split bar.

Splitting Windows

Saving Files

As you work with a file, everything you do is stored in only one place: *random access memory* or *RAM*. The contents of RAM are a lot like the light in a lightbulb—as soon as you turn it off or pull the plug, it's gone. Your hard disk or a floppy disk provides a much more permanent type of storage area. You use the Save command to copy the workbook file in RAM to disk.

✔ Tip

■ It's a very good idea to save documents frequently as you work to prevent data loss in the event of a computer problem.

To save a workbook file for the first time

1. Choose Save or Save As from the File menu (**Figure 34**) or press ⌃⌘⑤.

   or

   Click the Save button on the Standard toolbar.

2. Use the Save As dialog box that appears (**Figure 49**) to navigate to the folder (and disk, if necessary) in which you want to save the file:

   ▲ Use the directory pop-up menu near the top of the dialog box (**Figure 50**) to back out of the current folder.

   ▲ Double-click a folder to open it.

   ▲ Click the New button to create a new folder within the current folder. Enter the name for the folder in the New Folder dialog box (**Figure 51**) and click the Create button.

3. Enter a name for the file in the Save as edit box.

4. Click the Save button.

   The file is saved to disk. Its name appears in the window's title bar (**Figure 52**).

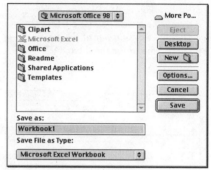

Figure 49. *The Save As dialog box.*

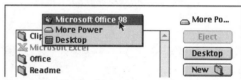

Figure 50. *Use the directory pop-up menu to back out of the current folder.*

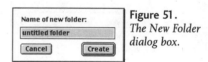

Figure 51. *The New Folder dialog box.*

Figure 52. *The file's name appears in the title bar.*

Figure 53.
Use the Save File as Type pop-up menu to save the document as a template or another type of file.

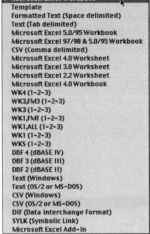

Figure 54.
Excel double-checks to make sure you want to overwrite a file with the same name.

✔ Tips

■ You can use the Save File as Type pop-up menu at the bottom of the Save As dialog box (**Figure 53**) to specify a format for the file or active sheet. This enables you to save the document as an Excel 98 template or in a format that can be opened and read by other versions of Excel or other applications.

■ Macintosh file names can be up to 31 characters long and can contain any character except a colon (:).

■ If you save a file with the same name and same disk location as another file, a dialog box appears, asking if you want to replace the file (**Figure 54**).

▲ Click the Replace button to replace the file already on disk with the file you are saving.

▲ Click the Cancel button to return to the Save As dialog box where you can enter a new name or specify a new disk location.

To save changes to a file

Choose Save from the File menu (**Figure 34**) or press ⌃⌘⑤.

or

Click the Save button on the Standard toolbar.

The file is saved with the same name in the same location on disk.

To save a file with a different name or in a different location

1. Choose Save As from the File menu (**Figure 34**).

2. Follow steps 2 and/or 3 on the previous page to select a new disk location and/or enter a different name for the file.

3. Click the Save button.

Saving Files

To set save options

1. Click the Options button in the Save As dialog box (**Figure 49**) to display the Save Options dialog box (**Figure 55**).

2. To tell Excel to always save the previous version of the file as a backup copy every time you save the file, turn on the Always create backup check box.

3. Set File sharing options as desired:

   ▲ **Password to open** enables you to specify a password that must be entered to open the file. **Figure 56** shows the dialog box that appears when you attempt to open a file with this option set.

   ▲ **Password to modify** enables you to specify a password that must be entered to save modifications to the file. **Figure 57** shows the dialog box that appears when you attempt to open a file with this option set.

   ▲ **Read-only recommended**, when turned on, tells Excel to display a dialog box (**Figure 58**) or Office Assistant balloon that recommends that the file be opened as a read-only file. If the file is opened as read-only, changes to the file must be saved in a file with a different name or in a different disk location.

3. Click OK to save your settings.

✔ Tip

■ If you set a password in the File sharing options, don't forget the password or you may be locked out of the file!

Figure 55. *Use the Save Options dialog box to set backup, password, and read-only options.*

Figure 56. *A dialog box like this appears when you attempt to open a file that requires a password to open.*

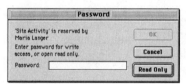

Figure 57. *A dialog box like this appears when you attempt to open a file that requires a password to modify.*

Figure 58. *A dialog box like this appears when you attempt to open a file that has the Read-only recommended option enabled.*

Figure 59. *The Open dialog box.*

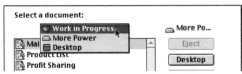

Figure 60. *Use the directory pop-up menu to back out of the current folder.*

Figure 61. *You can narrow down or expand the list of files shown by choosing an option from the List Files of Type pop-up menu.*

Opening Existing Files

Once a file has been saved on disk, you can reopen it to read it, modify it, or print it.

To open an existing file

1. Choose Open from the File menu **(Figure 34)** or press ⌘O.

   or

   Click the Open button on the Standard toolbar.

2. Use the Open dialog box that appears **(Figure 59)** to locate the file that you want to open:

   ▲ Use the directory pop-up menu near the top of the dialog box **(Figure 60)** to back out of the current folder.

   ▲ Double-click a folder to open it.

3. Select the file that you want to open and click the Open button.

   or

   Double-click the file that you want to open.

✔ Tips

■ To view only specific types of files in the Open dialog box, select a format from the List Files of Type pop-up menu at the bottom of the dialog box **(Figure 61)**.

■ If you select All Files from the List Files of Type pop-up menu **(Figure 61)**, you can open just about any kind of file. Be aware, however, that a file in an incompatible format may not appear the way you expect when opened.

■ Use the Find File button in the Open dialog box to search for a file based on criteria you specify.

■ You can open a recent file by selecting it from the list of recently opened files at the bottom of the File menu **(Figure 34)**.

Opening Files

USING FUNCTIONS IN FORMULAS 5

	A	B	C
1	*Product Inventory*		
2			
3	**Item Name**	**Item No.**	**Qty**
4	Dogzilla	D-439	159
5	Oceanic	O-571	341
6	Delayed Impact	D-845	415
7	Mask of Zero	M-482	167
8	Genus II	G-058	684
9	Eisenhower	E-473	218
10	Men in White	M-400	189
11	Loaded Weapon IV	L-108	581
12			

Figure 1. *Using the SUM function makes it easier to add up a column of numbers.*

Function name   Arguments

SUM(number1,number2,…)

Figure 2. *The parts of a function. Bold components are required.*

Functions

A function is a predefined formula for making a specific kind of calculation. Functions make it quicker and easier to write formulas.

For example, say you need to add up a column of numbers like the one in **Figure 1**. It's perfectly acceptable to write a formula using cell references separated by the addition operator (+) like this:

$$=C4+C5+C6+C7+C8+C9+C10+C11$$

But rather than enter a lengthy formula, you can use the SUM function to add up the same numbers like this:

$$=SUM(C4:C11)$$

The SUM function is only one of over 200 functions built into Excel. I list all functions in **Appendix B**.

Anatomy of a Function

As shown in **Figure 2**, each function has two main parts.

- The *function name* determines what the function does.
- The *arguments* determine what values or cell references the function should use in its calculation. Arguments are enclosed in parentheses and, if there's more than one, separated by commas.

✔ Tips

- If a function comes at the beginning of a formula, it must begin with an equal sign (=).
- Some arguments are optional. In the SUM function, for example, you can have only one argument, like a reference to a single range of cells.

Arguments

The argument component of a function can consist of any of the following:

- **Numbers (Figure 3)**. Like any other formula, however, the result of a function that uses values for arguments will not change unless the formula is changed.

- **Text (Figure 4)**. Excel includes a number of functions just for text. I tell you about them later in this chapter.

- **Cell references (Figures 4 through 8)**. This is a practical way to write functions, since when you change cell contents, the results of functions that reference them change automatically.

- **Formulas (Figures 6 and 7)**. This lets you create complex formulas that perform a series of calculations at once.

- **Functions (Figures 7 and 8)**. When a function includes another function as one of its arguments, it's called *nesting functions*.

- **Error values (Figure 8)**. You may find this useful to "flag" errors or missing information in a worksheet.

- **Logical values**. Some function arguments require TRUE or FALSE values.

Figure 3. *This example uses numbers as arguments for the DATE function.*

	A	B	C	D
1	**Commissions Report**			
2				
3		Rates		
4	Over $400	15%		
5	Up to $400	10%		
6				
7		Sales	Amt. Due	Comment
8	John	443.16	66.47	Good Work!
9	Jean	512.84	76.93	Good Work!
10	Joe	328.69	32.87	Try harder.
11	Joan	401.98	60.3	Good Work!

=IF(B8>400,"Good Work!","Try harder.")

Figure 4. *This example uses cell references, numbers, and text as arguments for the IF function.*

Figure 5. *This example shows two different ways to use cell references as arguments for the SUM function.*

	A	B
1	**Commissions R**	
2		
3		Rates
4	Over $400	15%
5	Up to $400	10%
6		
7		Sales
8	John	443.16
9	Jean	512.84
10	Joe	328.69
11	Joan	401.98
12	**Total**	1686.67

=SUM(B8:B11) *or*
=SUM(B8,B9,B10,B11)

	A	B	C	D
1	**Commissions Report**			
2				
3		Sales	Rate	Amt. Due
4	John	443.16	15%	66.47
5	Joan	512.84	10%	

Figure 6. *This example uses a formula as an argument for the ROUND function.*

=ROUND(B4*C4,2)

	A	B	C
1	**Commissions Report**		
2			
3		Rates	
4	Over $400	15%	
5	Up to $400	10%	
6			
7		Sales	Amt. Due C
8	John	443.16	66.47
9	Joan	512.84	

=ROUND(IF(B8>400,B8*B4,B8*B5),2)

Figure 7. *This example uses the ROUND and IF functions to calculate commissions based on a rate that changes according to sales.*

Figure 8. *This example uses three functions (IF, COUNTBLANK, and SUM), cell references, and error values to either indicate missing information or add a column of numbers.*

	A	B
1	**Commissions R**	
2		
3		Rates
4	Over $400	15%
5	Up to $400	10%
6		
7		Sales
8	John	443.16
9	Jean	512.84
10	Joe	
11	Joan	401.98
12	**Total**	#N/A

=IF(COUNTBLANK(B8:B11)>0,#N/A,SUM(B8:B11))

Figure 9.
If you don't enter parentheses correctly, Excel can get confused.

Figure 10. *Sometimes, Excel knows just what the problem is.*

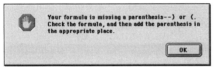

Figure 11. *The Formula AutoCorrect feature can fix common formula errors for you.*

Figure 12.
You can type in a function just like you type in any other formula.

	A	B
1	Commissions Re	
2		
3		Sales
4	John	443.16
5	Jean	512.84
6	Joe	328.69
7	Joan	401.98
8	Total	=SUM(B4:B7)

Figure 13.
When you press [Enter], the cell containing the function displays the result of the formula.

	A	B
1	Commissions R	
2		
3		Sales
4	John	443.16
5	Jean	512.84
6	Joe	328.69
7	Joan	401.98
8	Total	1686.67

Entering Functions

Excel offers several ways to enter a function:

- by typing
- by typing and clicking
- by using the Formula Palette

There is no "best" way—use the methods that you like most.

✔ Tips

- Function names are not case sensitive. *Sum* or *sum* is the same as *SUM*. Excel converts all function names to upper-case characters.

- Do not include spaces when writing formulas.

- When writing formulas with nested functions, it's important that you properly match parentheses. Excel helps you by boldfacing parentheses as you type them. If parentheses don't match, Excel either displays an error message (**Figures 9** and **10**) or offers to correct the error for you (**Figure 11**). Sometimes Excel will simply fix the error without displaying a message.

To enter a function by typing

1. Begin the formula by typing an equal sign (=).

2. Type in the function name.

3. Type an open parenthesis character.

4. Type in the value or cell reference for the first argument.

5. If entering more than one argument, type each of them in with commas between them.

6. Type a closed parenthesis character (**Figure 12**).

7. Press [Return] or [Enter] or click the Enter button on the formula bar.

   The result of the function is displayed in the cell (**Figure 13**).

To enter a function by typing & clicking

1. Begin the formula by typing an equal sign (=).

2. Type in the function name.

3. Type an open parenthesis character.

4. Type in a value or click on the cell whose reference you want to include as the first argument (**Figure 14**).

5. If entering more than one argument, type a comma, then type in a value or click on the cell for the next reference (**Figure 15**). Repeat this step for each argument in the function.

6. Type a closed parenthesis character (**Figure 16**).

7. Press (Return) or (Enter) or click the Enter button on the formula bar.

   The result of the function is displayed in the cell (**Figure 13**).

✔ Tips

■ To include a range by clicking, in step 4 or 5 above, drag the mouse pointer over the cells you want to include (**Figure 17**).

■ Be careful where you click or drag when entering a function or any formula. Each click or drag may add references to the formula! If you click on a cell by mistake, you can press ∂   to delete each character of the incorrectly added reference or click the Cancel button on the formula bar to start over from scratch.

Figure 14. *After typing the beginning of the function, you can click on cell references for arguments.*

Figure 15. *Type a comma before clicking to enter additional cell references for arguments.*

Figure 16. *Be sure to type a closed parenthesis character at the end of the function.*

Figure 17. *You can always enter a range in a formula by dragging, even when the range is an argument for a function.*

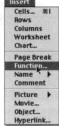

Figure 18.
Choosing Function from the Insert menu.

Figure 19. *The Paste Function dialog box.*

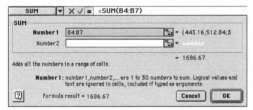

Figure 20. *The Formula Palette.*

Figure 21.
The Functions pop-up menu at the far left end of the formula bar.

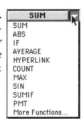

To enter a function with the Formula Palette

1. Choose Function from the Insert menu (**Figure 18**) or click the Paste Function button on the Standard toolbar.

2. In the Paste Function dialog box that appears (**Figure 19**), click to select a category in the Function category list on the left side of the dialog box.

3. Click to select a function from the Function name scrolling list on the right side of the dialog box. You may have to use the scroll bar to locate the function name you want.

4. Click OK.

    The Formula Palette appears beneath the formula bar (**Figure 20**). It provides information about the function you selected and may include one or more entries for the argument(s).

5. Enter a value or cell reference in the appropriate edit box for each required argument.

6. When you are finished entering function arguments, click OK.

    The Formula Palette closes and the result of the function is displayed in the cell (**Figure 13**).

✔ Tips

■ You can also open the Formula Palette by clicking the Edit Formula button in the formula bar. (This enables you to use the Formula Palette to enter or edit any formula, even if it doesn't include a function.) To paste a function into the Formula Palette, choose a specific function or More Functions from the Functions pop-up menu at the far left end of the formula bar (**Figure 21**).

continued on next page...

Using the Formula Palette

continued from previous page

■ In step 2, if you're not sure what category a function is in, select All. The Function name scrolling list displays all the functions Excel has to offer.

■ In step 5, you can click or drag in the worksheet window to enter a cell reference or range. To see obstructed worksheet cells, click the Hide Formula Palette button to collapse the Formula Palette (**Figure 22**). When you're finished selecting the cell or range, click the Display Formula Palette button to expand the Formula Palette and continue working with it.

■ In step 5, you can enter a function as an argument by clicking in the argument's edit box and choosing a specific function or More Functions from the Functions pop-up menu at the far left end of the formula bar (**Figure 21**). Although the Formula Palette only shows function options for one function at a time, you can view and edit the entire formula in the formula bar (**Figure 23**).

■ As you enter arguments in the Formula Palette, the calculated value of your entries appears at the bottom of the Formula Palette (**Figure 20**).

Figure 22. *You can collapse the Formula Palette to see and select cell references in the worksheet window.*

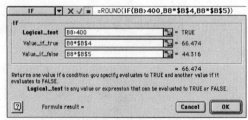

Figure 23. *Only one function's options appear in the Formula Palette at a time, but you can view and edit the entire formula in the formula bar.*

Figure 24.
When you click the AutoSum button, Excel writes a formula, guessing which cells you want to sum.

	A	B	
1		Southwes	
2		First Qua	
3		Jan	F
4	John	1254	
5	Jean	1865	
6	Joe	1614	
7	Joan	1987	
8	Totals	=SUM(B4:B7)	
9			

Math & Trig Functions

Excel's math and trig functions perform standard mathematical and trigonometric calculations. On the next few pages, I tell you about the most commonly used ones, starting with one so popular it even has its own toolbar button: SUM.

The SUM Function

The SUM function (**Figure 5**) adds up numbers. It uses the following syntax:

SUM(number1,number2,...)

Although the SUM function can accept up to 30 arguments separated by commas, only one is required.

To use the AutoSum button

1. Select the cell below the column or to the right of the row of numbers you want to add.

2. Click the AutoSum button on the Standard toolbar once.

   Excel examines the worksheet and makes a "guess" about which cells you want to add. It writes the corresponding formula and puts a marquee around the range of cells it used (**Figure 24**).

3. If the range in the formula is incorrect, type or select the correct range. Since the reference for the range of cells is selected in the formula, anything you type or select will automatically replace it.

4. When the formula is correct, press (Return) or (Enter), click the Enter button on the formula bar, or click the AutoSum button on the Standard toolbar a second time.

   The formula is entered and its results appear in the cell.

SUM & Using the AutoSum Button

To use the AutoSum button on multiple cells

1. Select a range of cells adjacent to the columns or rows you want to add (**Figure 25**).

2. Click the AutoSum button once. Excel writes the formulas in the cells you selected (**Figure 26**).

or

1. Select the cells containing the columns you want to add (**Figure 27**).

2. Click the AutoSum button once. Excel writes all the formulas in the row of cells immediately below the ones you selected (**Figure 28**).

or

1. Select the cells containing the columns and rows you want to add, along with the empty row beneath them and the empty column to the right of them (**Figure 29**).

2. Click the AutoSum button once. Excel writes all the formulas in the bottom and rightmost cells (**Figure 30**).

✔ Tip

■ Be sure to check the formulas Excel writes when you use the AutoSum button. Excel is smart, but it's no mind-reader. The cells it includes may not be the ones you had in mind!

Figure 25. *Select the cells adjacent to the columns (or rows) of cells that you want to add.*

Figure 26. *When you click the AutoSum button, Excel enters the appropriate formulas in the cells.*

Figure 27. *Select the cells containing the columns that you want to add.*

Figure 28. *When you click the AutoSum button, Excel enters the appropriate formulas in the cells beneath the selected cells.*

Figure 29. *Select the cells you want to add, along with the cells in which you want the totals to appear.*

Figure 30. *When you click the AutoSum button, Excel enters the appropriate formulas in the empty cells of the selection.*

	A	B	C	D	E	F
1	Item	Cost	Markup	Qty	Value	
2	Product A	1.54	115%	152	269.192	=PRODUCT(B2:D2)
3	Product B	3.58	250%	142	1270.9	=PRODUCT(B3,C3,D3)

Figure 31. *Two ways to use the PRODUCT function. The formulas in column E are shown in column F.*

	A	B	C	D	E	F
1		Sales	Rate	Amount Due	Rounded	
2	John	14528.16	15%	2179.224	2179.22	=ROUND(D2,2)
3	Jean	45284.48	20%	9056.896	9056.9	=ROUND(D3,2)
4	Joe	36547.19	15%	5482.0785	5482.08	=ROUND(D4,2)
5	Joan	27582.43	15%	4137.3645	4137.36	=ROUND(D5,2)

Figure 32. *Use the ROUND function to round numbers to the number of decimal places you specify. The formulas in column E are shown in column F.*

	A	E	F	G
1		**Total**	**Rounded**	
2	Sales	154258.65	154300	=ROUND(E2,-2)
3	Cost	59042.97		

Figure 33. *You can also use the ROUND function to round numbers to the left of the decimal point. The formula in cell F2 is shown in cell G2.*

	A	B	C	D	E
1		**Sales**	**Rate**	**Amount Due**	
2	John	14528.16	15%	2179.22	=ROUND(B2*C2,2)
3	Jean	45284.48	20%	9056.9	=ROUND(B3*C3,2)
4	Joe	36547.19	15%	5482.08	=ROUND(B4*C4,2)
5	Joan	27582.43	15%	4137.36	=ROUND(B5*C5,2)

Figure 34. *You can also use the ROUND function to round the results of another formula or function. The formulas in column D are shown in column E.*

The PRODUCT Function

The PRODUCT function (**Figure 31**) multiplies its arguments much like the SUM function adds them. It uses the following syntax:

PRODUCT(number1,number2,…)

Although the PRODUCT function can accept up to 30 arguments separated by commas, only one is required.

The ROUND Function

The ROUND function (**Figure 32**) rounds a number to the number of decimal places you specify. It uses the following syntax:

ROUND(number,num_digits)

Both arguments are required. The num_digits argument specifies how many decimal places the number should be rounded to. If 0, the number is rounded to a whole number. If less than 0, the number is rounded on the left side of the decimal point (**Figure 33**).

✔ Tips

- Rather than make a calculation in one cell and round it in another as shown in **Figures 32** and **33**, combine the two formulas in one cell (**Figure 34**).
- The ROUNDUP function works like the ROUND function, but it always rounds up to the next higher number. The num_digits argument is not required; if omitted, the number is rounded to the next highest whole number.
- The ROUNDDOWN function works just like the ROUNDUP function, but it always rounds down.

PRODUCT & ROUND

The EVEN & ODD Functions

The EVEN function (**Figure 35**) rounds a number up to the next even number. It uses the following syntax:

EVEN(number)

The number argument, which is required, is the number you want to round.

The ODD function works exactly the same way, but rounds a number up to the next odd number.

The INT Function

The INT function (**Figure 36**) rounds a number down to the nearest whole number or integer. It uses the following syntax:

INT(number)

The number argument, which is required, is the number you want to convert to an integer.

The ABS Function

The ABS function (**Figure 37**) returns the absolute value of a number—it leaves positive numbers alone but turns negative numbers into positive numbers. (Is that high school math coming back to you yet?) It uses the following syntax:

ABS(number)

The number argument, which is required, is the number you want to convert to an absolute value.

	A	B	C	D	E
1	Number	Even		Odd	
2	159.487	160	=EVEN(A2)	161	=ODD(A2)
3	1647.1	1648	=EVEN(A3)	1649	=ODD(A3)
4	-14.48	-16	=EVEN(A4)	-15	=ODD(A4)
5					

Figure 35. *Use the EVEN and ODD functions to round a number up to the next even or odd number. The formulas in columns B and D are shown in columns C and E.*

	A	B	C
1	Number	Integer	
2	159.487	159	=INT(A2)
3	1647.1	1647	=INT(A3)
4	-14.48	-15	=INT(A4)
5			

Figure 36. *Use the INT function to round a number down to the next whole number. The formulas in column B are shown in column C.*

	A	B	C
1	Number	Absolute Value	
2	159.487	159.487	=ABS(A2)
3	1647.1	1647.1	=ABS(A3)
4	-14.48	14.48	=ABS(A4)
5			

Figure 37. *Use the ABS function to get the absolute value of a number. The formulas in column B are shown in column C.*

	A	B	C
1	Number	Square Root	
2	36	6	=SQRT(A2)
3	22	4.69041576	=SQRT(A3)
4	-10	#NUM!	=SQRT(A4)
5			

Figure 38. *Use the SQRT function to find the square root of a number.*

	A	B	C
1	Number	Square Root	
2	36	6	=SQRT(ABS(A2))
3	22	4.69041576	=SQRT(ABS(A3))
4	-10	3.16227766	=SQRT(ABS(A4))
5			

Figure 39. *By combining the SQRT and ABS functions, you can prevent #NUM! errors when calculating the square root of a negative number. The formulas in column B are shown in column C.*

Figure 40. *The PI function calculates π to 14 decimal places.*

3.14159265358979

	A	B	C	D
1	Low	High	Random	
2	0	1	0.71651404	=RAND()
3	0	1000	699.319814	=RAND()*(B3-A3)+A3
4	36	42	41.9043917	=RAND()*(B4-A4)+A4
5	3458	4835	3776.38449	=RAND()*(B5-A5)+A5
6				

Figure 41. *The RAND function can be used alone or as part of a formula to generate a random number within a range. The formulas in column C are shown in column D.*

The SQRT Function

The SQRT function (**Figure 38**) calculates the square root of a number. It uses the following syntax:

SQRT(number)

The number argument, which is required, is the number you want to find the square root of.

✔ Tip

- You'll get a #NUM! error message if you try to use the SQRT function to calculate the square root of a negative number (**Figure 38**). Prevent the error by using the ABS function in the formula (**Figure 39**).

The PI Function

The PI function (**Figure 40**) returns the value of π, accurate up to 15 digits. It uses the following syntax:

PI()

The RAND Function

The RAND (**Figure 41**) function generates a random number greater than or equal to 0 and less than 1 each time the worksheet is calculated. It uses the following syntax:

RAND()

✔ Tips

- Although there is no argument in either the PI or RAND function, if you fail to include the parentheses characters, you'll get a #NAME? error.

- To generate a random number between two numbers (low and high), write a formula like this:

    =RAND()*(high-low)+low

    See **Figure 41** for some examples.

- The calculated value of a formula using the RAND function will change each time the worksheet is recalculated.

SQRT, PI, & RAND

The RADIANS & DEGREES Functions

The RADIANS function converts degrees to radians. The DEGREES function converts radians to degrees. They use the following syntax:

RADIANS(angle)

DEGREES(angle)

The angle argument, which is required, is the angle you want converted. Use degrees in the RADIANS function and radians in the DEGREES function. Both functions are illustrated in Figure 42.

The SIN Function

The SIN function (**Figure 42**) calculates the sine of an angle. It uses the following syntax:

SIN(number)

The number argument, which is required, is the angle, in radians, for which you want the sine calculated.

The COS Function

The COS function (**Figure 42**) calculates the cosine of an angle. It uses the following syntax:

COS(number)

The number argument, which is required, is the angle, in radians, for which you want the cosine calculated.

The TAN Function

The TAN function (**Figure 42**) calculates the tangent of an angle. It uses the following syntax:

TAN(number)

The number argument, which is required, is the angle, in radians, for which you want the tangent calculated.

	A	B	C	D	E
1		Radians		Degrees	
2	Entry	1		45	
3					
4	Convert to Radians			0.78539816	=RADIANS(D2)
5	Convert to Degrees	57.2957795	=DEGREES(B2)		
6					
7	Sine	0.84147098	=SIN(D2)	0.70710678	=SIN(RADIANS(D2))
8	Arcsine	1.57079633	=ASIN(D2)	0.90333911	=ASIN(RADIANS(D2))
9	Cosine	0.54030231	=COS(D2)	0.70710678	=COS(RADIANS(D2))
10	Arccosine	0	=ACOS(D2)	0.66745722	=ACOS(RADIANS(D2))
11	Tangent	1.55740772	=TAN(D2)	1	=TAN(RADIANS(D2))
12	Arctangent	0.78539816	=ATAN(D2)	0.66577375	=ATAN(RADIANS(D2))

Figure 42. *This example shows several trig functions in action. The formulas for columns B and D are shown in columns C and E.*

✔ **Tip**

■ To calculate the arcsine, arccosine, or arctangent of an angle, use the ASIN, ACOS, or ATAN function (**Figure 42**). Each works the same as its counterpart.

RADIANS, DEGREES, SIN, COS, & TAN

	A	B	C
1	*Product Inventory*		
2			
3	**Item Name**	**Price**	
4	Dogzilla	14.99	
5	Oceanic	15.99	
6	Delayed Impact	8.99	
7	Mask of Zero	24.99	
8	Genus II	19.99	
9	Eisenhower	19.99	
10	Men in White	22.99	
11	Loaded Weapon IV	13.99	
12			
13	**Average**	17.74	=AVERAGE(B4:B11)
14	**Median**	17.99	=MEDIAN(B4:B11)
15	**Mode**	19.99	=MODE(B4:B11)
16	**Minimum**	8.99	=MIN(B4:B11)
17	**Maximum**	24.99	=MAX(B4:B11)

Figure 43. *This example shows a few of Excel's statistical functions at work. The formulas for column B are shown in column C.*

Statistical Functions

Excel's statistical functions make it easy to perform complex statistical analyses. Here's a handful of the functions I think you'll use most.

The AVERAGE Function

The AVERAGE function (**Figure 43**) calculates the average or mean of its arguments. It uses the following syntax:

>   AVERAGE(number1,number2,...)

The MEDIAN Function

The MEDIAN function (**Figure 43**) calculates the median of its arguments. The median is the "halfway point" of the numbers—half the numbers have higher values and half have lower values. The MEDIAN function uses the following syntax:

>   MEDIAN(number1,number2,...)

The MODE Function

The MODE function (**Figure 43**) returns the mode of its arguments. The mode is the most common value. The MODE function uses the following syntax:

>   MODE(number1,number2,...)

If there are no repeated values, Excel returns a #NUM! error.

The MIN & MAX Functions

The MIN function (**Figure 43**) returns the minimum value of its arguments while the MAX function returns the maximum value of its arguments. They use the following syntax:

>   MIN(number1,number2,...)
>   MAX(number1,number2,...)

✔ Tips

- Excel's AVERAGE function does not include empty cells when calculating the average for a range of cells.

- Although the AVERAGE, MEDIAN, MODE, MIN and MAX functions can each accept up to 30 arguments separated by commas, only one argument is required.

AVERAGE, MEDIAN, MODE, MIN, & MAX

The COUNT & COUNTA Functions

The COUNT function counts how many numbers are referenced by its arguments. The COUNTA function counts how many values are referenced by its arguments. Although this may sound like the same thing, it isn't—COUNT includes only numbers or formulas resulting in numbers while COUNTA includes any non-blank cell. **Figure 44** shows an example that clarifies the difference.

The COUNT and COUNTA functions use the following syntax:

COUNT(number1,number2,...)

COUNTA(number1,number2,...)

Although either function can accept up to 30 arguments separated by commas, only one is required.

The STDEV & STDEVP Functions

Standard deviation is a statistical measurement of how much values vary from the average or mean for the group. The STDEV function calculates the standard deviation based on a random sample of the entire population. The STDEVP function calculates the standard deviation based on the entire population. **Figure 45** shows an example of each.

The STDEV and STDEVP functions use the following syntax:

STDEV(number1,number2,...)

STDEVP(number1,number2,...)

Although either function can accept up to 30 arguments separated by commas, only one is required.

✔ Tip

■ To get accurate results from the STDEVP function, the arguments must include data for the entire population.

Figure 44. *This example of the COUNT and COUNTA functions illustrates that while the COUNT function counts only cells containing numbers (including dates and times), the COUNTA function counts all non-blank cells. The formulas in column B are shown in column C.*

Figure 45. *In this example, the STDEV function assumes that the range is a random sample from a larger population of information. The STDEVP function assumes that the same data is the entire population. That's why the results differ. The formulas in column B are shown in column C.*

COUNT, COUNTA, STDEV, & STDEVP

	A	B	C
1	*Depreciation Comparison*		
2			
3	Cost	$ 5,000.00	
4	Salvage Value	$ 250.00	
5	Life (in years)	5	
6			
7	Year	1	
8	Straight Line	$950.00	=SLN(B3,B4,B5)
9	Declining Balance	$2,255.00	=DB(B3,B4,B5,B7)
10	Double Declining Balance	$2,000.00	=DDB(B3,B4,B5,B7)
11	Sum of the Year's Digits	$1,583.33	=SYD(B3,B4,B5,B7)

Figure 46. *A simple worksheet lets you compare different methods of depreciation using the SLN, DB, DDB, and SYD functions. The formulas in column B are shown in column C.*

Financial Functions

Excel's financial functions enable you to calculate depreciation, evaluate investment opportunities, or calculate the monthly payments on a loan. On the next few pages, I tell you about a few of the functions I think you'll find useful.

The SLN Function

The SLN function (**Figure 46**) calculates straight line depreciation for an asset. It uses the following syntax:

SLN(cost,salvage,life)

Cost is the acquisition cost of the asset, salvage is the salvage or scrap value, and life is the useful life expressed in years or months. All three arguments are required.

The DB Function

The DB function (**Figure 46**) calculates declining balance depreciation for an asset. It uses the following syntax:

DB(cost,salvage,life,period,month)

The cost, salvage, and life arguments are the same as for the SLN function. Period, which must be expressed in the same units as life, is the period for which you want to calculate depreciation. These first four arguments are required. Month is the number of months in the first year of the asset's life. If omitted, 12 is assumed.

The DDB Function

The DDB function (**Figure 46**) calculates the double-declining balance depreciation for an asset. It uses the following syntax:

DDB(cost,salvage,life,period,factor)

The cost, salvage, life, and period arguments are the same as for the DB function and are required. Factor is the rate at which the balance declines. If omitted, 2 is assumed.

The SYD Function

The SYD function (**Figure 46**) calculates the sum-of-years' digits depreciation for an asset. It uses the following syntax:

SYD(cost,salvage,life,period)

The cost, salvage, life, and period arguments are the same as for the DB and DDB functions. All arguments are required.

SLN, DB, DDB, & SYD

The PMT Function

The PMT function calculates the periodic payment for an annuity based on constant payments and interest rate. This function is commonly used for two purposes: to calculate the monthly payments on a loan and to calculate the monthly contribution necessary to reach a specific savings goal.

The PMT function uses the following syntax:

PMT(rate,nper,pv,fv,type)

Rate is the interest rate per period, nper is the total number of periods, and pv is the present value or current worth of the total payments. These three arguments are required. The fv argument is the future value or balance desired at the end of the payments. If omitted, 0 is assumed. Type indicates when payments are due: use 0 for payments at the end of the period and 1 for payments at the beginning of the period. If omitted, 0 is assumed.

To calculate loan payments

1. Enter the text and number values shown in **Figure 47** in a worksheet. If desired, use your own amounts.

2. Enter the following formula in cell *B5*: =PMT(B2/12,B3,B1)

   This formula uses only the first three arguments of the PMT function. The rate argument is divided by 12 to arrive at a monthly interest rate since the number of periods is expressed in months and payments will be made monthly (all time units must match).

3. Press Return or Enter or click the Enter button on the formula bar.

The result of the formula appears in the cell as a negative number (**Figure 48**) because it is an outgoing cash flow. (A minus sign or parentheses indicates a negative number.)

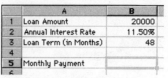

	A	B
1	Loan Amount	20000
2	Annual Interest Rate	11.50%
3	Loan Term (in Months)	48
4		
5	Monthly Payment	

Figure 47. *A basic structure for a worksheet that calculates loan payments.*

	A	B
1	Loan Amount	20000
2	Annual Interest Rate	11.50%
3	Loan Term (in Months)	48
4		
5	Monthly Payment	($521.78)

Figure 48. *The loan payment worksheet after entering a formula with the PMT function.*

	A	B
1	Loan Amount	25000
2	Annual Interest Rate	11.50%
3	Loan Term (in Months)	48
4		
5	Monthly Payment	($652.23)

Figure 49. *Playing "what-if." In this example, I increased the loan amount to see how much more the monthly payment would be.*

✔ Tips

- If you prefer, you can use the Formula Palette to write the formula in step 2. Be sure to include the formula *B2/12* in the rate edit box. Leave the fv and type edit boxes blank.

- You can calculate loan payments without creating a whole worksheet—simply enter values rather than cell references as arguments for the PMT function. But using cell references makes it easy to play "what-if"—see how payments change when the loan amount, rate, and number of periods changes. **Figure 49** shows an example.

	A	B	C	D
1	Loan Amount	20000		
2	Annual Interest Rate	11.50%		
3	Loan Term (in Months)	48		
4				
5	Monthly Payment	($521.78)		
6				
7		Payment Number	Beg Balance	Interest	Principal
8		1			
9		2			
10		3			
11		4			

Figure 50. *To create an amortization table, start with this simple worksheet.*

	A	B	C	D
1	Loan Amount	20000		
2	Annual Interest Rate	11.50%		
3	Loan Term (in Months)	48		
4				
5	Monthly Payment	($521.78)		
6				
7		Payment Number	Beg Balance	Interest	Principal
8		1	20000	191.67	$330.11
9		2	$19,669.89		
10		3			
11		4			

Figure 51. *Add formulas to calculate interest, principal, and beginning balance.*

	A	B	C	D
1	Loan Amount	20000		
2	Annual Interest Rate	11.50%		
3	Loan Term (in Months)	48		
4				
5	Monthly Payment	($521.78)		
6				
7		Payment Number	Beg Balance	Interest	Principal
8		1	20000	191.67	$330.11
9		2	$19,669.89	188.5	$333.28
10		3	$19,336.61	185.31	$336.47
11		4	$19,000.14	182.08	$339.70
12		5	$18,660.44	178.83	$342.95
13		6	$18,317.49	175.54	$346.24
14		7	$17,971.25	172.22	$349.56

Figure 52. *Then copy the formulas down each column for all months of the loan term.*

To create an amortization table

1. Create a loan payment worksheet following the steps on the previous page.

2. Enter text and number values for headings as shown in **Figure 50**. Make sure there is a row with a payment number for each month of the loan term in cell *B3*.

3. In cell *B8*, enter *=B1*.

4. In cell *C8*, enter the following formula: *=ROUND(B8*$B$2/12,2)*

   This formula calculates the interest for the period and rounds it to two decimal places.

5. In cell *D8*, enter the following formula: *=-$B$5-C8*

   This formula calculates the amount of principal paid for the current month.

6. In cell *B9*, enter the following formula: *=ROUND(B8-D8,2)*

   This formula calculates the current month's beginning balance, rounded to two decimal places.

   At this point, your worksheet should look like the one in **Figure 51**.

7. Use the fill handle to copy the formula in cell *B9* down the column for each month.

8. Use the Fill handle to copy the formulas in cells *C8* and *D8* down the columns for each month.

   Your amortization table is complete. It should look like the one in **Figure 52**.

✔ Tip

- If desired, you can add column totals at the bottom of columns *C* and *D* to total interest (you may be shocked) and principal (which should match cell *B1*).

To calculate contributions to reach a savings goal

1. Enter the text and number values shown in **Figure 53** in a worksheet. If desired, use your own amounts.

2. Enter the following formula in cell *B5*:
   =PMT(B2/12,B3,,B1)

   This formula uses the first four arguments of the PMT function, although the pv argument is left blank—that's why there are two commas after *B3*. The rate argument is divided by 12 to arrive at a monthly interest rate.

3. Press [Return] or [Enter] or click the Enter button on the formula bar.

   The result of the formula is expressed as a negative number (**Figure 54**) because it is an outgoing cash flow. (A minus sign or parentheses indicates a negative number.)

✔ Tips

■ If you prefer, you can use the Formula Palette to write the formula in step 2. Be sure to include the formula *B2/12* in the rate edit box. Leave the pv and type edit boxes blank.

■ You can calculate the amount of a monthly contribution to reach a savings goal without creating a whole worksheet—simply enter values rather than cell references as arguments for the PMT function. But using cell references makes it easy to play "what-if"—see how contributions change when the desired amount, rate, and number of periods changes. **Figure 55** shows an example.

■ To force an outgoing cash flow to be expressed as a positive number, simply include a minus sign (-) right after the equals sign (=) at the beginning of the formula.

	A	B
1	Desired Amount	50000
2	Annual Interest Rate	8.25%
3	Months	120
4		
5	Monthly Contribution	

Figure 53. *A basic structure for a worksheet to calculate contributions to reach a savings goal.*

	A	B
1	Desired Amount	50000
2	Annual Interest Rate	8.25%
3	Months	120
4		
5	Monthly Contribution	($269.51)

Figure 54. *The PMT function calculates the monthly contribution.*

	A	B
1	Desired Amount	30000
2	Annual Interest Rate	8.25%
3	Months	120
4		
5	Monthly Contribution	($161.71)

Figure 55. *Change one value and the result of the formula changes.*

	A	B
1	Monthly Payment	150
2	Annual Interest Rate	8.50%
3	Number of Months	12
4		
5	Future Value	($1,871.81)
6		=FV(B@/12,B3,B1)
7		

Figure 56. *Use the FV function to calculate the future value of constant cash flows, like those of periodic payroll savings deductions. The formula in cell B5 is shown in cell B6.*

	A	B
1	Initial Investment	-25000
2		
3	Monthly Cash In	200
4	Annual Interest Rate	9%
5	Number of Months	360
6		
7	Present Value	($24,856.37)
8		=PV(B4/12,B5,B3)
9		

Figure 57. *This example uses the PV function to determine whether an investment is a good one. (It isn't because the present value is less than the initial investment.) The formula in cell B7 is shown in cell B8.*

	A	B
1	Year 1	-500
2	Year 2	150
3	Year 3	100
4	Year 4	125
5	Year 5	135
6	Year 6	200
7		
8	Internal Rate of Return:	12%
9		=IRR(B1:B6)
10		

Figure 58. *This worksheet calculates the internal rate of return of an initial $500 investment that pays out cash over the next few years. The formula in cell B8 is shown in cell B9.*

The FV Function

The FV function (**Figure 56**) calculates the future value of an investment with constant cash flows and a constant interest rate. It uses the following syntax:

FV(rate,nper,pmt,pv,type)

Rate is the interest rate per period, nper is the total number of periods, and pmt is the amount of the periodic payments. These three arguments are required. The pv argument is the present value of the payments. Type indicates when payments are due: use 0 for payments at the end of the period and 1 for payments at the beginning of the period. If either optional argument is omitted, 0 is assumed.

The PV Function

The PV function (**Figure 57**) calculates the total amount that a series of payments in the future is worth now. It uses the following syntax:

PV(rate,nper,pmt,fv,type)

The rate, nper, pmt, and type arguments are the same in the FV function. Only the first three are required. The fv argument is the amount left after the payments have been made. If omitted, 0 is assumed.

The IRR Function

The IRR Function (**Figure 58**) calculates the internal rate of return for a series of periodic cash flows. It uses the following syntax:

IRR(values,guess)

The values argument, which is required, is a range of cells containing the cash flows. The guess argument, which is optional, is for your guess of what the result could be. Although seldom necessary, guess could help Excel come up with an answer when performing complex calculations.

FV, PV, & IRR

Logical Functions

You can use Excel's logical functions to evaluate conditions and act accordingly. here's the most useful one: IF.

The IF Function

The IF function evaluates a condition and returns one of two different values depending on whether the condition is met (true) or not met (false). It uses the following syntax:

IF(logical_test,value_if_true,value_if_false)

The logical_test argument is the condition you want to meet. This argument is required. The value_if_true and value_if_false arguments are the values to return if the condition is met or not met. If omitted, the values TRUE and FALSE are returned.

To use the IF function

This example uses the IF function to calculate commissions based on two different commission rates.

1. Create a worksheet with text and number values as shown in **Figure 59**.

2. In cell *C6*, enter the following formula:
   *=IF(B6>400,$B$2*B6,$B$3*B6)*

   This formula begins by evaluating the sales amount to see if it's over $400. If it is, it moves to the value_if_true argument and multiplies the higher commission rate by the sales amount. If it isn't, it moves on to the value_if_false argument and multiplies the lower commission rate by the sales amount.

3. Press Return or Enter or click the Enter button on the formula bar to complete the formula (**Figure 60**).

4. Use the fill handle to copy the formula down the column for the rest of the salespeople (**Figure 61**).

	A	B	C
1		Rates	
2	Over $400	15%	
3	Up to $400	10%	
4			
5		Sales	Amt. Due
6	John	443.16	
7	Jean	512.84	
8	Joe	328.69	
9	Joan	401.98	

Figure 59. *To try the IF function for yourself, start with a basic worksheet like this.*

	A	B	C
1		Rates	
2	Over $400	15%	
3	Up to $400	10%	
4			
5		Sales	Amt. Due
6	John	443.16	66.474
7	Jean	512.84	
8	Joe	328.69	
9	Joan	401.98	

Figure 60. *Enter the formula with the IF function in cell C6.*

	A	B	C
1		Rates	
2	Over $400	15%	
3	Up to $400	10%	
4			
5		Sales	Amt. Due
6	John	443.16	66.474
7	Jean	512.84	76.926
8	Joe	328.69	32.869
9	Joan	401.98	60.297

Figure 61. *Then use the fill handle to copy the formula to the other cells.*

	A	B	C	D
1	Item Number :	L-108		
2	Price :	13.99	=VLOOKUP(B1,A5:D12,4,FALSE)	
3				
4	**Item Number**	**Qty**	**Item Name**	**Price**
5	D-439	159	Dogzilla	14.99
6	D-845	341	Delayed Impact	8.99
7	E-473	415	Eisenhower	19.99
8	G-058	167	Genus II	19.99
9	L-108	684	Loaded Weapon IV	13.99
10	M-400	218	Men in White	22.99
11	M-482	189	Mask of Zero	24.99
12	0-571	581	Oceanic	15.99

Figure 62. *This example illustrates the VLOOKUP function. When you enter an item number in cell B1, the formula in B2 attempts to match it to a value in the first column of the lookup table below it (A5:D12). If it finds a match, it returns the value in the fourth column of the same row as the match. The formula in cell B2 is shown in cell C2.*

	A	B	C	D
1	Item Number :	M-16		
2	Price :	#N/A	=VLOOKUP(B1,A5:D12,4,FALSE)	
3				
4	**Item Number**	**Qty**	**Item Name**	**Price**
5	D-439	159	Dogzilla	14.99
6	D-845	341	Delayed Impact	8.99
7	E-473	415	Eisenhower	19.99
8	G-058	167	Genus II	19.99
9	L-108	684	Loaded Weapon IV	13.99
10	M-400	218	Men in White	22.99
11	M-482	189	Mask of Zero	24.99
12	0-571	581	Oceanic	15.99

Figure 63. *If the formula in B2 doesn't find a match, it returns the #N/A error value, since the optional rage_lookup argument is set to FALSE.*

Lookup and Reference Functions

Excel's lookup and reference functions return values based on information stored elsewhere in the workbook or in a linked worksheet.

The VLOOKUP and HLOOKUP Functions

The VLOOKUP (**Figures 62** and **63**) and HLOOKUP functions return information based on data stored in a lookup table. The function attempts to match a value in one of its arguments to values in the first column (VLOOKUP) or first row (HLOOKUP) of the lookup table. If it finds a match, it returns the associated value.

The VLOOKUP and HLOOKUP functions use the following syntax:

> VLOOKUP(lookup_value,table_array, col_index_num,range_lookup)
>
> HLOOKUP(lookup_value,table_array, row_index_num,range_lookup)

Lookup_value is the value you want to match in the table. Table_array is the cell reference for the lookup table. Col_index_num or row_index_num is the number of the column or row, relative to the table, that contains the values you want returned. These three arguments are required. Range_lookup, which is not required, tells Excel what it should do if it can't match the lookup_value. There are two options for this argument: TRUE tells Excel to return the value associated with the next lowest value; FALSE tells Excel to return the #N/A error value. If omitted, TRUE is assumed.

✔ Tip

■ The first column or row of the lookup table must be sorted in ascending order for the VLOOKUP or HLOOKUP function to work properly.

Information Functions

Excel's information functions return information about other cells.

The IS Functions

Excel's IS functions (**Figure 64**) use the following syntax:

ISBLANK(value)

ISERR(value)

ISERROR(value)

ISLOGICAL(value)

ISNA(value)

ISNONTEXT(value)

ISNUMBER(value)

ISREF(value)

ISTEXT(value)

In each case, Excel tests for a different thing. The value argument is the value or cell reference to be tested.

✔ Tip

- Use an IS function in conjunction with the IF function to return a value based on the condition of a cell (**Figures 65** and **66**).

	A	B	C	D	E
1	Test		673.24	anchovy		#N/A
2	Blank Cell	FALSE	FALSE	TRUE	FALSE
3	Error other than #N/A	FALSE	FALSE	FALSE	FALSE
4	Any Error	FALSE	FALSE	FALSE	TRUE
5	Logical Value	FALSE	FALSE	FALSE	FALSE
6	#N/A Error	FALSE	FALSE	FALSE	TRUE
7	Not Text	TRUE	FALSE	TRUE	TRUE
8	Number	TRUE	FALSE	FALSE	FALSE
9	Cell Reference	TRUE	TRUE	TRUE	TRUE
10	Text	FALSE	TRUE	FALSE	FALSE

Figure 64. *In this example, the IS functions were used to evaluate the contents of the cells in row 1 of the worksheet. The results of each function appear below the value.*

	A	B
1	Enter Your Name :	
2		
3	Message :	You did not enter your name.

Figures 65 & 66. *In this silly example, the formula in cell B3, =IF(ISTEXT(B1),"Hello "B1,"You did not enter your name."), scolds the user for not entering a name (above), then greets her by name when she does enter it (below).*

	A	B
1	Enter Your Name :	Maria
2		
3	Message :	Hello Maria

IS Functions

You Enter	Excel "Sees"
10/15/99	34986
6/30/61	21000
2:45 PM	0.61458333
10:02:56 AM	0.4187037
1/1/1904	0
12:00 AM	0

Table 1. *Examples of how Excel interprets dates and times.*

Figure 67. *The Preferences dialog box enables you to switch the standard 1904 date system and the Windows 1900 date system.*

Date and Time Functions

Excel's date and time functions are designed specifically to work with dates and times. I tell you about the most useful ones here.

✔ Tips

- Excel treats dates and times as serial numbers. This means that although you may enter information as a date or time—like 10/15/99 or 2:45 PM—Excel converts what you type into a number for its own internal use (see **Table 1**). A date is the number of days since January 1, 1904. A time is the portion of a day since midnight. Excel's formatting makes the number look like a date or time. I tell you about cell formatting in **Chapter 6**.

- You can change Excel's date system from the Macintosh 1904 system to the Windows 1900 system. Choose Preferences from the Tools menu, click the Calculation tab, and turn off the 1904 date system check box (**Figure 67**). This will change the serial numbers for dates for all worksheets in the current workbook. I tell you more about the Preferences dialog box in **Chapter 13**.

- Excel is Year 2000-ready. In fact, if you enter a date early in the 21st century, such as *5/15/04*, Excel assumes the year is 2004, not 1904.

The DATE Function

The DATE function (**Figure 3**) returns the serial number for a date. It uses the following syntax:

=DATE(year,month,day)

The year argument is the year number, the month argument is the month number, and the day argument is the day number. All arguments are required.

To calculate the number of days between two dates

Enter the two dates into separate cells of a worksheet, then write a formula using the subtraction operator (-) to subtract the earlier date from the later date (**Figure 68**).

or

In a worksheet cell, write a formula using the date function, like this:
=DATE(99,10,15)-DATE(99,5,8)

The NOW & TODAY Functions

The NOW and TODAY functions (**Figure 69**) return the serial number for the current date and time (NOW) or current date (TODAY). Results are automatically formatted and will change each time the worksheet is recalculated or opened. They use the following syntax:

NOW()

TODAY()

Although there are no arguments, the parentheses characters must be included.

The DAY, WEEKDAY, MONTH, & YEAR Functions

The DAY, WEEKDAY, MONTH, and YEAR functions (**Figure 70**) return the day of the month, the day of the week, the month number, or the year number for a serial number. They use the following syntax:

DAY(serial_number)

WEEKDAY(serial_number)

MONTH(serial_number)

YEAR(serial_number)

The serial_number argument can be a cell reference, number, or date written as text, like *10/15/99* or *15-Apr-04*.

	A	B
1	First Date	6/3/98
2	Second Date	4/15/01
3	Days Between	1047
4		=B2-B1

Figure 68. *Calculating the number of days between two dates is as simple as subtracting the contents of one cell from another. The formula in cell B3 is shown in cell B4.*

6/4/98 13:14	=NOW()
6/4/98	=TODAY()

Figure 69. *The NOW function returns the current date and time while the TODAY function returns just the current date.*

	A	B	C
1		6/30/01	
2	Day	30	=DAY(B1)
3	Weekday	7	=WEEKDAY(B1)
4	Month	6	=MONTH(B1)
5	Year	2001	=YEAR(B1)

Figure 70. *The DAY, WEEKDAY, MONTH, and YEAR functions extract portions of a date. The formulas in column B are shown in column C.*

	A	B	C
1	Original Text	This IS an eXample.	
2	Lowercase	this is an example.	=LOWER(B1)
3	Uppercase	THIS IS AN EXAMPLE.	=UPPER(B1)
4	Title Case	This Is An Example.	=PROPER(B1)

Figure 71. *Use the LOWER, UPPER, and PROPER functions to change the case of text. The formulas in column B are shown in column C.*

	A	B	C
1	Original Text	Mississippi	
2	First 4 characters	Miss	=LEFT(B1,4)
3	Last 4 characters	ippi	=RIGHT(B1,4)
4	4 characters starting with 3rd character	ssis	=MID(B1,3,4)
5			

Figure 72. *Use the LEFT, RIGHT, and MID functions to extract characters from text. The formulas in column B are shown in column C.*

Text Functions

Excel's text functions enable you to extract, convert, concatenate, and get information about text. I tell you about a few of the more commonly used ones here.

The LOWER, UPPER, & PROPER Functions

The LOWER, UPPER, and PROPER functions (**Figure 71**) convert text to lowercase, uppercase, and title case. They use the following syntax:

LOWER(text)

UPPER(text)

PROPER(text)

The text argument, which is required, is the text you want converted.

The LEFT, RIGHT, & MID Functions

The LEFT, RIGHT, and MID functions (**Figure 72**) return the leftmost, rightmost, or middle characters of a text string. They use the following syntax:

LEFT(text,num_chars)

RIGHT(text,num_chars)

MID(text,start_num,num_chars)

The text argument, which is required, is the text from which characters should be extracted. The num_chars argument is the number of characters you want extracted. If omitted from the LEFT or RIGHT function, 1 is assumed. The MID function has an additional argument, start_num, which is the number of the first character from which you want to extract text. The MID function requires all arguments.

Text Functions

The CONCATENATE Function

The CONCATENATE function (**Figure 73**) joins or concatenates two or more strings of text. It uses the following syntax:

CONCATENATE(text1,text2,...)

Each text argument can include single cell references, text, or numbers you want to join. The CONCATENATE function can accept up to 30 arguments, but only two are required.

✔ Tips

- Excel recognizes the ampersand character (&) as a concatenation operator in formulas. You can concatenate text by including an ampersand between cells or text strings in a formula, like this: *=B2&" "&A2*

- If you want spaces between the strings, be sure to include the space character, between double quote characters, as an argument (**Figure 73**).

- Creative use of the CONCATENATE function or operator makes it possible to give documents a personal touch. **Figure 74** shows an example.

	A	B	C
1	Last Name	First Name	Full Name
2	Twain	Mark	Twain Mark
3			=CONCATENATE(A2," ",B2)

Figure 73. *Use the CONCATENATE function to join strings of text. The formula in cell C2 is shown in cell C3.*

	A	B	C	D
1	Amount Due	124.95		
2	Date Due	8/16/98		
3				
4	The total amount due is $124.95. Please pay by 08/16/98.			

Figure 74. *The formula in cell A4, =*"The total amount due is "&DOLLAR(B1)&". Please pay by "&TEXT(B2,"mm/dd/yy")&".", *writes a sentence using the contents of two cells, the concatenate operator, and two text functions.*

Formatting
Worksheet Cells 6

Southwest Division			
First Quarter Sales			
	Jan	Feb	Mar	Total
John	1254	1256	2435	4945
Jean	1865	1736	1905	5506
Joe	1614	1284	2509	5407
Joan	1987	1908	2890	6785
Totals	6720	6184	9739	22643

Figure 1. *While content should be more important than appearance, you can bet that this worksheet won't get as much attention...*

Southwest Division First Quarter Sales			
	Jan	Feb	Mar	Total
John	$ 1,254	$ 1,256	$ 2,435	$ 4,945
Jean	1,865	1,736	1,905	5,506
Joe	1,614	1,284	2,509	5,407
Joan	1,987	1,908	2,890	6,785
Totals	$ 6,720	$ 6,184	$ 9,739	$22,643

Figure 2. *...as this one.*

Formatting Basics

To paraphrase an old Excel mentor of mine, formatting a worksheet is like putting on its makeup. The worksheet's contents may be perfectly correct, but by applying formatting, you can increase its impact to make an impression on the people who see it (**Figures 1** and **2**).

Excel offers a wide range of formatting options you can use to beautify your worksheets:

- **Number formatting** lets you change the appearance of numbers, dates, and times.
- **Alignment** lets you change the way cell contents are aligned within the cell.
- **Font formatting** lets you change the appearance of text and number characters.
- **Borders** let you add lines around cells.
- Patterns let you add color, shading, and patterns to cells.
- **Column and row formatting** let you change column width and row height.

You can apply formatting to cells using a variety of techniques: with toolbar buttons, shortcut keys, menu commands, or the Conditional Formatting or AutoFormat features.

✔ Tip
- Excel may automatically apply formatting to cells, depending on what you enter. For example, if you use a date function, Excel formats the results of the function as a date. You can change Excel's formatting at any time to best meet your needs.

Formatting Basics

93

Number Formatting

By default, Excel applies the General number format to worksheet cells. This format displays numbers just as they're entered (**Figure 3**).

Excel offers a wide variety of predefined number formatting options for different purposes:

- **Number** formats are used for general number display.

- **Currency** formats are used for monetary values.

- **Accounting** formats are used to line up columns of monetary values.

- **Date** formats are used to display dates.

- **Time** formats are used to display times.

- **Percentage** formats are used to display percentages.

- **Fraction** formats are used to display decimal values as fractions.

- **Scientific** format is used to display values in scientific notation.

- **Text** format is used to display cell contents as text, the way it was entered.

- **Special** formats include a variety of special purpose formatting options.

- **Custom** lets you create your own number format using formatting codes.

You can change number formatting with toolbar buttons or the Format Cells dialog box.

1548.36	
12458	
14.2	
-354.85	
116.028	
0.2	
1.25459E+14	

Figure 3. *General formatting displays the numbers just as they're typed in and uses scientific notation when they're very big.*

Number 1	1.5049	$	1.50
Number 2	3.504	$	3.50
	5.0089	$	5.01

Figure 4. *The two columns contain identical values, but the column on the right is formatted with the Currency style. Because Excel performs calculations with the numbers underlying any formatting, the total on the right appears incorrect!*

General	0.15	163.2	-12.785
Currency	$ 0.15	$ 163.20	$ (12.79)
Percent	15%	16320%	-1279%
Comma	0.15	163.20	(12.79)
Increase Decimal	0.150	163.20	-12.7850
Decrease Decimal	0.2	163	-12.79

Figure 5. *Three different numbers, each with one of the Formatting toolbar's number formats applied.*

Figure 6. *The Format menu offers access to most of the formatting commands discussed in this chapter.*

✔ Tips

- If the integer part of a number is longer than the width of the cell or 11 digits, General number format displays it in scientific notation (**Figure 3**).

- Number formatting changes only the appearance of a number. Although formatting may remove decimal places from displayed numbers, it does not round numbers. **Figure 4** illustrates this. Use the ROUND function, which I discuss in **Chapter 5**, to round numbers in formulas.

- If you include characters like dollar signs or percent symbols with a number you enter, Excel automatically assigns an appropriate built-in format to the cell.

Figures 7, 8, 9, & 10. *Examples of options in the Number tab of the Format Cells dialog box.*

To format numbers with toolbar buttons

1. Select the cell(s) containing the number(s) you want to format.

2. Click the Formatting toolbar button for the number format you want to apply:

   ▲ **Currency Style** displays the number as currency, with a dollar sign, commas, and two decimal places.

   ▲ **Percent Style** displays the number as a percentage with a percent symbol.

   ▲ **Comma Style** displays the number with commas and two decimal places.

   ▲ **Increase Decimal** displays an additional digit after the decimal point.

   ▲ **Decrease Decimal** displays one less digit after the decimal point.

   Figure 5 shows examples of these formats.

To format numbers with the Format Cells dialog box

1. Select the cell(s) containing the number(s) you want to format.

2. Choose Cells from the Format menu (**Figure 6**) or press ⌘ ⌘ 1.

3. In the Format Cells dialog box that appears, click the Number tab to display its options (**Figure 7**).

4. Choose a number format category from the Category scrolling list.

5. Set options in the dialog box. The options vary for each category; **Figures 8**, **9**, and **10** show examples. Check the Sample area to see the number in the active cell with the formatting options you selected applied.

6. Click OK to apply the formatting.

Applying Number Formatting

Alignment

Excel offers a wide variety of options to set the way characters are positioned within a cell (**Figure 11**):

- **Text alignment** controls the alignment of cell contents in relation to the edge of a cell:
    - ▲ **Horizontal** positions the text between the left and right sides of the cell or selection.
    - ▲ **Vertical** positions the text between the top and bottom of the cell.
    - ▲ **Indent** determines the amount of space between the cell contents and the left side of the cell.
- **Orientation** controls the angle at which text appears within the cell.
- **Text control** offers other options for text in cells:
    - ▲ **Wrap text** allows word wrap between the cell's left and right sides. (This may increase the height of the cell's row.)
    - ▲ **Shrink to fit** reduces the size of characters to fit within the cell.
    - ▲ **Merge cells** combines multiple selected cells into one cell.

You can change alignment options with toolbar buttons or the Format Cells dialog box.

✔ Tips

- By default, within each cell, Excel left aligns text and right aligns numbers. This is called General alignment.
- Although it's common to center headings over columns containing numbers, the worksheet may actually look better with headings right aligned. **Figure 12** shows an example.

Figure 11. *Examples of cells with different alignment options applied.*

Jan	Feb
1,254	1,256
1,865	1,736
1,614	1,284
1,987	1,908
6,720	6,184

Figure 12. *Headings sometimes look better when they're right aligned (right) rather than centered (left) over columns of numbers.*

- Alignment is applied to cells, not cell contents. If you use the Clear Contents command or ⌃⌘B shortcut to clear a cell, the formatting remains and will be applied to whatever data is next entered into it.

Figure 13. *The Alignment tab of the Format Cells dialog box.*

Figure 14.
Options on the Horizontal pop-up menu.

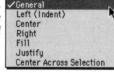

Figure 15.
Options on the Vertical pop-up menu.

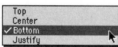

To align cell contents with toolbar buttons

1. Select the cell(s) whose contents you want to align.

2. Click the Formatting toolbar button for the alignment you want to apply:

   ▲ **Align Left** aligns cell contents against the left side of the cell.

   ▲ **Center** centers cell contents between the left and right sides of the cell.

   ▲ **Align Right** aligns cell contents against the right side of the cell.

   The cell contents shift accordingly.

To align cell contents with the Format Cells dialog box

1. Select the cell(s) whose contents you want to align.

2. Choose Cells from the Format menu (**Figure 6**) or press ⌘①.

3. The Format Cells dialog box appears. If necessary, click the Alignment tab to display its options (**Figure 13**).

4. Select options from the Horizontal (**Figure 14**) and Vertical (**Figure 15**) pop-up menus to set alignment as desired.

5. Click OK.

Aligning Cell Contents

To indent cell contents

1. Select the cell(s) whose contents you want to indent (**Figure 16**).

2. Choose Cells from the Format menu (**Figure 6**) or press ⌘⌘①.

3. In the Format Cells dialog box that appears, click the Alignment tab to display its options (**Figure 13**).

4. Choose Left (Indent) from the Horizontal pop-up menu (**Figure 14**).

5. In the Indent edit box, enter the number of characters by which you want to indent cell contents (**Figure 17**).

6. Click OK.

   The cell's contents are indented to your specifications (**Figure 18**).

To merge and center cells

1. Select the cell(s) whose contents you want to center, along with the cells of the columns to the right that you want to center across (**Figure 19**).

2. Click the Merge and Center button on the Formatting toolbar.

or

1. Select the cell(s) whose contents you want to center, along with the cells of the columns to the right that you want to center across (**Figure 19**).

2. Choose Cells from the Format menu (**Figure 6**) or press ⌘⌘①.

3. In the Format Cells dialog box that appears, click the Alignment tab to display its options (**Figure 13**).

4. Choose Center from the Horizontal pop-up menu (**Figure 14**).

5. Turn on the Merge cells check box.

6. Click OK.

The cell contents shift so they're centered between the left and right sides of the selected area (**Figure 20**).

	A	B
1	Southwest Division	
2	First Quarter Sales	
3		Jan
4	John	$ 1,254
5	Jean	1,865
6	Joe	1,614
7	Joan	1,987
8	Totals	$ 6,720

Figure 16. *Select the cell for which you want to indent the contents.*

Figure 17. *To indent text, set Text alignment options like this.*

	A	B
1	Southwest Division	
2	First Quarter Sales	
3		Jan
4	John	$ 1,254
5	Jean	1,865
6	Joe	1,614
7	Joan	1,987
8	Totals	$ 6,720

Figure 18. *The cell's contents are indented.*

	A	B	C	D	E
1	Southwest Division				
2	First Quarter Sales				
3		Jan	Feb	Mar	Total
4	John	$ 1,254	$ 1,256	$ 2,435	$ 4,945
5	Jean	1,865	1,736	1,905	5,506

Figure 19. *Select the cells you want to merge and center.*

	A	B	C	D	E
1			Southwest Division		
2	First Quarter Sales				
3		Jan	Feb	Mar	Total
4	John	$ 1,254	$ 1,256	$ 2,435	$ 4,945
5	Jean	1,865	1,736	1,905	5,506

Figure 20. *The cells are merged together and the cell contents are centered in the merged cell.*

✔ Tip

■ You can get similar results by choosing Center Across Selection from the Horizontal pop-up menu (**Figure 14**) in step 4 and skipping step 5. The cells, however, are not merged, so an entry into one of the adjacent cells could obscure the centered contents.

Indenting & Merging Cell Contents

Figure 21. *Select the cells for which you want to change orientation.*

Vertical Orientation button

Figure 22. *Set options using the orientation area of the Format Cells dialog box.*

Figure 23. *The orientation of selected cells changes.*

To change the orientation or rotation of cell contents

1. Select the cell(s) whose orientation you want to change (**Figure 21**).

2. Choose Cells from the Format menu (**Figure 6**) or press ⌃⌘1.

3. In the Format Cells dialog box, click the Alignment tab (**Figure 13**).

4. Set Options in the Orientation area (**Figure 22**) using one of these methods:

   ▲ To display text characters one above the other, click the Vertical Orientation button.

   ▲ To display text characters at an angle, drag the red diamond in the rotation area to match the angle you want.

   ▲ To display text characters at an angle, enter an angle value in the Degrees box.

5. Click OK.

   The cell's contents change orientation (**Figure 23**). If necessary, the entire row's height changes to accommodate the shifted characters.

✔ Tips

■ You cannot set orientation options if Center Across Selection is chosen from the Horizontal pop-up menu (**Figure 14**). Choose another option before you set orientation.

■ You can enter either a positive or negative value in the Degrees box (**Figure 22**).

■ Rotated text appears better when printed than it does on screen.

■ Rotating the text in column headings often enables you to decrease column width, thus enabling you to fit more information on screen or on paper. I tell you how to change column width later in this chapter.

Changing Cell Orientation & Rotation

To fit cell contents within a cell

1. Select the cell(s) whose contents you want to fit within the cell (**Figure 24**).

2. Choose Cells from the Format menu (**Figure 6**) or press ⌘⌘1.

3. In the Format Cells dialog box, click the Alignment tab (**Figure 13**).

4. Turn on one of the following check boxes:

   ▲ **Wrap text** forces word wrap to occur within the cell. This increases the row height (**Figure 25**).

   ▲ **Shrink to fit** reduces the size of font characters to squeeze them into the cell. This may make cell contents difficult to read (**Figure 26**).

5. Click OK.

✔ Tips

■ To benefit from either of these options, the text within the cell must be too wide to fit into the cell. I tell you how to change column width and row height later in this chapter.

■ You cannot use the Wrap text and Shrink to fit options together.

To merge cells

1. Select the cells you want to merge into one cell.

2. Choose Cells from the Format menu (**Figure 6**) or press ⌘⌘1.

3. In the Format Cells dialog box, click the Alignment tab (**Figure 13**).

4. Turn on the Merge cells check box.

5. Click OK.

6. If more than one of the cells is not empty, Excel displays a dialog box or Office Assistant balloon (**Figure 27**) to warn you that only the upper-left cell will retain its data. If this is OK, click OK to merge the cells. Otherwise, click Cancel and reconsider the merge.

Figure 24. *Select a cell with much information.*

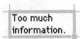

Figure 25. *Here's the cell from* **Figure 24** *with wrap text applied.*

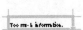

Figure 26. *Here's the cell from* **Figure 24** *with Shrink to fit applied.*

Figure 27. *Excel warns you when merging cells could result in data loss.*

✔ Tip

■ The cell reference for merged cells is the cell reference for the upper-left cell in the original selection.

Using Text Control Options

	A	B	C	D	E
1		Southwest Division			
2		First Quarter Sales			
3		*Jan*	*Feb*	*Mar*	*Total*
4	John	$ 1,254	$ 1,256	$ 2,435	$ 4,945
5	Jean	1,865	1,736	1,905	5,506
6	Joe	1,614	1,284	2,509	5,407
7	Joan	1,987	1,908	2,890	6,785
8	Totals	$ 6,720	$ 6,184	$ 9,739	$ 22,643

Figure 28. *This example shows font, font size, and font style applied to the contents of cells.*

Figure 29. *You can also select individual characters within a cell...*

Figure 30. *...and apply formatting to them.*

Font Formatting

Excel uses 9 point Geneva as the default font or typeface for worksheets. You can apply a variety of font formatting options to cells, some of which are shown in **Figure 28**:

- **Font** is the typeface used to display characters. This includes all fonts properly installed in your system.

- **Font style** is the weight or angle of characters. Options usually include Regular, Bold, Italic, and Bold Italic.

- **Size** is the size of characters, expressed in points.

- **Underline** is character underlining. Don't confuse this with borders, which can be applied to the bottom of a cell, regardless of its contents.

- **Color** is character color.

- **Effects** are special effects applied to characters.

You can apply font formatting with toolbar buttons, shortcut keys, and the Format Cells dialog box.

✔ Tip

- You can change the formatting of individual characters within a cell by double-clicking the cell to make it active, selecting the characters you want to change (**Figure 29**), and then using the appropriate font formatting technique to change the characters (**Figure 30**).

Font Formatting Basics

To change a font with the Formatting toolbar

1. Select the cell(s) or character(s) whose font you want to change.

2. Click on the arrow beside the Font box on the Formatting toolbar to display a menu of all fonts installed in your system (**Figure 31**) and choose the font you want to apply.

   or

   Click on the Font box to select its contents (**Figure 32**), type in the name of the font you want to apply (**Figure 33**), and press $\boxed{\text{Return}}$ or $\boxed{\text{Enter}}$.

   The font you chose is applied to the selected cell(s).

To change font size with the Formatting toolbar

1. Select the cell(s) or character(s) whose font size you want to change.

2. Click on the arrow beside the Font Size box on the Formatting toolbar to display a menu of sizes (**Figure 34**) and choose the size you want to apply.

   or

   Click on the Font Size box to select its contents, type in a size (**Figure 35**), and press $\boxed{\text{Return}}$ or $\boxed{\text{Enter}}$.

   The font size you chose is applied to the selected cell(s).

✔ Tip

■ Font size must be between 1 and 409 points in half-point increments. (In case you're wondering, 72 points equals 1 inch.)

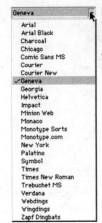

Figure 31.
The Font menu on the Formatting toolbar lists all the fonts properly installed in your system.

Figure 32. *Click the font name to select it…*

Figure 33. *…then type in the name of the font that you want to apply.*

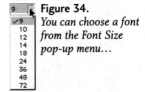

Figure 34.
You can choose a font from the Font Size pop-up menu…

Figure 35. *…or enter any size you like in the Font Size edit box.*

To change font style with the Formatting toolbar or shortcut keys

1. Select the cell(s) whose font style you want to change.

2. Click the Formatting toolbar button for the style you want to apply:

   ▲ **Bold** (or ⌃⌘ Shift B) makes characters in the selected cell(s) appear in a bold style.

   B

   ▲ *Italic* (or ⌃⌘ Shift I) makes characters in the selected cell(s) appear in an italic style.

   I

   ▲ <u>Underline</u> (or ⌃⌘ Shift U) puts a single underline under characters in the selected cell(s).

   <u>U</u>

3. The button you click turns dark to indicate that it's selected and the formatting changes accordingly.

✔ Tips

■ You can apply more than one style to selected cells or characters.

■ Use border formatting or accounting underlines rather than the Underline button to put lines at the bottom of columns being totalled. I tell you about border formatting and accounting underlines later in this chapter.

Applying Font Formatting

To change font formatting with the Format Cells dialog box

1. Select the cell(s) or character(s) whose font you want to change.

2. Choose Cells from the Format menu (**Figure 6**) or press ⌘⌘①.

3. In the Format Cells dialog box that appears, click the Font tab to display its options (**Figure 36**).

4. Set options as desired:

   ▲ Select a font from the Font scrolling list or type a font name into the edit box above the list.

   ▲ Select a style from the Font style scrolling list or type a style name into the edit box above the list.

   ▲ Select a size from the Size scrolling list or type a size into the edit box above the list.

   ▲ Choose an underline option from the Underline pop-up menu (**Figure 37**).

   ▲ Choose a font color from the Color pop-up menu (**Figure 38**).

   ▲ Turn on check boxes in the Effects area to apply font effects.

5. When the sample text in the Preview area looks just the way you want, click OK.

✔ Tips

■ To return a selection to the default font, turn on the Normal font check box in the Format Cells dialog box (**Figure 36**).

■ The accounting underline options in the Underline pop-up menu (**Figure 37**) stretch almost the entire width of the cell.

Figure 36. *The Font tab of the Format Cells dialog box.*

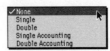

Figure 37. *Excel offers several underlining options.*

Figure 38. *The Color pop-up menu in the Format Cells dialog box…*

Figure 39. *…and the Font Color pop-up menu on the Formatting toolbar offer two ways to apply color to font characters.*

■ The Automatic color option in the Color pop-up menu (**Figure 38**) allows color to be determined by formatting options on the Number tab, which I discuss earlier in this chapter.

■ You can also change font color with the Font Color menu on the Formatting toolbar (**Figure 39**).

Applying Font Formatting

104

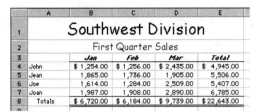

	A	B	C	D	E
1	Southwest Division				
2	First Quarter Sales				
3		*Jan*	*Feb*	*Mar*	*Total*
4	John	$ 1,254.00	$ 1,256.00	$ 2,435.00	$ 4,945.00
5	Jean	1,865.00	1,736.00	1,905.00	5,506.00
6	Joe	1,614.00	1,284.00	2,509.00	5,407.00
7	Joan	1,987.00	1,908.00	2,890.00	6,785.00
8	Totals	$ 6,720.00	$ 6,184.00	$ 9,739.00	$ 22,643.00

Figure 40. *Use borders to place lines under headings and above and below column totals.*

Figure 41.
The Borders menu on the Formatting toolbar.

Borders

Excel offers a number of different border styles that you can apply to separate cells or a selection of cells (**Figure 40**). Use the Formatting toolbar or the Format Cells dialog box to add borders.

To add borders with the Borders button

1. Select the cell(s) to which you want to add borders.

2. Click on the Borders button to apply the border style illustrated on the button.

   or

   Click on the triangle on the right side of the Borders button to display a menu of border styles (**Figure 41**) and choose the style you want.

   The border is applied.

✔ Tips

- Most border styles on the Borders menu apply borders to each cell in the selection. The last two styles apply borders around just the outside of the selection.

- The Borders button displays the last border selection you made from the Borders menu, making it easy to apply the same border style again.

- To remove borders from a selection, choose the first (top left) border style. If the border does not disappear, it may be applied to a cell adjoining the one you selected.

- The accounting underline options on the Underline pop-up menu in the Format Cells dialog box (**Figure 37**) are not the same as borders. They do not stretch the entire width of the cell and they only appear when the cell is not blank.

Adding Borders

105

To add borders with the Format Cells dialog box

1. Select the cell(s) to which you want to add borders.

2. Choose Cells from the Format menu (**Figure 6**) or press ⌃⌘1.

3. In the Format Cells dialog box that appears, click the Border tab to display its options (**Figure 42**).

4. Select a line style in the Line area.

5. If desired, select a color from the Color pop-up menu, which looks just like the one in **Figure 38**.

6. Set individual borders for the selected cells using one of these methods:

   ▲ Click one of the buttons in the Presets area to apply a predefined border. (None removes all borders from the selection.)

   ▲ Click a button in the Border area to add a border to the corresponding area.

   ▲ Click between the lines in the illustration in the Border area to place corresponding borders.

7. Repeat steps 4, 5, and 6 until all the desired borders for the selection are set.

8. Click OK.

   The borders are applied.

✔ Tip

■ To get the borders in your worksheet to look just the way you want, be prepared to make several selections and trips to either the Borders button on the Formatting toolbar or the Border tab of the Format Cells dialog box.

Figure 42. *The Border tab of the Format Cells dialog box.*

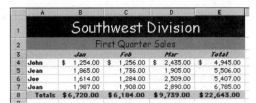

Figure 43. *Use Excel's pattern feature to add fill colors and patterns to cells.*

Figure 44.
The Fill Color pop-up menu on the Formatting toolbar.

Fill Colors & Patterns

Excel's pattern feature lets you add color to cells **(Figure 43)**, either with or without patterns. Although the Fill Color menu on the Formatting toolbar just lets you add color to cell backgrounds, the Format Cells dialog box offers far more flexibility.

✔ Tips

- By combining two colors with a pattern, you can create various colors and levels of shading.

- Be careful when adding colors to cells! If the color is too dark, cell contents may not be legible.

- To improve the legibility of cell contents in colored cells, try making the characters bold.

- For a different look, use a dark color for the cell and make its characters white.

To add color with the Fill Color button

1. Select the cell(s) to which you want to add color.

2. Click on the Fill Color button to apply the color shown on the button.

   or

   Click on the triangle on the right side of the Fill Color button to display a menu of colors **(Figure 44)** and choose the style you want.

   The color is applied.

✔ Tips

- The Fill Color button displays the last color selection you made from the Fill Color menu, making it easy to apply the same color again.

- To remove colors from a selection, choose No Fill from the Fill Color menu **(Figure 44)**.

Adding Color

To add fill color & pattern with the Format Cells dialog box

1. Select the cell(s) to which you want to add colors, patterns, or shading.

2. Choose Cells from the Format menu (**Figure 6**) or press ⌃⌘①.

3. In the Format Cells dialog box that appears, click the Patterns tab to display its options (**Figure 45**).

4. Select a color from the Color palette in the Cell shading area of the dialog box. This is the background color.

5. If desired, choose a foreground color and pattern from the Pattern pop-up menu (**Figure 46**).

6. When the Sample area of the dialog box looks just the way you want your selection to look, click OK.

   The options you selected are applied.

Figure 45. *The Patterns tab of the Format Cells dialog box.*

Figure 46.
Use the Pattern pop-up menu to choose a pattern and a foreground color.

Styles

Once you get the hang of using Excel's formatting options, check out its Style feature. This advanced feature, which is beyond the scope of this book, lets you combine formats into named styles that you can apply to any cell in the workbook. This can save time and ensure consistency.

✔ Tips

■ Excel's style feature works a lot like Word's style feature.

■ You can access the style feature by choosing Style from the Format menu (**Figure 6**).

Conditional Formatting

Excel's new Conditional Formatting feature enables you to set up special formatting that is automatically applied by Excel only when cell contents meet certain criteria.

For example, say you have a worksheet containing the total sales for each member of your company's sales staff. You want to display all sales over $5,000 in bold, blue type with a yellow background. You can use Conditional Formatting to automatically apply the desired formatting in cells containing values over $5,000 (**Figure 47**).

To apply Conditional Formatting

1. Select the cells to which you want to apply conditional formatting.

2. Choose Conditional Formatting from the Format menu (**Figure 6**) to display the Conditional Formatting dialog box (**Figure 48**).

3. Use the pop-up menus and edit boxes in the Condition 1 part of the dialog box to set up the criteria for applying formatting. **Figure 49** shows an example.

4. Click the Format button to display a special version of the Format Cells dialog box that offers tabs for Font, Border, and Patterns only (**Figure 50**). Use the dialog box to set formatting options for cells meeting the condition.

5. To add another condition for applying the formatting, click the Add button. The dialog box expands to offer an additional condition set (**Figure 51**). Repeat steps 3 and 4.

6. Repeat step 5 for each condition you want to add.

7. When you're finished specifying conditions and formatting, click OK.

   If any cells meet the condition(s) you specified, the formatting you specified is applied.

Figure 47.
Conditional Formatting instructs Excel to format cells based on their contents.

	A	B
1	**National J Company**	
2	First Quarter Sales	
3		
4	John	$5,843.00
5	Jean	3,584.00
6	Joe	4,259.00
7	Joan	6,841.00
8	Jerry	3,954.00
9	Jack	4,856.00
10	Jason	5,012.00
11	Jeremy	8,423.00
12	Jane	2,384.00
13		$ 45,156.00

Figure 48. *The Conditional Formatting dialog box.*

Figure 49. *This condition set applies formatting to selected cells containing values greater than 5000.*

Figure 50. *Formatting options for Conditional Formatting are slightly limited.*

Figure 51. *The Conditional Formatting dialog box expands so you can add more conditions.*

The Format Painter

The Format Painter lets you copy cell formatting and apply it to other cells. This can help you format worksheets quickly and consistently.

To use the Format Painter

1. Select a cell with the formatting you want to copy.

2. Click the Format Painter button on the Standard toolbar. The mouse pointer turns into a little plus sign with a paintbrush beside it and a marquee appears around the original selection (**Figure 52**).

3. Use the Format Painter pointer to select the cells you want to apply the formatting to (**Figure 53**). When you release the mouse button, the formatting is applied (**Figure 54**).

✔ Tips

■ You can double-click the Format Painter button in step 1 to keep applying a copied format throughout the worksheet. Press Esc or click the Format Painter button again to stop applying the format and return the mouse pointer to normal.

■ You can also use the Copy and Paste Special commands under the Edit menu (**Figure 55**) to copy the formatting of selected cells and paste it into other cells.

	1,614.00	1,284.00
	1,987.00	1,908.00
s	**$6,720.00**	6184

Figure 52. *When you click the Format Painter button a marquee appears around the original selection and the mouse pointer turns into the Format Painter pointer.*

	1,614.00	1,284.00	2,309.00	3,407.00
	1,987.00	1,908.00	2,890.00	6,785.00
ls	**$6,720.00**	6184	9739	22643

Figure 53. *Drag to select the cells to which you want to copy formats.*

	1,614.00	1,284.00	2,309.00	3,407.00
	1,987.00	1,908.00	2,890.00	6,785.00
ls	**$6,720.00**	**$6,184.00**	**$9,739.00**	**$22,643.00**

Figure 54. *When you release the mouse button, the formatting is applied.*

Edit	
Undo Paste Special	⌘Z
Can't Repeat	⌘Y
Cut	⌘X
Copy	⌘C
Paste	⌘V
Paste Special...	
Paste as Hyperlink	
Fill	▶
Clear	▶
Delete...	⌘K
Delete Sheet	
Move or Copy Sheet...	
Find...	⌘F
Replace...	⌘H
Go To...	
Publishing	▶
Links...	
Object	

Figure 55. *You can also use the Copy and Paste Special commands under the Edit menu to copy and paste formatting.*

Figure 56. *When text doesn't fit in a cell, it appears to overlap into the cell beside it…*

| Total for all s | 14982 |

Figure 57. *…unless the cell beside it isn't blank.*

| ###### |

Figure 58. *When a number doesn't fit in a cell, the cell fills with # signs.*

| $14,982.00 |

Figure 59. *You can make the number fit by making the cell wider…*

| $ 14,982 |

Figure 60. *…or by changing the number's formatting to remove decimal places.*

Column Width & Row Height

If the data you enter into a cell doesn't fit, you can make the column wider to accommodate all the characters. You can also make columns narrower to use worksheet space more efficiently. And although Excel automatically adjusts row height when you increase the font size of cells within the row, you can increase or decrease row height as desired.

Excel offers two ways to change column width and row height: with the mouse and with Format menu commands.

✔ Tips

- If text typed into a cell does not fit, it appears to overlap into the cell to its right (**Figure 56**). Even though the text may appear to be in more than one cell, all of the text is really in the cell in which you typed it. (You can see for yourself by clicking in the cell to the right and looking at the formula bar—it will not contain any part of the text!) If the cell to the right of the text is not blank, the text appears truncated (**Figure 57**). Don't let appearances fool you. The text is still all there. The missing part is just hidden by the contents of the cell beside it.

- If a number doesn't fit in a cell, the cell fills up with pound signs (#) (**Figure 58**). To display the number, make the column wider (**Figure 59**) or change the number formatting to omit symbols and decimal places (**Figure 60**). I tell you how to make columns wider on the next page and how to change number formatting earlier in this chapter.

- Setting column width or row height to 0 (zero) hides the column or row.

To change column width or row height with the mouse

1. Position the mouse pointer on the line right after the column letter(s) (**Figure 61**) or right below the row number (**Figure 62**) of the column or row you want to change. The mouse pointer turns into a line with two arrows coming out of it.

2. Press the mouse button down and drag.

   ▲ To make a column narrower, drag to the left.

   ▲ To make a column wider, drag to the right.

   ▲ To make a row taller, drag down.

   ▲ To make a row shorter, drag up.

   As you drag, a dotted line moves along with the mouse pointer and the width or height of the column or row appears in a yellow box (**Figure 63**).

3. Release the mouse button. The column width or row height changes.

✔ Tips

■ When you change column width or row height, you change the width or height for the entire column or row, not just selected cells.

■ To change column width or row height for more than one column or row at a time, select multiple columns or rows and drag the border of one of them.

■ If you drag a column or row border all the way to the left or all the way up, you set the column width or row height to 0. The column or row disappears from view. I tell you more about hiding columns and rows on the next page.

■ To quickly set the width or height of a column or row to fit its contents, double-click the column or row heading border. I tell you more about this AutoFit feature later in this chapter.

Figure 61. *Position the mouse pointer on the right border of a column heading...*

Figure 62. *...or on the bottom border of a row heading.*

Figure 63. *Drag to reposition the border.*

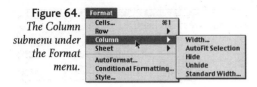

Figure 64. *The Column submenu under the Format menu.*

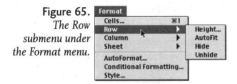

Figure 65. *The Row submenu under the Format menu.*

Figures 66 & 67. *The Column Width (left) and Row Height (right) dialog boxes.*

Figure 68. *Select the column that you want to hide.*

Figure 69. *When you choose the Hide command, the column disappears.*

Figure 70. *Select the rows above and below the hidden row.*

Figure 71. *When you choose the Unhide command, the hidden row reappears.*

To change column width or row height with menu commands

1. Select the column(s) or row(s) whose width or height you want to change.

2. Choose Width from the Column submenu under the Format menu (**Figure 64**) or choose Height from the Row submenu under the Format menu (**Figure 65**).

3. In the Column Width dialog box (**Figure 66**) or Row Height dialog box (**Figure 67**), enter a new value. Column width is expressed in standard font characters while row height is expressed in points.

4. Click OK to change the selected columns' width or rows' height.

To hide columns or rows

1. Select the column(s) (**Figure 68**) or row(s) you want to hide.

2. Choose Hide from the Column submenu (**Figure 64**) or the Row submenu (**Figure 65**) under the Format menu.

   The selected column(s) or row(s) disappear (**Figure 69**).

✔ Tip

- Hiding a column or row is not the same as deleting it. Data in a hidden column or row still exists in the worksheet and can be referenced by formulas.

To unhide columns or rows

1. Select the columns or rows on both sides of the hidden column(s) or row(s) (**Figure 70**).

2. Choose Unhide from the Column submenu (**Figure 64**) or the Row submenu (**Figure 65**) under the Format menu.

   The hidden columns(s) or rows(s) reappear (**Figure 71**).

Changing Column Width & Row Height

AutoFit

Excel's AutoFit feature automatically adjusts a column's width or a row's height so it's only as wide or as high as it needs to be to display the information within it. This is a great way to adjust columns and rows to use worksheet space more efficiently.

To use AutoFit

1. Select the column(s) or row(s) for which you want to change the width or height (**Figure 72**).

2. Choose AutoFit Selection from the Column submenu (**Figure 64**) or AutoFit from the Row submenu under the Format menu (**Figure 65**).

   or

   Double-click on the border to the right of the column heading (**Figure 61**) or below the row heading (**Figure 62**).

   The column width or row height changes to fit cell contents (**Figure 73**).

✔ Tips

- To adjust a column's width without taking every cell into consideration—for example, to exclude a cell containing a lot of text—select only the cells for which you want to adjust the column (**Figure 74**). When you choose AutoFit Selection from the Column submenu under the Format menu (**Figure 64**), only the cells you selected are measured for the AutoFit adjustment (**Figure 75**).

- Use the Wrap text and AutoFit features to keep your columns narrow. I tell you about Wrap text earlier in this chapter.

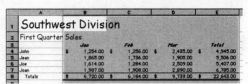

Figure 72. *Select the columns for which you want to change the width.*

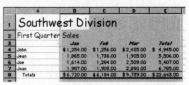

Figure 73. *When you choose the AutoFit Selection command, the width of the columns changes so they're only as wide as they need to be to fit cell contents.*

Figure 74. *Select the cells that you want Excel to measure for the AutoFit feature.*

Figure 75. *When you choose the AutoFit Selection command, Excel resizes the entire column based on the width of the contents in the selected cells.*

Figure 76. *Select the part of the worksheet you want to format.*

Figure 77. *The AutoFormat dialog box.*

AutoFormat

Excel's AutoFormat feature offers a quick way to dress up tabular data in worksheets by applying predefined formats. If you're like me and like to leave design for designers, you'll welcome this feature.

To use AutoFormat

1. Select the portion of the worksheet you want to format (**Figure 76**).

2. Choose AutoFormat from the Format menu (**Figure 6**) to display the AutoFormat dialog box (**Figure 77**).

3. Choose a format from the Table format scrolling list. A preview of the format appears in the Sample area so you can decide whether you like it before you apply it.

4. When you're satisfied with your selection, click OK or press Return or Enter. Your worksheet is formatted instantly (**Figure 78**).

✔ Tip

■ To pick and choose among the different kinds of formatting automatically applied, click the Options button in the AutoFormat dialog box. The box expands to display check boxes for each type of formatting (**Figure 79**). To exclude a type of change from the AutoFormat process, turn off its check box.

Southwest Division First Quarter Sales				
	Jan	Feb	Mar	Total
John	1254	1256	2435	4945
Jean	1865	1736	1905	5506
Joe	1614	1284	2509	5407
Joan	1987	1908	2890	6785
Totals	6720	6184	9739	22643

Figure 78. *The worksheet in Figure 76 with the Classic 3 AutoFormat applied.*

Figure 79. *Clicking the Options button expands the AutoFormat dialog box so you can select which parts of the format should be applied.*

AutoFormat

Cell Comments

Excel lets you add comments to any cell. You can use comments to annotate your worksheets, providing background information for complex calculations or important information.

✔ Tip

■ Cell comments were known as cell notes in previous versions of Excel.

To add a cell comment

1. Select the cell to which you want to add a comment.

2. Choose Comment from the Insert menu (**Figure 80**).

3. A yellow comment box with your name in it appears (**Figure 81**). Enter the text for the comment.

4. Click in the worksheet window outside the comment box.

   The box disappears as the comment is saved. A red comment indicator mark appears in the upper-right corner of the selected cell (**Figure 82**).

To view a cell comment

Position the mouse pointer over a cell containing a comment.

An arrow and yellow box containing the comment appear (**Figure 83**).

To edit a comment

1. Select the cell containing the comment you want to edit.

2. Choose Edit Comment from the Insert menu (**Figure 84**).

3. A yellow comment box containing the comment appears (**Figure 85**). Edit the comment as desired.

4. Click in the worksheet window outside the comment box to save your changes.

Figure 80.
You can find the Comment command under the Insert menu.

Figure 81. *Enter a comment in a comment box.*

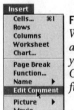

Figure 82.
A red mark appears in the corner of a cell containing a comment.

Figure 83. *Point to a cell containing a comment to view the comment.*

Figure 84.
When a cell containing a comment is selected, you can choose the Edit Comment command from the Insert menu.

Figure 85. *You can edit a comment in the comment box.*

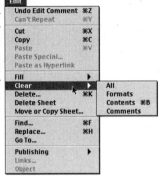

Figure 86.
The Clear submenu under the Edit menu enables you to clear just the formats or comments in cells.

Removing Formatting & Comments from Cells

You can use options on the Clear submenu under the Edit menu (**Figure 86**) to remove only formatting or comments from selected cells. Values or formulas in the cells are not removed.

✔ Tips

- When you remove formats from a cell, you return font formatting to the normal font and number formatting to the General format. You also remove borders or colors added to the cell.

- Removing formatting does not affect column width or row height.

	A	B	C	D
1		Southwest Divis		
2		First Quarter Sal		
3		*Jan*	*Feb*	*M.*
4	John	$ 1,254	$ 1,256	$ 2.
5	Jean	1,865	1,736	1.
6	Joe	1,614	1,284	2.
7	Joan	1,987	1,908	2.
8	Totals	$ 6,720	$ 6,184	$ 9

Figure 87. *Select the cells from which you want to remove just the formatting.*

To remove only formatting from cells

1. Select the cell(s) from which you want to remove just the formatting (**Figure 87**).

2. Choose Formats from the Clear submenu under the Edit menu (**Figure 86**).

   The formats are removed (**Figure 88**).

	A	B	C	D
1		Southwest Divis		
2		First Quarter Sal		
3		Jan	*Feb*	*M.*
4	John	1254	$ 1,256	$ 2.
5	Jean	1865	1,736	1.
6	Joe	1614	1,284	2.
7	Joan	1987	1,908	2.
8	Totals	6720	$ 6,184	$ 9

Figure 88. *All the formatting—but nothing else—is removed from selected cells.*

To remove only comments from cells

1. Select the cell(s) from which you want to remove just the comments.

2. Choose Comments from the Clear submenu under the Edit menu (**Figure 86**).

   The comments and red comment indicator marks are removed.

DRAWING & FORMATTING OBJECTS 7

Figure 1. *When you click the Drawing button, it turns dark gray.*

Figure 1. *When you click the Drawing button, it turns dark gray.*

Drawing Objects

Excel's Drawing toolbar (**Figure 2**) includes a wide range of tools you can use to add lines, arrows, shapes, and text boxes to your worksheets and charts. Through creative use of these tools, you can add impact and improve appearance for all of your Excel documents.

Draw menu | Free Rotate | Line | Rectangle | Text Box | Fill Color | Font Color | Dash Style | Shadow

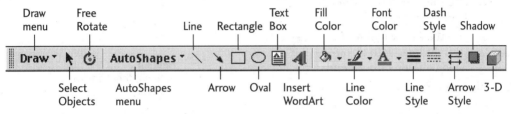

Select Objects | AutoShapes menu | Arrow | Oval | Insert WordArt | Line Color | Line Style | Arrow Style | 3-D

Figure 2. *The Drawing toolbar.*

To display the Drawing toolbar

Click the Drawing button on the Standard toolbar . The button turns dark gray (**Figure 1**) and the Drawing toolbar appears (**Figure 2**).

✔ Tip

- If your Drawing toolbar doesn't look exactly like this one, don't panic. Although the Drawing toolbar is docked at the bottom of the screen by default, it may have been floated the last time it was used—Excel remembers the position of all toolbars. I tell you more about floating and docking toolbars in **Chapter 1**.

To hide the Drawing toolbar

Click the Drawing button on the Standard toolbar.

Drawing Objects

Many of the tools on the Drawing toolbar let you draw *objects*—lines or shapes—in worksheet or chart windows. Excel lets you draw lines, rectangles, squares, ovals, circles, shapes, and text boxes. Objects you draw can be selected, resized, moved, or copied at any time.

To draw a line or arrow

1. Click the appropriate Drawing toolbar button once to select it:

   ▲ Use the Line tool to draw straight lines.

   ▲ Use the Arrow tool to draw straight lines with arrow-heads on one or both ends.

   When you click the tool's button the mouse pointer turns into a crosshairs pointer (**Figure 3**).

2. Position the crosshairs where you want to begin drawing the line.

3. Press the mouse button down and drag. As you move the mouse, a line is drawn (**Figure 4**).

4. Release the mouse button to complete the line. The line appears with selection handles on either end (**Figures 5 and 6**). I tell you more about selection handles later in this chapter.

✔ Tips

■ To draw a line or arrow that's perfectly vertical, horizontal, or at a 45° angle, hold down Shift in step 3.

■ To force the line's end to snap to the worksheet grid, hold down ⌘ in step 3.

■ To draw multiple lines with the same tool, double-click the tool's button to select it. The tool remains active until you either click the button again, click another button, or press Esc.

Figure 3.
When you click a drawing tool's button, the mouse pointer changes into a crosshairs pointer.

Figure 4.
Drag to draw a line.

Figure 5.
A freshly drawn line.

Figure 6.
A freshly drawn arrow.

Drawing Lines & Arrows

Figure 7.
Drag to draw a shape.

Figure 8.
A freshly drawn rectangle.

Figure 9.
A freshly drawn oval.

To draw a rectangle, square, oval, or circle

1. Click the appropriate Drawing toolbar button once to select it:

   ▲ Use the Rectangle tool to draw rectangles or squares.

   ▲ Use the Oval tool to draw ovals and circles.

   When you click the tool's button the mouse pointer turns into a crosshairs pointer (**Figure 3**).

2. Position the crosshairs where you want to begin drawing the shape.

3. Press the mouse button down and drag. As you move the mouse, the shape begins to take form (**Figure 7**).

4. Release the mouse button to complete the shape. The shape appears with selection handles around it (**Figures 8 and 9**). I tell you more about selection handles later in this chapter.

✔ Tips

- When you draw with the rectangle or ellipse tool, you draw from corner to corner.

- To draw a square or a circle, click the Rectangle or Ellipse button, then hold down (Shift) in step 3. The drawing movements are restricted so only perfectly square or perfectly round shapes can be drawn.

- To force the shape's sides or corners to snap to the worksheet grid, hold down (⌘) in step 3.

- To draw multiple shapes with the same tool, double-click the tool's button to select it. The tool remains active until you either click the button again, click another button, or press (Esc).

Drawing Simple Shapes

To draw an AutoShape

1. Choose a shape or line from one of the submenus (**Figure 10**) on the Drawing toolbar's AutoShapes menu. The mouse pointer turns into a crosshairs pointer (**Figure 3**).

2. Position the crosshairs where you want to begin drawing the shape or line.

3. Press the mouse button down and drag. As you move the mouse, the shape or line begins to take form (**Figure 11**).

4. Release the mouse button to complete the shape. The shape appears with selection handles around it (**Figure 12**). I tell you more about selection handles on the next page.

✔ Tips

- The AutoShapes feature makes it easy to draw complex lines and shapes.

- The Connectors submenu offers options for creating lines that connect two shapes.

- The AutoShapes menu (**Figure 13**) and its submenus (**Figure 10**) can be dragged off the toolbar to create a separate floating toolbar (**Figure 14**).

Figure 10. *Choose a shape from one of the submenus under the AutoShapes menu.*

Figure 11. *Drag to draw the shape.*

Figure 12. *A freshly drawn shape.*

Figure 13. *The AutoShapes menu on the Drawing toolbar.*

Figure 14. *When you drag the AutoShapes menu away from the toolbar, it turns into a floating menu.*

Drawing AutoShapes

Figure 15. *When you position the mouse pointer on an object, the mouse pointer turns into a selection pointer.*

Figure 16. *Selection handles appear around selected objects.*

Selecting Objects

To move or modify a drawn object, you must first select it.

To select an object

1. Position the mouse pointer on the object. The mouse pointer turns into a selection pointer (**Figure 15**) rather than the standard worksheet pointer.

2. Click. Selection handles appear around the object (**Figure 16**).

✔ Tips

■ If a shape does not have any fill, you must click on its border to select it. I tell you about fill color later in this chapter.

■ To change the mouse pointer into a selection pointer so the standard worksheet pointer doesn't appear while you're working with drawing objects, click the Select Objects button on the Drawing toolbar. The button turns dark gray and the mouse pointer changes to an arrow. To get the regular pointer back, click the Drawing Selection button again, double-click any worksheet cell, or press (Esc) once or twice.

To deselect an object

Click on any other object or anywhere else in the window. The selection handles disappear.

To select multiple objects

1. Follow the instructions on the previous page to select the first object (**Figure 17**).

2. Hold down (Shift) and continue to select objects until all have been selected (**Figure 18**).

or

1. Click the Select Objects button on the Drawing toolbar to activate the selection pointer.

2. Use the pointer to drag a rectangle that completely surrounds all the objects you want to select (**Figure 19**).

   When you release the mouse button, selection handles appear around each object (**Figure 20**).

✔ Tips

■ To select all the objects on a worksheet, click the Select Objects button on the Drawing toolbar and press (Ⅽ)(⌘)(A).

■ To deselect objects from a multiple selection, hold down (Shift) while clicking on the objects you want to deselect.

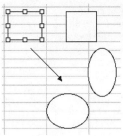

Figure 17.
Select the first object.

Figure 18.
Then hold down (Shift) and click to select other objects.

Figure 19.
You can use the selection pointer to draw a boundary box that completely surrounds the objects you want to select.

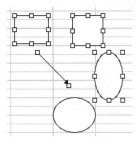

Figure 20.
When you release the mouse button, the objects within the boundary are selected.

Selecting Multiple Objects

Figure 21.
*The Drawing
toolbar's Draw
menu.*

Grouping Objects

To keep multiple objects together, you can group them. This enables you to select, move, and modify all of the objects in the group by clicking any one of them.

To group objects

1. Select all the objects you want to include in the group (**Figure 20**).
2. Choose Group from the Drawing toolbar's Draw menu (**Figure 21**).

   The objects are grouped together, with only one set of selection handles (**Figure 22**).

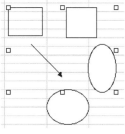

Figure 22.
*The objects selected
in* **Figure 20** *after
grouping them.*

To ungroup objects

1. Select the grouped objects you want to ungroup (**Figure 22**).
2. Choose Ungroup from the Drawing toolbar's Draw menu (**Figure 21**).

   Separate selection handles appear for each object (**Figure 20**).

✔ Tip

- In addition to grouping individual objects, you can also group groups of objects.

Moving, Copying, & Deleting Objects

Objects (or groups of objects) can be moved, copied, or deleted.

Figure 23.
Position the selection pointer on the object.

To move an object by dragging

1. Position the mouse pointer on the object so that the selection pointer appears (**Figure 23**).

2. Press the mouse button down and drag. An outline of the object moves along with the mouse pointer (**Figure 24**).

3. When the object's outline is in the desired position, release the mouse button. The object moves.

Figure 24.
Drag to move the object.

✔ Tips

- To restrict an object's movement so that it moves only horizontally or vertically, hold down (Shift) while dragging.

- To restrict an object's movement so that it snaps to the worksheet gridlines, hold down (⌘) while dragging.

Figure 25.
The Edit menu.

To move an object with the Cut & Paste commands

1. Select the object you want to move.

2. Choose Cut from the Edit menu (**Figure 25**), press (⌘)(X), or click the Cut button on the Standard toolbar. The object disappears.

3. To paste the object into a different sheet, switch to that sheet.

4. Choose Paste from the Edit menu (**Figure 25**), press (⌘)(V), or click the Paste button on the Standard toolbar. The object appears.

5. If necessary, drag the object into the desired position on the sheet.

✔ Tip

- This technique is most useful when moving an object to another sheet.

Moving Objects

Figure 26.
Hold down
Option *while*
dragging…

Figure 27.
…to copy an
object.

Figure 28.
The Clear
submenu under
the Edit menu
when an object
is selected.

To copy an object by dragging

1. Position the mouse pointer on the object so that the selection pointer appears (**Figure 23**).

2. While holding down Option, press the mouse button down and drag. An outline of the object moves along with the mouse pointer, which displays a plus sign beside it (**Figure 26**).

3. When you release the mouse button a copy of the object appears at the outline (**Figure 27**).

To copy an object with the Copy & Paste commands

1. Select the object you want to copy.

2. Choose Copy from the Edit menu (**Figure 25**), press ⌘C, or click the Copy button on the Standard toolbar.

3. To paste the object into a different sheet, switch to that sheet.

4. Choose Paste from the Edit menu (**Figure 25**), press ⌘V, or click the Paste button on the Standard toolbar.

To delete an object

1. Select the object(s) or group of objects you want to delete.

2. Press Delete or Del.

   or

   Choose All from the Clear submenu under the Edit menu (**Figure 28**) or press ⌘B.

   The object(s) disappear.

Modifying Objects

Any object you draw in Excel can be modified to change its size, shape, and formatting.

To resize an object

1. Select the object you want to resize.

2. Position the mouse pointer on a selection handle. The mouse pointer turns into a double-headed arrow (**Figure 29**).

3. Press the mouse button down and drag to stretch or shrink the object. The mouse pointer turns into a crosshairs and an outline of the edge of the object moves with your mouse pointer as you drag (**Figure 30**).

4. When the outline of the object reflects the size you want, release the mouse button. The object is resized (**Figure 31**).

✔ Tips

■ To resize an object or group proportionally, hold down (Shift) while dragging a corner selection handle.

■ To resize the object so that the handle you drag snaps to the worksheet gridlines, hold down (⌃ ⌘) while dragging.

■ To resize multiple objects at the same time, select the objects, then resize one of them. All selected objects will stretch or shrink.

Figure 29.
Position the mouse pointer on a selection handle and it turns into a resizing pointer.

Figure 30.
Drag to stretch (or shrink) the object.

Figure 31.
When you release the mouse button, the object resizes.

Figure 32. *Select the AutoShape that you want to change.*

Figure 33. *Choose a new shape from one of the Change AutoShape submenus.*

To change an AutoShape

1. Select the AutoShape object that you want to change (**Figure 32**).

2. Choose a new shape from one of the Change AutoShape submenus under the Drawing toolbar's Draw menu (**Figure 33**).

   The shape changes (**Figure 34**).

✔ Tips

- You cannot change an AutoShape line to an AutoShape shape or change an AutoShape shape to an AutoShape line.

- The new shape is the same size as the original shape.

Figure 34. *The AutoShape changes to the shape you chose.*

To customize an AutoShape

1. Select the AutoShape object that you want to customize.

2. Position the mouse pointer on the yellow diamond handle. The mouse pointer turns into a hollow white arrowhead pointer.

Figures 35 & 36. *Drag the yellow diamond (left) to customize the AutoShape (right).*

3. Drag the yellow diamond. As you drag, the outline of the customized shape moves with the mouse pointer (**Figures 35** and **37**).

4. Release the mouse button.

   The shape changes (**Figures 36** and **38**).

✔ Tip

- This technique can only be used on AutoShape lines or shapes that display a yellow diamond when selected.

Figures 37 & 38. *You can even turn a smile (left) into a frown (right).*

Changing AutoShapes

To format lines & shapes with the Drawing toolbar

1. Select the line or shape you want to format.

2. Use button menus on the Drawing toolbar to format the selected object:

   ▲ To change the fill color of a shape, choose an option from the Fill Color button menu **(Figure 39)**.

   ▲ To change the line color of a line or shape border, choose an option from the Line Color button menu **(Figure 40)**.

   ▲ To change the line thickness of a line or shape border, choose an option from the Line Style button menu **(Figure 41)**.

   ▲ To change the style of a dashed line or dashed shape border, choose an option from the Dash Style button menu **(Figure 42)**.

   ▲ To add, change, or remove arrow components for a line or arrow, choose an option from the Arrow Style button menu **(Figure 43)**.

   ▲ To add, remove, or change the shadow of a line or shape, choose an option from the Shadow button menu **(Figure 44)**.

   ▲ To add, change, or remove three dimensional effects for a simple shape, choose an option from the 3-D button menu **(Figure 45)**.

✔ Tips

■ The formatting options that are available depend on the line or shape that is selected.

■ You can combine as many formatting options as you like to customize the appearance of lines and shapes.

Figure 39. *The Fill Color button menu.*

Figure 40. *The Line Color button menu.*

Figure 41. *The Line Style button menu.*

Figure 42. *The Dash Style button menu.*

Figure 43. *The Arrow Style button menu.*

Figure 44. *The Shadow button menu.*

Figure 45. *The 3-D button menu.*

Figure 46.
With a line or shape selected, choose AutoShape from the Format menu.

Figure 47. *The Format AutoShape dialog box for a shape,...*

Figure 48. *...for a line or arrow,...*

Figure 49. *...and for a connector.*

To format lines & shapes with the Format AutoShape dialog box

1. Select the line or shape you want to format and choose AutoShape from the Format menu (**Figure 46**) or press ⌃⌘1.

   or

   Double-click the line or shape you want to format.

2. The Format AutoShape dialog box appears. Click the Colors and Lines tab to display its options (**Figures 47, 48,** and **49**).

3. Set options as desired:

   ▲ To change the fill color, choose an option from the Color pop-up menu in the Fill area of the dialog box (**Figure 47**). The options are the same as those on the Fill Color button menu (**Figure 39**).

   ▲ To enable objects to be seen through a fill color, turn on the Semitransparent check box in the Fill area of the dialog box (**Figure 47**).

   ▲ To change the line color, choose an option from the Color pop-up menu in the Line area of the dialog box (**Figures 47, 48,** and **49**). The options are the same as those on the Line Color button menu (**Figure 40**).

   ▲ To change the dashed style, choose an option from the Dashed pop-up menu in the Line area of the dialog box (**Figures 47, 48,** and **49**). The options are the same as those on the Dash Style button menu (**Figure 42**).

   ▲ To change a connector's style, choose an option from the Connector pop-up menu (**Figure 50**) in the Line area of the dialog box (**Figure 49**).

continued on next page...

Formatting Lines & Shapes

continued from previous page

▲ To change the line style, choose an option from the Style pop-up menu in the Line area of the dialog box (**Figure 48**). The options are the same as those on the Line Style button menu (**Figure 41**).

▲ To change the line weight, enter a value in pixels in the Weight edit box in the Line area of the dialog box (**Figures 47**, **48**, and **49**).

▲ To change the style of arrowheads on a line or arrow, choose options from the Begin style and End style pop-up menus (**Figure 51**) in the Arrows area of the dialog box (**Figures 48** and **49**). When you choose an arrow style, you can also set the arrow size by choosing options from the Begin size and End size pop-up menus (**Figure 52**).

4. When you're finished setting options in the dialog box, click OK.

✔ Tips

■ As shown in **Figures 47**, **48**, and **49**, the formatting options that are available in the dialog box depend on the line or shape that is selected.

■ You can combine as many formatting options as you like to customize the appearance of lines and shapes.

Figure 50. *The Connector pop-up menu.*

Figure 51. *The Begin style pop-up menu. The End style pop-up menu looks the same, but the arrows point the other way.*

Figure 52. *The End size pop-up menu. The Begin size pop-up menu looks the same, but the arrows point the other way.*

Formatting Lines & Shapes

Figure 53. *Because each object is drawn in a separate layer, objects can be obscured by other objects "on top" of them.*

Figure 54. *To change an object's layer, start by selecting it.*

Figure 55. *The Order submenu under the Drawing toolbar's Draw menu.*

Figure 56. *A selected object can be brought to the top layer...*

Figure 57. *...or sent to the bottom layer.*

Stacking Order

Each time you draw a shape, Excel puts it on a new drawing layer. When you draw a shape that overlaps another shape, the first shape may be partially obscured by the one "on top" of it (**Figure 53**).

To change stacking order

1. Select the object(s) you want to move to another layer (**Figure 54**).

2. Choose an option from the Order submenu on the Drawing toolbar's Draw menu (**Figure 55**):

   ▲ **Bring to Front** moves the object(s) to the top layer (**Figure 56**).

   ▲ **Send to Back** moves the object(s) to the bottom layer (**Figure 57**).

   ▲ **Bring Forward** moves the object(s) up one layer.

   ▲ **Send Backward** moves the object(s) down one layer.

✔ Tips

- Once you've gotten objects in the order you want, consider grouping them so they stay just the way you want them to. I tell you how to group objects earlier in this chapter.

- You cannot move graphic objects behind the worksheet layer.

Text Boxes

A text box is like a little word processing document within an Excel sheet. Once created, you can enter and format text within it.

✔ Tip

■ Text boxes offer more flexibility than worksheet cells when entering long passages of text.

To add a text box

1. Click the Text Box button on the Drawing toolbar. The mouse pointer turns into a special crosshairs pointer (**Figure 58**).

2. Position the crosshairs where you want to begin drawing the text box.

3. Press the mouse button down and drag. As you move the mouse, the text box begins to take form (**Figure 59**).

4. Release the mouse button to complete the text box. An insertion point appears within it (**Figure 60**).

5. Enter the text you want in the text box (**Figure 61**).

✔ Tips

■ You can move, copy, resize, and delete a text box just like any other object.

■ To edit text in a text box, double-click inside it to select one or more characters. Then use the arrow keys to move the insertion point. Use standard editing techniques to modify text.

■ To format a selected text box or selected contents, choose Text Box from the Format menu (**Figure 62**). Then use tabs on the Format Text Box dialog box that appears (**Figure 63**) to set formatting options. Click OK to save your settings.

Figure 58.
The mouse pointer turns into a special crosshairs pointer when you click the Text Box button.

Figure 59.
Drag to draw a text box.

Figure 60.
When you release the mouse button, the text box appears with a blinking insertion point inside it.

Figure 61.
You can type whatever text you like in the text box.

Figure 62. *When a text box is selected, the Text Box command appears under the Format menu.*

Figure 63. *You can use options in the Format Text Box dialog box to format a selected text box or selected text box contents.*

Adding Text Boxes

Figure 64. *Here's a company logo created in Photoshop being copied to the Clipboard.*

Chase Consulting Services

Southwest Division

First Quarter Sales

	Jan	Feb	Mar	Total
John	$ 1,254.00	$ 1,256.00	$ 2,435.00	$ 4,945.00
Jean	1,865.00	1,736.00	1,905.00	5,506.00
Joe	1,614.00	1,284.00	2,509.00	5,407.00
Joan	1,987.00	1,908.00	2,890.00	6,785.00
Totals	$ 6,720.00	$ 6,184.00	$ 9,739.00	$ 22,643.00

Figure 65. *Here's the same logo pasted into a worksheet to add visual appeal and emphasize corporate identity.*

Other Graphics

You can add graphics created with other programs to your Excel sheets. This enables you to include graphics that are more complex that those you can draw with Excel's drawing tools—like a company logo, stylized text, or clip art.

✔ Tip

- You can move, copy, or resize externally created graphic images like any graphic image created within Excel.

To paste in graphic objects

1. Open the file containing the graphic you want to use.
2. Select the graphic (**Figure 64**).
3. Choose Copy from the Edit menu to copy the object to the Clipboard.
4. Switch to the sheet in which you want to paste the object.
5. Choose Paste from the Edit menu (**Figure 25**), press ⌘V, or click the Paste button on the Standard toolbar. The object appears.
6. Drag the object into the desired position on the sheet (**Figure 65**).

✔ Tips

- Once you put a graphic object in an Excel sheet, it can be moved, copied, or resized just like any other graphic object.
- Use the Scrapbook (available under the Apple menu) to store graphics you use often. Excel documents aren't the only ones into which you can paste graphics!

Pasting in Graphic Objects

To insert clip art

1. Choose Clip Art from the Picture submenu under the Insert menu (**Figure 66**) to display the Microsoft Clip Gallery window (**Figure 67**).
2. Click a tab to select the type of clip you want to insert.
3. Click a category name in the list on the left side of the window to display only those clips within a certain category.
4. Click to select the clip that you want to insert.
5. Click the Insert button. The clip is inserted in the active sheet (**Figure 68**).

✔ Tips

- Only the Clip Art tab of the Microsoft Clip Gallery window includes content. The other tabs are empty. You can add content by clicking the Import Clip button to open and import a file into the currently displayed tab.
- To change a clip art image, double click it to reopen the Microsoft Clip Gallery window. Then follow steps 2 through 5.
- When a clip art image is selected, the Picture toolbar (**Figure 69**) automatically appears. You can use this toolbar to modify the appearance of pictures.

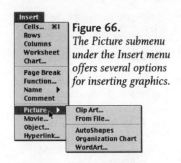

Figure 66.
The Picture submenu under the Insert menu offers several options for inserting graphics.

Figure 67. *The Microsoft Clip Gallery window.*

Figure 68.
One of the dozens of clip art pictures that comes with Excel.

Insert Picture From File, More Contrast, More Brightness, Crop, Format Picture, Reset Picture, Image Control, Less Contrast, Less Brightness, Line Style, Set Transparent Color

Figure 69. *The Picture toolbar.*

Inserting Clip Art

Figure 70. *The WordArt Gallery offers many stylized text options.*

Figure 71. *Enter your text in the Edit WordArt Text dialog box.*

Figure 72. *A WordArt image inserted in a worksheet.*

WordArt

WordArt is an application that comes with Excel. It enables you to convert any text into a colorful, three-dimensional image.

To insert WordArt

1. Choose WordArt from the Picture submenu under the Insert menu (**Figure 66**).

   or

   Click the Insert WordArt button on the Drawing toolbar to display the WordArt Gallery dialog box (**Figure 70**).

2. Click to select a WordArt style.

3. Click OK.

4. In the Edit WordArt Text dialog box that appears next (**Figure 71**), change the sample text to the text that you want to display. You can also select a different font and font size and turn on bold and/or italic formatting.

5. Click OK. The WordArt image appears in the sheet (**Figure 72**).

✔ Tips

- To change a WordArt image, double-click it to reopen the Edit WordArt Text dialog box. Then follow steps 4 and 5.

- When a WordArt image is selected, the WordArt toolbar (**Figure 73**) automatically appears. You can use this toolbar to work with WordArt images.

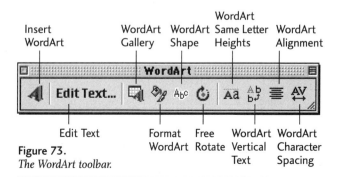

Figure 73.
The WordArt toolbar.

CREATING & FORMATTING CHARTS

Figure 1. *Here's a 3-D pie chart embedded in a worksheet file.*

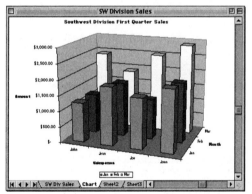

Figure 2. *Here's a 3-D column chart on a chart sheet of its own.*

Charts

A chart is a graphic representation of data. A chart can be embedded in a worksheet (**Figure 1**) or can be a chart sheet of its own (**Figure 2**).

With Excel, you can create many different types of charts. The 3-D pie chart and 3-D column chart shown here (**Figures 1** and **2**) are only two examples. Since each type of chart has at least one variation and you can customize any chart you create, there's no limit to the number of ways you can present data graphically with Excel.

✔ Tips

- Include charts with worksheets whenever you want to emphasize worksheet results. Charts can often communicate information like trends and comparative results better than numbers alone.

- A skilled chartmaker can, through choice of data, chart format, and scale, get a chart to say almost anything about the data it represents!

The Chart Wizard

Excel's Chart Wizard walks you step-by-step through the creation of a chart. It uses illustrated dialog boxes to prompt you for information. In each step of the Chart Wizard, you get to see what your chart looks like. At any point, you can go back and make changes to selections. When you're finished, your chart appears. You can then use a variety of chart formatting commands and buttons to change the look of your chart.

Charts & the Chart Wizard

To use the Chart Wizard

1. Select the data you want to include in the chart (**Figure 3**).

2. Choose Chart from the Insert menu (**Figure 4**) or click the Chart Wizard button on the Standard toolbar.

3. In the Chart Wizard – Chart Type dialog box (**Figure 5**), click to select one of the chart types in the scrolling list. Then click to select one of the chart sub-types on the right side of the dialog box. Click Next.

4. In the Chart Wizard – Chart Source Data dialog box (**Figure 6**), check the contents of the Data Range edit box to assure that it indicates the data you want to chart. You can see which data range will be charted by clicking the Collapse Dialog button so you can see the sheet behind the dialog box (**Figure 7**). If incorrect, select the correct range. If necessary, click the Expand Dialog button to display the entire dialog box again. You can also select a different Series radio button to change the way data is charted. Then click Next.

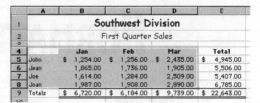

Figure 3. *Select the data you want to chart.*

Figure 4.
Choose Chart from the Insert menu.

Figure 5. *The first step of the Chart Wizard enables you to select a chart type.*

Figure 6. *The second step of the Chart Wizard enables you to check and, if necessary, change the range to be charted.*

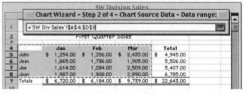

Figure 7. *You can collapse the Chart Wizard dialog box to see what range is selected.*

Figure 8. *Chart Wizard Title options.*

Figure 9. *Chart Wizard Axes options.*

Figure 10. *Chart Wizard Gridlines options.*

Figure 11. *Chart Wizard Legend options.*

Figure 12. *Chart Wizard Data Labels options.*

Figure 13. *Chart Wizard Data Table options.*

5. In the Chart Wizard – Chart Options dialog box, use the tabs at the top of the dialog box to set a variety of formatting options:

▲ **Titles** (**Figure 8**) enables you to set a chart title and axes titles.

▲ **Axes** (**Figure 9**) enables you to select which axes you want to display.

▲ **Gridlines** (**Figure 10**) enables you to select which gridlines to display.

▲ **Legend** (**Figure 11**) enables you to show and position or hide the legend.

▲ **Data Labels** (**Figure 12**) enables you to set the type of data labels that should be displayed.

▲ **Data Table** (**Figure 13**) enables you to include a data table with the chart.

Set options as desired. When you change a setting, the sample chart changes accordingly. When you are finished, click Next.

Using the Chart Wizard

6. In the Chart Wizard — Chart Location dialog box **(Figure 14)**, select the radio button to set the location for the chart:

 ▲ As **new sheet** puts the chart on a new chart sheet. You can enter a name in the edit box to name the new sheet when you create it.

 ▲ As **object in** puts the chart on another sheet in the workbook. You can use the pop-up menu to select the sheet.

7. Click Finish.

 Excel creates and inserts the chart with the settings and in the location you specified.

✔ Tips

■ At any time while using the Chart Wizard, you can click the Back button to move to a previous step. Any changes you make in a previous step are carried forward when you continue.

■ In step 3, to see what your data would look like when charted with the chart type and sub-type you select, click and hold down the Press and Hold to View Sample button **(Figure 15)**.

■ In step 3, you can select one of the custom chart types by clicking the Custom Types tab **(Figure 16)**. Then follow the instructions in step 3 for that tab.

■ In step 4, you can add, modify, or delete data series for the chart in the Series tab **(Figure 17)**. I tell you about working with data series later in this chapter.

■ I explain all the options in step 5 throughout this book.

Figure 14. *The final step of the Chart Wizard.*

Figure 15. *You can preview what your chart will look like with the chart type and sub-type you selected by clicking a button in the first window of the Chart Wizard.*

Figure 16. *The Chart Wizard also allows you to select some custom chart types from the Chart Gallery.*

Using the Chart Wizard

Figure 17. *You can also add, modify, or remove data series from a chart within the Chart Wizard.*

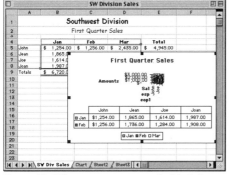

Figure 18. *When you create an embedded chart, Excel just plops it on the worksheet.*

Figure 19. *You can move and resize a chart to improve its appearance.*

- In step 5, axes and gridlines options are only available for charts that have axes or gridlines. Pie charts, for example, have neither axes nor gridlines.

- A chart embedded in a worksheet or a chart sheet is a special kind of graphic. You can move, copy, resize, or delete it just like any other graphic object. I tell you how to work with graphics in **Chapter 7**.

- If an embedded chart is too small to properly display data (**Figure 18**), resize it. The larger the chart, the better it will display (**Figure 19**).

- You can also improve the appearance of an embedded chart by resizing or removing chart elements such as legends, axes labels, and data tables.

- You're not stuck with the formatting you select in the Chart Wizard. I tell you about chart formatting options throughout this chapter.

- Don't be afraid to experiment with the Chart Wizard. Try different options to see what effects you can achieve. You can always delete the chart and start fresh. Deleting a chart does not change data.

To reuse the Chart Wizard

1. Activate the chart by switching to its chart sheet or, if it's an embedded chart, by clicking within it.

2. Click the Chart Wizard button on the Standard toolbar.

3. Follow the steps on the previous pages to set or change Chart Wizard options for the chart.

Worksheet & Chart Links

When you create a chart based on worksheet data, the worksheet and chart are linked. Excel knows exactly which worksheet and cells it should look at to plot the chart. If the contents of one of those cells changes, the chart changes accordingly (**Figures 20** and **21**).

Figures 20 & 21. *A linked worksheet and chart before (top) and after (bottom) a change to a cell's contents. When you change one, the other changes automatically.*

✔ Tips

- The link works both ways. With some chart types, you can drag a data point to change the data in the source worksheet (**Figure 22**). This makes a good planning tool for businesses interested in maintaining trends.

- Excel's Range Finder feature places a color-coded box around ranges in a selected chart (**Figure 23**), making them easy to spot.

- You can see (and edit) the links between a chart and a worksheet by activating the chart, selecting one of the data series, and looking at the formula bar. You should see a formula with a SERIES function that specifies the sheet name and absolute cell references for the range making up that series. **Figure 23** shows an example.

- If you delete worksheet data or an entire worksheet that is linked to a chart, Excel warns you with a dialog box like the one in **Figure 24**. If you removed the data by mistake, choose Undo Delete from the Edit menu, click the Undo button on the Standard toolbar, or press ⌘Z to get the deleted data back.

Figure 22. *Dragging a data point changes the data in the linked cell.*

Figure 23. *This illustration shows both the Range Finder feature and the SERIES formula.*

Figure 24. *If you delete cells linked to a chart, you may see a dialog box like this.*

Figure 25. *When you activate a chart, Range Finder frames appear around each data series.*

Figure 26. *Drag a Range Finder handle to change the size of the series.*

Figure 27. *When you release the mouse button, the series—and the chart— changes.*

Data Series & Points

A *data series* is a group of related data in a chart. A data series normally corresponds to the values in a linked range of cells in a single column or row of a single worksheet. When plotted on a chart, each data series is assigned its own color or pattern.

Each cell within a data series is called a *data point*. Data points are individually plotted on a chart.

You can change data series included in a chart at any time using four different methods:

- Use Range Finder handles to modify a series in an embedded chart.

- Use the Source Data dialog box to add, modify, or remove a series.

- Use the Copy and Paste commands to paste in a new series.

- Use drag and drop editing to drag in a new series.

I tell you about all these techniques next.

To modify a data series with Range Finder handles

1. Click the chart to activate it. Range Finder frames with handles appear around each data series (**Figure 25**).

2. Position the mouse pointer on the handle for the series you want to change. The mouse pointer turns into a thick crosshairs pointer.

3. Press the mouse button down, and drag to stretch or shrink the series (**Figure 26**).

4. When you release the mouse button, the series (and any related series) changes, thus changing the information plotted in the chart (**Figure 27**).

✔ Tip

- You can only use this method with an embedded chart.

To modify data series with the Data Source dialog box

1. Activate the chart by switching to its chart sheet or, if it's an embedded chart, by clicking within it.

2. Choose Source Data from the Chart menu (**Figure 28**) to display the Source Data dialog box (**Figures 29** and **30**).

3. Click the Data Range tab (**Figure 29**):

   ▲ To change the range of data plotted in the chart, select a new data range. As you select the range, it is automatically entered in the Data range edit box for you.

   ▲ To switch the series from column to row or row to column, select the appropriate Series in radio button.

   or

   Click the Series tab (**Figure 30**):

   ▲ To add a data series, click the Add button, then drag in the worksheet to enter a range in the Name and Values edit boxes.

   ▲ To modify a data series, select the name of the series you want to change, then drag in the worksheet to modify the range in the Name and/or Values edit boxes.

   ▲ To remove a data series, select the name of the series you want to remove and click the Remove button.

4. Consult the sample chart in the dialog box to see the affect of your changes. When the chart reflects the correct data ranges, click OK.

✔ Tips

■ The Source Data dialog box looks (and works) just like the second step of the Chart Wizard (**Figures 6** and **17**). In fact, you can use the Chart Wizard to make any of the changes discussed on this page.

Figure 28.
The Chart menu appears only when a chart is active.

Figure 29. *The Data Range tab of the Source Data dialog box.*

Figure 30. *The Series tab of the Source Data dialog box.*

■ You can click the Collapse Dialog or Expand Dialog buttons to change the size of the Source Data dialog box.

■ Removing a data series does not delete data from the source worksheet.

Using the Data Series Dialog Box

Figure 31. *Select the data that you want to add to the chart.*

Figure 32.
The Edit menu includes the Copy, Paste, and Paste Special commands, which you can use to add data to a chart.

Figure 33. *When you paste in the data, the chart changes accordingly.*

Figure 34.
The Paste Special dialog box offers additional options for pasting data into charts.

To add a data series with the Copy & Paste commands

1. In the worksheet, select the data you want to add to the chart (**Figure 31**). Be sure to include column or row headings if they should be included as labels.

2. Choose Copy from the Edit menu (**Figure 32**), press ⌃⌘C or click the Copy button on the Standard toolbar.

    A marquee appears around the selected cells.

3. Activate the chart to which you want to add the data by switching to its chart sheet or, if it's an embedded chart, by clicking within it.

4. Choose Paste from the Edit menu (**Figure 32**), press ⌃⌘V, or click the Paste button on the Standard toolbar.

    The chart changes to include the additional data (**Figure 33**).

✔ Tips

- In order for this technique to work properly, the data you add must be the same kind of data originally charted. For example, if you originally plotted totals to create a pie chart, you can't successfully add a series of numbers that aren't totals to the chart.

- For additional control over how data is pasted into a chart, choose Paste Special from the Edit menu (**Figure 32**) in step 4 above. The Paste Special dialog box (**Figure 34**) will sometimes appear on its own when you paste a range into a chart.

Adding a Data Series with Copy & Paste

To add a data series with drag & drop

1. In the worksheet, select the data you want to add to the chart (**Figure 35**). Be sure to include column or row headings if they should be included as labels.

2. Position the mouse pointer on the border of the selection. The mouse pointer turns into an arrow.

3. Press the mouse button down and drag the selection on top of the chart. The mouse pointer gets a little plus sign next to it and the chart border changes (**Figure 36**).

4. Release the mouse button.

   The chart changes to include the additional data (**Figure 37**).

✔ Tips

■ In order for this technique to work properly, the data you add must be the same kind of data originally charted. For example, if you originally plotted totals to create a pie chart, you can't successfully add a series of numbers that aren't totals to the chart.

■ This technique only works for charts that are embedded in the worksheet containing the original data.

■ To add data contained in noncontiguous ranges, use one of the other methods discussed in this section.

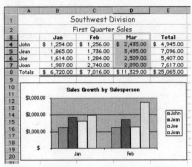

Figure 35. *Select the data you want to add to the chart.*

Figure 36. *Drag the selection onto the chart.*

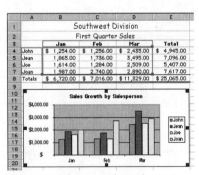

Figure 37. *When you release the mouse button, the data is added to the chart.*

Adding a Data Series with Drag & Drop

Figure 38.
Select the series you want to remove.

Figure 39.
Choose Series from the Clear submenu under the Edit menu.

Figure 40.
All trace of the series is removed from the chart.

Figure 41.
Chart tips identify the chart elements and values you point to.

Figure 42. *The name of a selected element appears in the Name Box on the formula bar.*

To remove a data series

1. Click to select the series you want to remove. Selection handles appear at each data point in the series (**Figure 38**).

2. Choose Series from the Clear submenu under the Edit menu (**Figure 39**), press ⌘⌥B, or press Del.

   The series disappears (**Figure 40**). If the chart included a legend, it is revised to exclude the deleted data.

✔ Tips

- Removing a series from a chart does not delete data from the source worksheet.

- You can also remove a data series with the Source Data dialog box (**Figure 30**). I tell you how earlier in this chapter.

Chart Elements

Each chart is made up of multiple elements, each of which can be selected, then modified or formatted to fine-tune the appearance of a chart.

To identify a chart element

Point to the element you want to identify. Excel displays the name (and values, if appropriate) for the element in a yellow Chart Tip box (**Figure 41**).

To select a chart element

Click the element you want to select. Selection handles or a selection box (or both) appear around it (**Figure 42**).

✔ Tips

- To select a single data point, first click to select the data series, then click the point to select it.

- Excel displays the name of a selected chart element in the Name Box on the formula bar (**Figure 42**).

Chart Type

Excel includes dozens of standard and custom chart types. You select the chart type when you create a chart with the Chart Wizard, but you can change the type at any time. You can also add your formatted charts to the chart gallery so you can use them to create future charts.

To change the chart type

1. Activate the chart by switching to its chart sheet or, if it's an embedded chart, by clicking within it.

2. Choose Chart Type from the Chart menu (**Figure 28**) to display the Chart Type dialog box.

3. Click the Standard Types tab (**Figure 43**):

   ▲ To select a standard chart type, select a Chart type, then select a Chart sub-type.

   ▲ To apply a chart type to a selected data series, turn on the Apply to selection check box.

   ▲ To remove formatting you have applied to the chart, turn on the Default formatting check box.

   or

   Click the Custom Type tab:

   ▲ To select a built-in chart type, select the Built-in radio button (**Figure 44**), then select a Chart type.

   ▲ To select a user-defined chart type, select the User-defined radio button (**Figure 45**), then select a Chart type.

4. Click OK to apply the chart type.

✔ Tip

■ The Chart Type dialog box looks (and works) just like the first step of the Chart Wizard (**Figures 5** and **15**). In fact, you can use the Chart Wizard to make any of the changes discussed on this page.

Figure 43. *The Standard Types tab of the Chart Types dialog box.*

Figure 44. *The Custom Types tab of the Chart Types dialog box with Built-in selected.*

Figure 45. *The Custom Types tab of the Chart Types dialog box with User-defined selected.*

Figure 46. *Use the Add Custom Chart Type dialog box to enter a name and description for a chart type.*

Figure 47. *The chart type you added appears in the User-defined Chart type list.*

To set the default chart type

1. Choose Chart Type from the Chart menu (**Figure 28**) to display the Chart Type dialog box.

2. Click the Standard Types tab (**Figure 43**).

3. Select the Chart type and sub-type you want to set as the default chart type.

4. Click the Set as Default Chart button.

5. Click OK.

✔ Tip

■ The default chart type is the one automatically selected for creating a new chart.

To add a user-defined chart to the Chart Type dialog box

1. Activate the formatted chart you want to add by switching to its chart sheet or, if it's an embedded chart, by clicking within it.

2. Choose Chart Type from the Chart menu (**Figure 28**) to display the Chart Type dialog box.

3. Click the Custom Type tab.

4. Select the User-defined radio button (**Figure 45**)

5. Click the Add button.

6. In the Add Custom Chart Type dialog box that appears (**Figure 46**), enter a name and description for the chart in the appropriate edit boxes.

7. Click OK.

   The chart appears in the User-defined Chart type list (**Figure 47**).

8. Click OK.

✔ Tip

■ This feature makes it easy to create the same basic charts over and over again with different data—like you might have to do for a monthly report.

Setting Default & Adding Chart Types

Chart Options

Chart options refer to the inclusion and basic formatting of chart elements such as titles, axes, gridlines, legend, data labels, and data tables. You set chart options with the Chart Options dialog box.

To use the Chart Options dialog box

1. Activate the chart by switching to its chart sheet or, if it's an embedded chart, by clicking within it.

2. Choose Chart Options from the Chart menu (**Figure 28**) to display the Chart Options dialog box (**Figure 48**).

3. Click the tab for the type of option you want to set.

4. Set options as desired.

5. Repeat steps 3 and 4 for each type of option you want to set.

6. Click OK to apply your settings.

✔ Tips

- I provide details on all options on the following pages.

- The Chart Options dialog box looks (and works) just like the third step of the Chart Wizard (**Figures 8** through 13). In fact, you can use the Chart Wizard to make any of the changes discussed on this page.

- Each time you make a change in the Chart Options dialog box, the effect of your change is reflected in the chart preview within the dialog box. Use this feature to check your changes before clicking OK to apply them to the chart.

- The options available in the Chart Options dialog box vary based on the type of chart that is selected. If a specific option is not available, it will either not appear or it will appear in gray within the dialog box.

Figure 48. *The Titles tab of the Chart Options dialog box for a 3-D column chart. The sample illustration shows all titles set.*

Titles

Titles are textual labels that appear in specific locations on the chart.

To set chart titles

1. In the Chart Options dialog box click the Titles tab to display its options (**Figure 48**).

2. Enter titles in the desired edit boxes:

   ▲ **Chart title** is the chart's main title. It appears at the top of the chart.

   ▲ **Category (X) axis** is the category axis title. Available for most 2-D and 3-D chart types, it appears along the bottom (front) axis.

   ▲ **Series (Y) axis** is the series axis title. Available for most chart types, it appears down the left side of a 2-D chart and along the bottom (back) axis of 3-D chart.

   ▲ **Value (Z) axis** is the value axis title. Available only for 3-D chart types, it appears down the left side of the chart.

To remove a chart title

1. In the Chart Options dialog box click the Titles tab to display its options (**Figure 48**).

2. Clear the edit box(es) for the titles you want to remove.

Setting & Removing Chart Titles

Axes

Axes are the bounding lines of a chart. 2-D charts have two axes: X and Y. 3-D charts have three axes: X, Y, and Z. Pie and doughnut charts do not have axes at all.

✔ Tip

- In case you're wondering, *axes* (pronounced *ax-eez*) is the plural of *axis*. While axes are also tools for chopping wood, you can't chop wood with Excel.

To set axes options

1. In the Chart Options dialog box click the Axes tab to display its options (**Figure 49**).

2. Turn on the check boxes for the axes you want to display:

   ▲ **Category (X) axis** appears along the bottom (front) axis.

   ▲ **Series (Y) axis** appears down the left side of a 2-D chart and along the bottom (back) axis of 3-D chart.

   ▲ **Value (Z) axis**, which is available only for 3-D chart types, appears down the left side of the chart.

3. If you turned on the Category (X) axis option in step 2, select one of the formatting option radio buttons:

   ▲ **Automatic** instructs Excel to check the formatting of the category data to determine whether it should use time-scale or category formatting.

   ▲ **Category** instructs Excel to use the category data for the X axis.

   ▲ **Time-Scale** instructs Excel to create a time scale for the X axis.

Figure 49. *The Axes tab of the Chart Options dialog box for a 3-D column chart. The sample illustration shows all axes displayed.*

Figure 50. *The Gridlines tab of the Chart Options dialog box for a 3-D column chart. The sample illustration shows only the major gridlines for the Value (Z) axis turned on.*

Gridlines

Gridlines are lines indicating major and minor scale points along a chart's walls. They can make it easier to follow chart points to corresponding values on a chart axis. Pie and doughnut charts do not have gridlines.

✔ Tip

- Although gridlines can make a chart's data easier to read, too many gridlines can clutter a chart's walls, making data impossible to read.

To set gridlines

1. In the Chart Options dialog box click the Gridlines tab to display its options (**Figure 50**).

2. Turn on the check boxes for the gridlines you want to display on each axis:
   ▲ **Major gridlines** correspond to major tickmark units for the axis scale.
   ▲ **Minor gridlines** correspond to minor tickmark units for the axis scale.

3. To apply a 2-D appearance to 3-D chart walls and gridlines, turn on the 2-D walls and gridlines check box. This option is only available for certain types of charts.

✔ Tips

- I explain how to set the scale for an axis later in this chapter.
- I define the three axes on the previous page.

Setting Gridlines

Legend

A legend is a box with color coded labels identifying a chart's data series. You can turn a legend on or off and set its position within the chart area.

✔ Tip

- Excel creates the legend based on cells selected as part of the data source. That's why it's a good idea to include column and/or row headings in the selected range when you create a chart.

To add a legend

1. In the Chart Options dialog box click the Legend tab to display its options (**Figure 51**).

2. Turn on the Show Legend check box.

3. Select one of the radio buttons for a legend position:

   ▲ **Bottom** displays the legend at the bottom-center of the chart.

   ▲ **Corner** displays the legend at the top-right corner of the chart.

   ▲ **Top** displays the legend at the top-center of the chart.

   ▲ **Right** displays the legend at the right-middle of the chart.

   ▲ **Left** displays the legend at the left-middle of the chart.

✔ Tips

- You can also move a legend by dragging it to a new position within the chart.

- The legend position can affect the size of a chart's plot area.

To remove the legend

1. In the Chart Options dialog box click the Legend tab to display its options (**Figure 51**).

2. Turn off the Show Legend check box.

Figure 51. *The Legend tab of the Chart Options dialog box for a 3-D column chart. The sample illustration shows a legend placed at the bottom of the chart.*

Figure 52. *The Data Labels tab of the Chart Options dialog box for a 3-D pie chart. The sample illustration shows percent data labels.*

Data Labels

Data labels provide additional information about specific data points.

✔ Tip

■ The Chart Options dialog box enables you to set data labels for all chart points. To set data labels for just a single data series or data point, select the series or point, then use the Format dialog box, which I tell you about later in this chapter.

To set data labels

1. In the Chart Options dialog box click the Data Labels tab to display its options (**Figure 52**).

2. Select one of the Data labels radio buttons:
   ▲ **None** removes all data labels.
   ▲ **Show value** displays the value for each data point.
   ▲ **Show percent** displays the percentage of the whole for each data point. This option is only available for pie and doughnut charts.
   ▲ **Show label** displays the legend label for each data point.
   ▲ **Show label and percent** displays the both the legend label and percentage of the whole for each data point. This option is only available for pie and doughnut charts.
   ▲ **Show bubble sizes** displays the size of bubbles in a bubble chart.

3. To show the legend color key beside a data label, turn on the Legend key next to label check box.

4. For a pie or doughnut chart, to display a line from the data point to the data label, turn on the Show leader lines check box.

Setting Data Labels

Data Table

A data table is the data plotted on the chart, in tabular format.

✔ Tips

- Data tables are more useful on chart sheets than on embedded charts, since embedded charts can include the worksheet on which the chart is based.

- Data tables are not available for pie and doughnut charts.

To add a data table

1. In the Chart Options dialog box click the Data Table tab to display its options (**Figure 53**).
2. Turn on the Show data table check box.
3. To show the legend color key in the data table, turn on Show legend keys check box.

To remove a data table

1. In the Chart Options dialog box click the Data Table tab to display its options (**Figure 53**).
2. Turn off the Show data table check box.

Figure 53. *The Data Table tab of the Chart Options dialog box for a 3-D column chart. The sample illustration shows a data table with legend keys turned on.*

Figure 54. *Formatting can make this boring, default chart...*

Figure 55. *...look interesting!*

Formatting Chart Elements

You can use the Format dialog box to apply a variety of formatting to chart elements:

- **Font** enables you to change the appearance of an element's font characters.

- **Number** enables you to change the number formatting of values.

- **Alignment** enables you to change the alignment and orientation of text.

- **Patterns** enables you to change an element's color and pattern. It also enables you to set axis tick mark styles.

- **Placement** enables you to set the position for a chart legend.

- **Scale** enables you to change the values that appear on an axis.

- **Shape** enables you to change the shape of data points.

- **Data Labels** enables you to set data labels for a single data series or data point. I discuss these options earlier in this chapter.

- **Series Order** enables you to change the order in which data series appear.

- **Options** enables you to set data series spacing options.

Figures 54 and **55** may give you an idea of what you can do with chart formatting.

In this section, I tell you how chart formatting works and discuss some of the formatting options available just for charts.

✔ Tip

- I discuss pattern, font, number, and alignment formatting in **Chapter 6**. I discuss legend position and data labels earlier in this chapter.

To use the Format dialog box

1. Select the chart element that you want to format and choose the first command under the Format menu (**Figures 56, 57,** and **58**).

   or

   Double-click the element that you want to format.

2. In the Format dialog box that appears, click the tab for the type of option you want to set.

3. Set options as desired.

4. Repeat steps 2 and 3 for each type of option you want to set.

5. Click OK to apply the formatting.

✔ Tips

- The exact name of the menu command in step 1 varies depending on the chart element that is selected. You can see this in **Figures 56, 57,** and **58**.

- The exact name of the Format dialog box in step 2 varies depending on the chart element that is selected. You can see this in **Figures 59** and **61**.

To set the data point shape

1. Open the Format Data Series dialog box for a selected data series.

2. Click the Shape tab to display its options (**Figure 59**).

3. Click to select the desired shape.

4. Click OK.

   The shape is applied to the seleted data series (**Figure 60**).

✔ Tip

- This option is only available for certain 3-D charts.

Figures 56, 57, & 58. *The first command under the Format menu enables you to format the selected chart element.*

Figure 59. *The Shape tab of the Format Data Series dialog box enables you to select a shape to apply to the selected series in a 3-D chart.*

Figure 60. *In this example, shape style #6 was applied to one data series.*

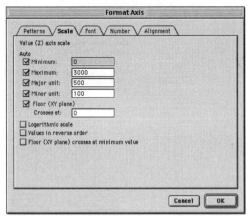

Figure 61. *The Scale tab of the Format Axis dialog box.*

To set the scale

1. Open the Format Gridlines or Format Axis dialog box for the gridline or axis for which you want to set the scale.
2. Click the Scale tab to display its options (**Figure 61**).
3. Enter the scale values you want to use in the edit boxes:
   - ▲ **Minimum** is the minimum value on the scale. It is normally set to 0.
   - ▲ **Maximum** is the maximum value on the scale. It is normally set to a round number larger than the highest value plotted.
   - ▲ **Major unit** is the unit corresponding to major gridlines and tick marks.
   - ▲ **Minor unit** is the unit corresponding to minor gridlines and tick marks.
   - ▲ **Floor (XY plane) Crosses at** is the value at which the X and Y axes cross each other. It is normally set to 0.
4. Turn on check boxes for special scale options as desired:
   - ▲ **Logarithmic scale** recalculates the values in the edit boxes as powers of 10.
   - ▲ **Values in reverse order** reverses the order in which the scale appears, putting the largest values at the bottom or left side of the axis.
   - ▲ **Floor (XY plane) crosses at minimum value** overrides the Floor (XY plane) Crosses at value and sets it to the minimum value.
5. Click OK.

✔ Tip

- ■ When you enter a value in an edit box, its corresponding check box should turn itself off automatically; you can turn it back on to use the default setting.

Setting Scale

To set tick marks

1. Open the Format Axis dialog box for the axis for which you want to set the tick marks.

2. Click the Patterns tab to display its options (**Figure 62**).

3. Select the radio button for the desired Tick mark labels option:

   ▲ **None** omits tick mark labels.

   ▲ **Low** displays tick mark labels at the bottom or to the right of the plot area.

   ▲ **High** displays tick mark labels that the top or to the left of the plot area.

   ▲ **Next to axis** displays tick mark labels next to the selected axis. This is the default option.

4. Select the radio buttons for the desired Major tick mark type and Minor tick mark type:

   ▲ **None** omits tick marks.

   ▲ **Inside** displays tick marks inside the plot area.

   ▲ **Outside** displays tick marks outside the plot area.

   ▲ **Cross** displays tick marks that cross the axis line.

5. If desired, use options in the Axis area to modify the appearance of the Axis.

6. Click OK.

Figure 62. *The Patterns tab of the Format Axis dialog box.*

Figure 63. *To move a chart element, drag it to its new position.*

Figure 64. *When you release the mouse button, it moves.*

Figure 65. *When you move a piece of a pie chart away from the rest of the pie…*

Figure 66. *…you get an "exploded" effect.*

Other Formatting Options

In addition to formatting individual chart elements, you can make other modifications to a chart to change the way it appears. Here are a few additional options you may find handy.

To move a chart element

1. Click the element to select it.
2. Position the mouse pointer on the element, press the mouse button down, and drag. As you drag, an outline of the element moves with the mouse pointer (**Figure 63**).
3. Release the mouse button. The element moves (**Figure 64**).

✔ Tip

■ You can use this technique with most chart elements.

To "explode" a pie chart

1. Select the data point for the pie piece you want to move.
2. Drag the pie piece away from the pie (**Figure 65**).
3. Release the mouse button. The piece moves away from the pie (**Figure 66**).

✔ Tip

■ If desired, you can drag more than one piece away from the pie.

Moving Elements, Exploding Pies

To rotate a 3-D chart

1. Activate the chart you want to rotate (**Figure 67**).

2. Choose 3-D View from the Chart menu (**Figure 28**).

3. In the 3-D View dialog box (**Figure 68**), click the Elevation, Rotation, and Perspective buttons to change the view of the chart.

4. When you're finished making changes, click OK. The chart rotates (**Figure 69**).

✔ Tips

■ You can click the Apply button in the 3-D View dialog box (**Figure 68**) to get a first-hand look at the modified chart without closing the dialog box. You may have to drag the Format 3-D View dialog box out of the way to see your chart.

■ You can click the Default button in the 3-D View dialog box to return the chart to its default rotation.

■ Some changes in the 3-D View dialog box may change the size of the chart.

To resize a chart element

1. Click the element to select it.

2. Position the mouse pointer on one of the resizing handles for the element, press the mouse button down, and drag. As you drag, the border of the element moves with the mouse pointer (**Figure 70**).

3. Release the mouse button. The element resizes (**Figure 71**).

✔ Tip

■ You can use this technique with most chart elements.

Figure 67. *A chart before rotation.*

Figure 68. *The 3-D view dialog box.*

Figure 69. *The chart from Figure 67 after rotation.*

Figure 70. *Drag a selection handle…*

Figure 71. *…to resize almost any chart element.*

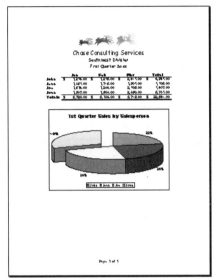

Figure 1. *Print Preview lets you see reports before you commit them to paper.*

Printing

In most cases, when you create a worksheet or chart, you'll want to print it. With Excel, you can print all or part of a sheet, multiple sheets, or an entire workbook—all at once. Excel gives you control over page size, margins, headers, footers, page breaks, orientation, scaling, page order, and content. Its Print Preview feature (**Figure 1**) shows you what your report will look like when printed, so you can avoid wasteful, time-consuming reprints.

Printing is basically a three-step process:

1. Use the Page Setup dialog box to set up your report for printing. You can skip this step if you set the report up the last time you printed it and don't need to change the setup.

2. Use the Print Preview feature to take a look at your report before committing it to paper. You can skip this step if you already know what the report will look like.

3. Use the Print command to send the desired number of copies to the printer for printing.

In this chapter, I tell you about each of these steps.

✔ Tip

- When you save a document, Excel saves many Page Setup and Print options with it.

Printer Drivers

Your computer uses a *printer driver* to communicate with your printer. A printer driver is a special kind of system file called a *Chooser extension*.

By default, a number of Apple printer drivers are installed in the Extensions folder inside your System Folder when you install the System software. If you buy a printer made by a company other than Apple (such as Hewlett-Packard or Epson), the printer comes with printer driver software that you must install before you can use the printer.

Figure 2. *Apple's Chooser, with the LaserWriter 8 driver and a PostScript printer selected.*

✔ Tips

■ Use Apple's Chooser (**Figure 2**) to select and set up your printer. You only have to do this once for all your programs—unless you have multiple printers and often switch from one to the other. Chances are, your printer has already been selected and is ready to use.

■ The appearance and options in the standard Page Setup and Print dialog boxes vary depending on the printer driver selected in the Chooser and the version of the System software installed on your computer. It is impossible to show all possibilities in this book. Instead, I provide specific information for only two commonly used printer drivers installed on a Mac OS 8.1 computer: the Color StyleWriter 2500 and LaserWriter 8. The options supported by your printer will be similar to one of these.

■ To learn more about the Chooser and the printing options supported by your printer, consult the documentation that came with Mac OS or your printer.

Printer Drivers

Figure 3. *The Page tab of Excel's Page Setup dialog box.*

Figure 4.
The File menu offers a number of printing-related commands.

The Page Setup Dialog Box

The Page Setup dialog box (**Figure 3**) lets you set up a document for printing. Setup options are organized under the following tabs:

- **Page (Figure 3)** lets you set the orientation, scaling, first page number, and print quality.

- **Margins (Figures 8** and **9)** lets you set the page margins, the distance the header and footer should be from the edge of the paper, and the positioning of the document on the paper.

- **Header/Footer (Figure 10)** lets you select a standard header and footer or create custom ones.

- **Sheet (Figure 16)** lets you specify the print area, print titles, items to print, and page order. If a chart sheet is active when you choose Page setup, you'll see a Chart tab **(Figure 23)** rather than a Sheet tab. Use it to specify the printed chart size and print quality.

✔ Tip

- You may have noticed that this Page Setup dialog box looks very different from the Apple standard. If you want to see the standard Apple Page Setup dialog box (**Figures 5** and **6**) for your printer, click the Options button in the Excel Page Setup dialog box.

To open Excel's Page Setup dialog box

Choose Page Setup from the File menu. (**Figure 4**).

or

Click the Setup button in the Print Preview window (**Figure 24**).

Page Setup Options

To set the paper size

1. Click the Options button on any tab in Excel's Page Setup dialog box (**Figure 3**).

2. In the standard Page Setup dialog box that appears (**Figures 5** and **6**), choose a paper size from the pop-up menu.

3. Click OK to dismiss the dialog box.

To set page options

1. In Excel's Page Setup dialog box, click the Page tab to display its options (**Figure 3**).

2. In the Orientation area, select the desired orientation radio button:

   ▲ **Portrait**, the default option for worksheets, prints vertically down the page.

   ▲ **Landscape**, the default option for chart sheets, prints horizontally across the page.

3. For a worksheet only, in the Scaling area, select the desired scaling radio button:

   ▲ **Adjust to** enables you to specify a percentage of the normal size for printing. Be sure to enter a value in the edit box. This option is selected by default with 100 in the edit box.

   ▲ **Fit to** instructs Excel to shrink the report so it fits on the number of pages you specify. Be sure to enter values in the two edit boxes.

4. If desired, in the First page number edit box, enter a value that should be used as the page number on the first page of the report. This enables you to start page numbering at a value other than 1.

5. Choose an option from the Print quality pop-up menu (**Figure 7**). The default value is High.

6. Click OK to save your settings.

Figure 5. *Apple's standard Page Setup dialog box for the LaserWriter 8 printer driver…*

Figure 6. *…and Color LaserWriter 2500 printer driver.*

Figure 7. *The Print quality pop-up menu with the LaserWriter 8 printer driver selected. Options on this menu can vary from one printer to another.*

✔ Tips

■ You can also change the page orientation in the Apple Page Setup dialog box (**Figures 5** and **6**).

■ Neither scaling option is available for chart sheets. You can change the scaling for a chart sheet on the Chart tab of the Page Setup dialog box, which I discuss later in this chapter.

Setting Paper Size & Page Options

Figure 8. *The Margins tab of the Page Setup dialog box for a worksheet...*

Figure 9. *...and for a chart sheet.*

To set margins & centering options

1. In Excel's Page Setup dialog box, click the Margins tab to display its options (**Figure 8** or **9**).

2. Enter values in the Top, Left, Right, and Bottom edit boxes to set the amount of space between the edge of the paper and the report content.

3. Enter values in the Header and Footer edit boxes to set the amount of space between the edge of the paper and the header and footer content.

4. For a worksheet only, turn on the desired Center on page check boxes:

    ▲ **Horizontally** centers the report content between the left and right margins.

    ▲ **Vertically** centers the report content between the top and bottom margins.

5. Click OK to save your settings.

✔ Tips

■ As you make changes in this window, the preview area changes accordingly. This helps you get an idea of what the document will look like when previewed or printed.

■ You can also set margins in the Print Preview window. I tell you how later in this chapter.

■ Do not set margins to smaller values than the Header and Footer values or Excel will print your report over the header or footer.

■ Some printers cannot print close to the edge of the paper. If part of your report is cut off when printed, increase the margin, header, and footer values.

Setting Margins & Centering Options

Adding & Removing Headers & Footers

To add built-in headers & footers

1. In Excel's Page Setup dialog box, click the Header/Footer tab to display its options (**Figure 10**).

2. Choose options from the Header and Footer pop-up menus (**Figure 11**).

    The option(s) you selected appear in the sample area(s) in the dialog box (**Figure 12**).

3. Click OK to save your settings.

✔ Tips

■ The pop-up menu for Footer is identical to the one for Header.

■ Excel gets your name and company name from entries you made when you installed Excel. You can change the name by choosing Preferences from the Tools menu, entering a new User name in the General tab, and clicking OK. You cannot change the company name without reinstalling Excel.

■ To change the formatting of text in the header or footer, you need to use the Custom Header or Custom Footer button in the Header/Footer tab of the Page Setup dialog box. I tell you about that next.

To add custom headers & footers

1. In Excel's Page Setup dialog box, click the Header/Footer tab to display its options (**Figure 10**).

2. To add a header, click the Custom Header button to display the Header dialog box (**Figure 13**).

3. Enter the text or codes that you want to appear in the header in the Left Section, Center Section, and Right Section edit boxes. You can use the buttons in **Table 1** to format selected text or insert codes for dynamic information. **Figure 14** shows an example.

Figure 10. *The Header/Footer tab of the Page Setup dialog box.*

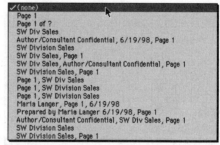
Figure 11. *The Header and Footer pop-up menus offer a number of predefined headers and footers.*

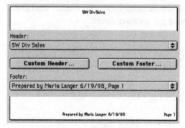
Figure 12. *The header and footer you select appear in the sample areas in the dialog box.*

Figure 13. *The Header dialog box.*

	Use the Font button to format selected text. I tell you about the Font dialog box in Chapter 6.
	Use the Page Number button to insert the &[Page] code. This inserts the page number.
	Use the Total Pages button to insert the &[Pages] code. This inserts the total pages number.
	Use the Date button to insert the &[Date] code. This inserts the print date.
	Use the Time button to insert the &[Time] code. This inserts the print time.
	Use the Filename button to insert the &[File] code. This inserts the workbook name.
	Use the Sheet Name button to insert the &[Tab] code. This inserts the sheet name.

Table 1. *Use these buttons to insert codes for dynamic information.*

Left Section:	Center Section:	Right Section:
&[File]	&[Tab]	Prepared by Maria Langer &[Date] at &[Time]

Figure 14. *An example of a custom header entered into the Header dialog box.*

SW Division Sales	SW Div Sales	Prepared by Maria Langer 6/19/98 at 10:21 AM

Header:
SW Division Sales, SW Div Sales, Prepared by Maria Langer6

Figure 15. *Here's the header from* **Figure 14** *in the Page Setup dialog box.*

4. Click OK to save your settings.

   The settings appear in the Page Setup dialog box **(Figure 15)**.

5. To add a footer, click the Custom Footer button. This displays the Footer dialog box, which looks and works just like the Header dialog box.

6. Repeat steps 3 and 4 for the footer.

7. Click OK in the Page Setup dialog box to save your settings.

✔ Tips

■ In step 3, to enter an ampersand (&) character in a header or footer, type && where you want it to appear.

■ To specify the starting page number to be printed in the header or footer, enter a value in the First page number edit box of the Page tab of the Page Setup dialog box **(Figure 3)**.

■ Dynamic information is information that changes automatically. For example the page number changes automatically for each page and the print date changes automatically each day you print the file. Using the buttons or codes for dynamic information **(Table 1)** ensures header and footer contents are accurate.

To remove headers & footers

1. In Excel's Page Setup dialog box, click the Header/Footer tab to display its options **(Figure 10)**.

2. Choose (none) from the Header and Footer pop-up menus **(Figure 11)**.

   The header and footer disappear from the dialog box.

3. Click OK to save your settings.

To set sheet options

1. In Excel's Page Setup dialog box, click the Sheet tab to display its options (**Figure 16**).

2. To print less than the entire worksheet, enter a range in the Print area edit box (**Figure 17**).

3. To display column or row titles on all pages of a lengthy report, enter row or column (or both) ranges in the Rows to repeat at top or Columns to repeat at left edit boxes (**Figure 17**). **Figures 18** through **20** show how this affects the printout.

4. Turn on check boxes in the center of the dialog box to set additional print options as desired:

   ▲ **Gridlines** prints the worksheet gridlines.

   ▲ **Black and white** prints the worksheet in black and white. This can save time if you print on a color printer.

   ▲ **Draft quality** reduces printing time by omitting gridlines and most graphics.

   ▲ **Row and column headings** prints the column letters and row numbers with the worksheet.

5. To print worksheet comments, choose an option other than (None) from the Comments pop-up menu (**Figure 21**).

6. Select a Page order option for a long or wide worksheet:

   ▲ **Down, then over** prints all rows of the first few columns first, then prints rows from subsequent columns.

   ▲ **Over, then down** prints all columns of the first bunch of rows first, then prints columns from subsequent rows.

7. Click OK to save your settings.

Figure 16. *The Sheet tab of the Page Setup dialog box.*

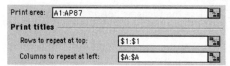

Figure 17. *This example shows the proper way to enter ranges for the Print area and Print titles.*

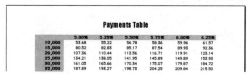

Figure 18. *Here's the first page of a lengthy report.*

Figure 19. *Without page titles, the headings don't appear on subsequent pages.*

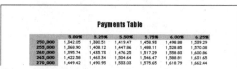

Figure 20. *But with page titles set as they are in* **Figure 17**, *headings appear on every page.*

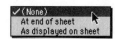

Figure 21. *The Comments pop-up menu.*

Figure 22. *Use options under the Print Area submenu to set or clear a print area.*

Figure 23. *The Chart tab of the Page Setup dialog box.*

✔ **Tip**

■ For the largest possible image, make sure Landscape is the selected orientation in the Page tab of the Page Setup dialog box (**Figure 3**). I tell you about orientation earlier in this chapter.

✔ **Tips**

■ In steps 2 and 3, you can enter each range manually by typing it into the edit box or have Excel enter it automatically for you by clicking in the edit box, then selecting the range in the worksheet window.

■ You can use the Collapse Dialog button to collapse the dialog box so you can see the worksheet behind it. You can then use the Expand Dialog button to restore the dialog box so you can finish working with it.

■ You can also specify the range of cells to print by selecting the range in the worksheet, then choosing Set Print Area from the Print Area submenu under the File menu (**Figure 22**). The Clear Print Area command clears any previously set print area.

To set chart options

1. In Excel's Page Setup dialog box, click the Chart tab to display its options (**Figure 23**).

2. Select one of the Printed chart size radio buttons:

   ▲ **Use full page** expands the chart so it fills the page. The size of chart objects may change, relative to each other.

   ▲ **Scale to fit page** expands the chart proportionally until it fills the space between one set of opposite margins.

   ▲ **Custom** uses the custom scale set in the Apple Page Setup dialog box (**Figures 5** and **6**).

3. To print the chart in black and white with patterns replacing colors, turn on the Print in black and white check box.

4. Click OK to save your settings.

Print Preview

Excel's Print Preview feature lets you see what a report will look like before you print it. If a report doesn't look perfect, you can use Setup, Margins, and Page Break Preview buttons right inside the Print Preview dialog box to make adjustments. When you're ready to print, click the Print button.

To preview a report

Choose Print Preview from the File menu (**Figure 4**).

or

Click the Print Preview button on the Standard toolbar.

or

Click the Print Preview button in the Page Setup or Print dialog box.

A preview of the current sheet appears (**Figure 24**). It reflects all Page Setup dialog box settings.

✔ Tips

- To view the other pages of the report, click the Next or Previous button.

- To zoom in to see report detail, click the Zoom button or click the mouse pointer (a magnifying glass) on the area you want to magnify.

- To open the Print dialog box and print, click the Print button. I tell you about the Print dialog box later in this chapter.

- To change Page Setup dialog box options, click the Setup button.

- To close the Print Preview dialog box, click the Close button.

Figure 24. *A worksheet with embedded chart in Print Preview.*

Print Preview

Figure 25. *When you click the Margins button, handles for margins, header, footer, and columns appear.*

Figure 26.
Position the mouse pointer on a handle and drag to change the measurement.

To change margin options & column widths

1. In the Print Preview window, click the Margins button.

   Handles for margins, header and footer locations, and column widths appear around the report preview (**Figure 25**).

2. Position the mouse pointer over the handle or guideline for the margin, header, footer, or column you want to change. The mouse pointer turns into a line with two arrows coming out of it (**Figure 26**).

3. Press down the mouse button and drag to make the change. A measurement for your change appears in the status bar as you drag.

4. Release the mouse button to complete the change. The report reformats automatically.

✔ Tips

- The changes you make by dragging handles in the Print Preview dialog box will be reflected in the appropriate edit boxes of the Page Setup dialog box.

- I tell how to change margins and header and footer locations with the Page Setup dialog box earlier in this chapter. I tell you how to change column widths in the worksheet window or with the Column Width dialog box in **Chapter 6**.

Setting Margin Options & Column Widths

To set page breaks

1. In normal view, choose Page Break Preview from the View menu (**Figure 27**).

   or

   In the Print Preview window (**Figure 24**), click the Page Break Preview button.

   The sheet appears in Page Break Preview view (**Figure 28**).

2. Position the mouse pointer over one of the dashed, blue page break lines. The mouse pointer turns into a line with two arrows coming out of it.

3. Press down the mouse button and drag to make the change. A dark line moves with the mouse pointer (**Figure 29**).

4. Release the mouse button.

   The page break shifts to the new position and turns into a solid blue line. Any automatic page break to its right or below it also shifts (**Figure 30**).

5. To return to Normal view, choose Normal from the View menu (**Figure 27**).

   or

   To return to Print Preview, choose Print Preview from the File menu (**Figure 4**) or click the Print Preview button on the Standard toolbar.

✔ Tips

■ The first time you use the Page Break Preview feature, a dialog box with instructions appears (**Figure 28**). You must click OK to dismiss the dialog box before you can drag page breaks. Turn on the check box within the dialog box if you don't want to see it again.

■ You may need to scroll within the window to see all the page breaks for a very large worksheet.

■ You can use this feature to change both vertical and horizontal page breaks.

Figure 27.
The View menu.

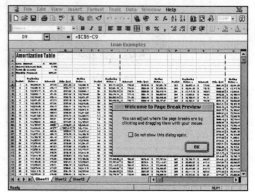

Figure 28. *Page Break Preview view, with its instruction dialog box.*

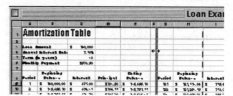

Figure 29. *Drag a page break to change it.*

Figure 30. *When you move one page break, the ones beyond it also move.*

Setting Page Breaks

Figure 31. *The Print dialog box for the LaserWriter 8 printer driver...*

Figure 32. *...and for the Color StyleWriter 2500 printer driver.*

The Print Dialog Box

You use the Print dialog box (**Figures 31** and **32**) to set a number of options for the print job, including:

■ **Copies** is the number of copies of the document you want to print.

■ **Collated** automatically collates multiple copies.

■ **Pages** is the range of document pages you want to print.

■ **Print Quality** is the printer's quality setting. This option is generally available only on dot-matrix and inkjet printers.

■ **Paper Source** is the location of the paper in the printer. This option is generally available only on printers with multiple feed methods.

After setting options, clicking the Print button sends the document to the printer.

✔ Tip

■ These are just a few of the options offered in the Print dialog box. I tell you about others on the next few pages. Remember, options vary greatly depending on the printer and printer driver.

To open the Print dialog box

Choose Print from the File menu (**Figure 4**) or press ⌘P.

or

Click the Print button on the Standard or Print Preview toolbar.

or

Click the Print button in the Page Setup dialog box (**Figure 3**) or Print Preview window (**Figure 24**).

To set General options

1. Open the Print dialog box (**Figures 31** and **32**).
2. Set options as desired.

To set Excel-specific options

1. Open the Print dialog box (**Figures 31** and **32**).
2. If necessary, choose Microsoft Excel from the pop-up menu at the top of the dialog box (**Figure 33**) to display Excel-specific options (**Figure 34**).
3. Select one of the Print radio buttons:
   ▲ **Selection** prints only selected cells, charts, or other objects.
   ▲ **Active Sheets** prints only the sheets with selected sheet tabs. (Normally, only one sheet is selected; I tell you how to select multiple sheets in **Chapter 1**.)
   ▲ **Entire Workbook** prints all sheets in the workbook.

To set other options

1. Open the Print dialog box (**Figures 31** and **32**).
2. If necessary, choose an option from the pop-up menu near the top of the dialog box (**Figure 33**) to display a different category of options (**Figures 35** through **39**).
3. Set options as desired.
4. Repeat steps 2 and 3 for each type of option you want to set.

✔ Tips

■ These other options are specific to your printer, not to Microsoft Excel.
■ I tell you about the Save as File options available for PostScript printers later in this chapter.

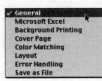

Figure 33.
Use this pop-up menu to switch from one type of option to another for a PostScript printer.

Figure 34. *The Microsoft Excel options in the Print dialog box.*

Figure 35. *The Background Printing options in the Print dialog box.*

Figure 36. *The Cover Page options in the Print dialog box.*

Figure 37. *The Color Matching options in the Print dialog box.*

Figure 38. *The Layout options in the Print dialog box.*

Figure 39. *The Error Handling options in the Print dialog box.*

Figure 40. *Excel confirms that it has saved print options.*

To save Print options

1. In the Print dialog box (**Figures 31** and **34** through **39**), click the Save Settings button.

2. A dialog box (**Figure 40**) or Office Assistant balloon appears to confirm that the settings have been saved for the printer.

✔ Tips

■ Using the Save Settings option automatically restores the current settings to the Print dialog box every time you print to the currently selected printer.

■ This option is not available for all printers.

To print

Click the Print button in the Print dialog box (**Figures 31**, **32**, and **34** through **39**).

One of two things happens:

■ If background printing is enabled, the document is sent to the print spooler on your hard disk. The print spooler will release the document to the printer when the printer is available. You can continue working while the document prints.

■ If background printing is disabled, the document is sent directly to the printer. You may have to wait until printing is complete before you can continue working.

✔ Tip

■ Background printing is supported by many—but not all—printers. If there is no background printing option in the Print dialog box for your printer, your printer does not support this feature.

Saving Print Options, Printing

Printing to a File

Most PostScript printers enable you to "print" a document as a PostScript file. Although this process creates a file on disk, it is created with the Print command rather than the Save command as discussed in **Chapter 4**.

✔ Tip

■ PostScript files are often used to output documents to high-resolution printing devices such as imagesetters.

To print to a file

1. Open the Print dialog box (**Figure 31**).

2. Choose File from the Destination pop-up menu (**Figure 41**).

3. Set options as desired in the various option categories of the dialog box.

4. Choose Save as File from the pop-up menu near the top of the dialog box (**Figure 33**) to display the Save as File options (**Figure 42**).

5. Choose an option from the Format pop-up menu (**Figure 43**) to specify the PostScript file format.

6. Use the radio buttons to set appropriate PostScript Level and Data Format options.

7. Choose an option from the Font inclusion pop-up menu (**Figure 44**) to specify which fonts (if any) should be included in the document.

8. Click Save.

9. Use the Save As dialog box that appears (**Figure 45**) to enter a name and specify a disk location for the file.

10. Click Save to save the PostScript file to disk.

Figure 41. *The Destination pop-up menu.*

Figure 42. *The Save as File options of the Laser-Writer 8 Print dialog box.*

Figure 43.
The Format pop-up menu.

Figure 44. *The Font inclusion pop-up menu.*

Figure 45. *Use a standard Save As dialog box to enter a name and specify a disk location for the PostScript file.*

✔ Tips

■ The Acrobat PDF option can only be used if the full Adobe Acrobat package (not just Acrobat Reader) is installed on your computer.

■ If you're not sure how to set options in this dialog box, set Font inclusion to All and leave the other options set to the defaults shown in **Figure 42**.

Printing to a File

WORKING WITH DATABASES

Databases

Excel's database features and functions help make it a flexible tool for creating, maintaining, and reporting data. With Excel, you can use a form to enter data into a list, filter information, sort records, and automatically generate subtotals. You can use Excel's calculating, formatting, charting, and printing features on your database, too.

In Excel, a database is any list of information with unique labels in the first row. You don't need to do anything special to identify a database—Excel is smart enough to know one when it sees it. **Figure 1**, for example, shows the first few rows of a list that Excel can recognize as a database.

A database is organized into fields and records. A *field* is a category of information. In **Figure 1**, *Product Code*, *Department*, and *Cost* are the first three fields. A *record* is a collection of fields for one thing. In **Figure 1**, *row 2* shows the record for the item with product code *KZH1517Q* and *row 3* shows the record for *GYM29L*.

✔ Tip

■ Fields are always in columns while records are aways in rows.

Figure 1. *The first few rows of a list that Excel can automatically recognize as a database.*

	Product Code	Department	Cost	Sale Price	Reorder Point	Qty on Hand	Time to Order?	Resale Value	Markup
1									
2	KZH1517Q	Men's Accessories	12.14	38.99	70	385		15,011	321%
3	GYM29L	Junior Clothes	15.46	64.99	160	77	Reorder Now!	5,004	420%
4	OYM66B	Automotive	12.79	69.99	60	105		7,349	547%
5	FZX1916K	Misses Clothes	8.58	46.99	100	280		13,157	548%
6	PPZ1219C	Garden	0.28	1.99	90	139		277	711%
7	NYL71A	Hardware	13.22	46.99	20	297		13,956	355%
8	VNX21141	Electronics	19.28	107.99	140	471		50,863	560%
9	NYW1123P	Hardware	0.32	1.99	40	174		346	622%
10	LOW1523T	Children's Accessories	19.34	37.99	130	328		12,461	196%

Inventory

Databases

181

To create a list

1. In a worksheet window, enter unique column titles for each of the fields in your list (**Figure 2**). These will be the field names.

2. Beginning with the row immediately below the one containing the column titles, enter the data for each record (**Figure 3**). Be sure to put the proper information in each column.

✔ Tips

- Use only one cell for each column title. If the field name is too long to fit in the cell, use the Alignment tab in the Font dialog box to wrap text in the cell (**Figure 4**). I tell you about alignment options in **Chapter 6**.

- Do not skip rows when entering information. A blank row indicates the end of the database above it.

- If the first few characters that you type into a cell match an existing entry in the same column, Excel automatically fills in the remaining characters for you (**Figure 5**). To accept the entry, press **Enter**. To type something else, continue typing.

- You can format your list any way you like (**Figure 4**). The formatting will not affect the way Excel recognizes and works with the list data.

- Your list can include formulas. Excel treats the results of the formulas like any other field.

Figure 2. *Enter unique field names in the first row of the list.*

Figure 3. *Enter the data, one record per row.*

Figure 4. *Formatting a list doesn't affect the way Excel works with data.*

Figure 5. *When the first few characters you type match an existing entry in the column, Excel fills in the remaining characters for you.*

Field name | Field containing a formula | Field containing a value | Record number indicator

Figure 6. *The data form offers another way to enter, edit, delete, and find records.*

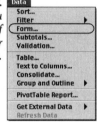

Figure 7. *The Data menu offers a number of commands for working with lists.*

Click here to see the previous record.

Click here to jump back 10 records.

Click here to jump forward 10 records.

Click here to see the next record.

Figure 8. *Use the scroll bar in the data form to browse records.*

Using the Data Form

Excel's data form feature creates a dialog box with custom edit boxes for fields (**Figure 6**). You can use this dialog box to enter, edit, delete, and find records in a database.

To open the data form

1. Select any cell in the list.
2. Choose Form from the Data menu (**Figure 7**).

To browse records

Use the scroll bar (**Figure 8**) as follows:

- To see the next record, click the down arrow on the scroll bar.
- To see the previous record, click the up arrow on the scroll bar.
- To jump ahead 10 records, click the scroll bar beneath the scroll box.
- To jump back 10 records, click the scroll bar above the scroll box.

To enter, edit, and delete data

To create a new record, click the New button and enter the information into the empty edit boxes for each field.

or

To edit a record, locate the record you want to edit and make changes in the appropriate edit boxes.

or

To delete a record, locate the record you want to delete and click the Delete button.

✔ Tips

- Excel records your changes when you move to another record or click the Close button to close the form.
- If a field contains a formula, Excel carries the formula forward from the previous record and performs the calculation.

To find records

1. In the data form, click the Criteria button. A criteria form appears (**Figure 9**).

2. Enter search criteria in the field(s) in which you expect to find a match (**Figure 10**).

3. Click the Find Next button to move forward through the list for records that match the criteria.

   or

   Click the Find Prev button to move backward through the list for records that match the criteria.

   Excel beeps when it reaches the end or beginning of the matches.

✔ Tips

- You can enter criteria in any combination of fields. If you enter criteria into multiple fields, Excel looks for records that match all criteria.

- The more fields you enter data into, the more specific you make the search and the fewer matches you'll find.

- You can use comparison operators (**Table 1**) and wildcard characters (**Table 2**) in conjunction with criteria. For example, *>100* finds records with values greater than 100 in the field in which the criteria is entered.

- You can also use Excel's AutoFilter feature to quickly locate and display all records that match search criteria. I tell you how next.

Figure 9. *The data form turns into a criteria form when you click the Criteria button.*

Department:	Computers

Figure 10. *Enter the search criteria in the field in which you expect to find a match.*

Operator	Meaning
=	Equal To
<>	Not Equal To
>	Greater Than
>=	Greater Than or Equal To
<	Less Than
<=	Less Than or Equal To

Table 1. *Comparison operators.*

Character	Meaning
?	Any single character
*	Any group of characters

Table 2. *Wildcard characters.*

Figure 11. *The AutoFilter submenu offers options for working with Excel's AutoFilter feature.*

Figure 12. *The AutoFilter feature creates a pop-up menu for each field.*

Figure 13. *Choose search criteria from a pop-up menu.*

Figure 14. *Excel displays only the records that match the criteria you chose.*

Figure 15. *Use the Top 10 AutoFilter to find the top or bottom number or percent of items.*

Using AutoFilter

The AutoFilter feature puts pop-up menus in the titles of each column (**Figure 12**). You can use these menus to choose criteria in the column and display only those records that match the criteria.

To display AutoFilter menus

1. Select any cell in the list.
2. Choose AutoFilter from the Filter submenu under the Data menu (**Figure 11**).

   Excel scans the data and creates pop-up menus for each field (**Figure 12**).

To find records with AutoFilter

1. Display the AutoFilter menus (**Figure 12**).
2. Use a pop-up menu to select criteria in a specific field (**Figure 13**).

   Only the records matching the criteria you selected are displayed (**Figure 14**).

✔ Tip

- To display all of the records again, choose Show All from the Filter submenu under the Data menu (**Figure 11**) or choose (All) from the pop-up list you used to filter the data (**Figure 13**).

To use the Top 10 AutoFilter

1. Display the AutoFilter menus (**Figure 12**).
2. Choose (Top 10…) from the pop-up menu for the field by which you want to filter information.
3. In the Top 10 AutoFilter dialog box (**Figure 15**), set options to locate the top or bottom items or percent based on the field you selected. Click OK.

   Excel filters the database and displays only the records that match the settings you entered.

Using AutoFilter

185

To set a custom AutoFilter

1. Choose (Custom…) from the pop-up menu for the field for which you want to set criteria (**Figure 13**).

   Custom AutoFilter dialog box (**Figure 16**) appears.

2. Use the pop-up menus (**Figure 17**) to choose one or two comparison operators.

3. Use the pop-up menus or edit boxes to enter one or two criteria.

4. Select the And or Or radio button to tell Excel whether it should match both criteria (And) or either criteria (Or).

5. Click OK.

   Only the records matching the criteria you entered are displayed (**Figure 18**).

✔ Tip

- Criteria can include wildcard characters (**Table 2**).

To use multiple AutoFilters

Choose filters from the pop-up menus for each of the fields for which you want to set criteria. Excel will display only the records that match all of the filters (**Figure 19**).

Figure 16. *The Custom AutoFilter dialog box.*

Figure 17.
Use this pop-up menu to select a comparison operator.

Figure 18. *In this example, the Custom AutoFilter was used to find all inventory items in the Junior Clothes or Misses Clothes department.*

Figure 19. *This example adds another filter to* **Figure 18***: Sale Price <10.*

Figure 20.
Create a criteria range with field names and values that you want to match.

	K	L
1	**Department**	**Markup**
2	Automotive	>250%
3	Hardware	>250%
4	Electronics	>250%

Figure 21.
The Advanced Filter dialog box, all set up to filter a list.

Advanced Filters

Advanced filters enable you to specify even more criteria than you can with AutoFilters. First set up a criteria range, then use the Advanced Filter dialog box to perform the search.

To use advanced filters

1. Create a criteria range by copying the data labels in the list to a blank area of the worksheet and then entering the criteria in the cells beneath it (**Figure 20**).

2. Choose Advanced Filter from the Filter submenu under the Data menu (**Figure 11**).

3. In the Advanced Filter dialog box (**Figure 21**), select a radio button to specify whether the matches should replace the original list (Filter the list, in-place) or be created elsewhere (Copy to another location).

4. In the List range edit box, confirm that the correct cell references for your list have been entered.

5. In the Criteria range edit box, enter the cell references for the range containing your criteria (including the field labels).

6. If you selected the Copy radio button in step 3 above, enter a cell reference for the first cell of the new list in the Copy to edit box.

7. To omit duplicate records from the results list, turn on the Unique records only check box.

8. Click OK.

   Excel searches for records that match the criteria and either replaces the original list or creates a new list with the matches (**Figure 22**).

Figure 22. *The criteria in* **Figure 21** *yielded these records.*

✔ Tip

■ You can enter a range into any of the edit boxes in the Advanced Filter dialog box by selecting the range you want to enter.

Using Advanced Filters

Sorting

You can sort lists by any column(s). Excel will quickly put database information in the order you specify.

To sort a list

1. Select any cell in the list.

2. Choose Sort from the Data menu (**Figure 7**) to display the Sort dialog box (**Figure 23**).

3. Choose a primary sort field from the Sort By pop-up menu (**Figure 24**).

4. Select a sort order radio button:

   ▲ **Ascending** is lowest to highest.

   ▲ **Descending** is highest to lowest.

5. If desired, repeat steps 3 and 4 for a secondary and tertiary sort field using options in the Then by areas.

6. If the list has column titles, select the Header row radio button; otherwise, select the No header row radio button.

7. Click OK.

   Excel sorts the list as you specified (**Figure 25**).

or

1. Select a cell in the column for the field by which you want to sort.

2. Click the Sort Ascending button to sort from lowest to highest value or the Sort Descending button to sort from highest to lowest value. (Both buttons are on the Standard toolbar.)

Figure 23. *The Sort dialog box, with a primary and secondary sort set up.*

Figure 24.
The Sort by (or Then by) pop-up menu lists all database fields.

Figure 25. *The beginning of a list sorted as shown in* **Figure 23**.

✔ Tips

- You can sort an entire list, a filtered list, or a list created with the Advanced Filter dialog box.

- The two Then by fields in the sort dialog box are "tie-breakers" and are only used if the primary sort field has more than one record with the same value. **Figures 23** and **25** show how they can be used.

- If the results of a sort are not what you expected, choose Undo from the Edit menu, press ⌃⌘Z, or click the Undo button on the Standard toolbar to restore the original sort order.

- If you make the wrong selection in the My list has area at the bottom of the dialog box, you could sort column titles along with the rest of the list. Undo the sort and try again.

- If you select a cell in the column by which you want to sort, that column is automatically referenced in the Sort dialog box when you open it.

- To sort by more than three columns, sort by the least important columns first, then by the most important ones. For example, to sort a list by columns A, B, C, D, and E, you'd sort first by columns D and E, then by columns A, B, and C.

- In order to use Excel's Subtotal feature, you must first sort the data by the column for which you want subtotals. I tell you about the Subtotal feature next.

Sorting Tips

Subtotals

Excel's Subtotal feature enters formulas with the SUBTOTAL function in sorted database lists. The SUBTOTAL function (**Figure 28**) returns a subtotal for a sorted list. It uses the following syntax:

SUBTOTAL(*function_num,ref*)

The function_num argument is a number that specifies which function to use. **Table 3** shows the valid values. (I tell you about most of these functions in **Chapter 5**.) The ref argument is the range of cells to subtotal.

Number	Function Name
1	AVERAGE
2	COUNT
3	COUNTA
4	MAX
5	MIN
6	PRODUCT
7	STDEV
8	STDEVP
9	SUM
10	VAR
11	VARP

Table 3. *Valid function_num values for the SUBTOTAL function.*

To subtotal a list

1. Sort the list by the field(s) for which you want subtotals and position the cellpointer in the list (**Figure 25**).

2. Choose Subtotals from the Data menu (**Figure 7**) to display the Subtotal dialog box (**Figure 26**).

3. Choose the name of the field to be grouped for subtotaling from the At each change in pop-up menu. The field you select will probably be one of the fields you sorted by.

4. Choose a function from the Use function pop-up menu (**Figure 27**).

5. In the Add subtotal to scrolling list, use the check boxes to choose the field(s) to subtotal.

6. If desired, use the check boxes at the bottom of the dialog box to set other options.

7. Click OK.

   Excel turns the list into an outline and enters row titles and subtotals (**Figure 28**).

✔ Tips

- To remove subtotals, click the Remove All button in the Subtotal dialog box (**Figure 26**).

Figure 26. *The Subtotal dialog box.*

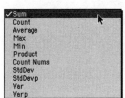

Figure 27.
Use this pop-up menu to choose a function for the Subtotal. In most cases, you'll choose Sum.

- Excel's outline feature groups information into different levels. You can show or hide information based on its level.

Outline buttons & bars

=SUBTOTAL(9,C2:C9)

Figure 28. *Here's part of the list in* **Figure 25** *with subtotals.*

To work with a subtotal outline

Click outline symbols on the left side of the window to display or hide detail:

- Click a minus sign button to collapse the outline for that section.

- Click a plus sign button to expand the outline for that section.

- Click one of the outline level numbers to collapse or expand the entire outline to that level.

Figure 29 shows an outline created by the Subtotal command partially collapsed. Note how the outline buttons and bars are set to the left of the data.

✔ Tip

- You can create an outline for virtually any spreadsheet data. Although creating outlines is beyond the scope of this book, here's a hint to get you started if you decide to explore this feature: Use commands on the Group and Outline submenu under the Data menu (**Figure 30**) to create and clear groups and outlines.

Figure 29. *Here's the outline from Figure 28 with some of the detail hidden.*

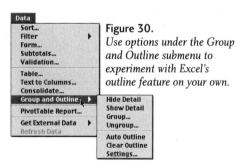

Figure 30.
Use options under the Group and Outline submenu to experiment with Excel's outline feature on your own.

Database Functions

Excel includes several database and list management functions. (SUBTOTAL, which I discuss earlier in this chapter, is one of them.) Here are a few of the most commonly used ones, along with their syntax:

DSUM(*database,field,criteria*)

DAVERAGE(*database,field,criteria*)

DCOUNT(*database,field,criteria*)

DCOUNTA(*database,field,criteria*)

DMAX(*database,field,criteria*)

DMIN(*database,field,criteria*)

The database argument is the cell references for a range containing the database or list. The field argument is the name of the field you want to summarize. The criteria argument is either the data you want to match or a range containing the data you want to match.

Figure 31 shows an example of these database functions in action, using the criteria range in **Figure 20**.

✔ Tips

- Each database function corresponds to a mathematical or statistical function and performs the same kind of calculation—but on records matching criteria only. I tell you about other functions in **Chapter 5**.

- You can enter database functions with the Formula Palette. I tell you how to use the Formula Palette in **Chapter 5**.

DSUM	595.05	=DSUM($A$1:$I$501,"Cost",$K$1:$L$4)
DAVERAGE	12.396875	=DAVERAGE($A$1:$I$501,"Cost",$K$1:$L$4)
DCOUNT	48	=DCOUNT($A$1:$I$501,"Cost",$K$1:$L$4)
DCOUNTA	48	=DCOUNTA($A$1:$I$501,"Cost",$K$1:$L$4)
DMAX	24.95	=DMAX($A$1:$I$501,"Cost",$K$1:$L$4)
DMIN	0.11	=DMIN($A$1:$I$501,"Cost",$K$1:$L$4)

Figure 31. *These formulas use database functions to summarize information based on criteria. The database is the 500-record list used throughout this chapter. The field is the Cost field, which is found in column C of the database. The criteria range is the range illustrated in **Figure 20**.*

ADVANCED TECHNIQUES

	A	B	C	D	E
1			Southwest Division		
2			First Quarter Sales		
3		Jan	Feb	Mar	Total
4	John	$ 1,254.00	$ 1,256.00	$ 2,435.00	$ 4,945.00
5	Jean	1,865.00	1,736.00	3,495.00	7,096.00
6	Joe	1,614.00	1,284.00	2,509.00	5,407.00
7	Joan	1,987.00	2,740.00	2,890.00	7,617.00
8	Totals	$ 6,720.00	$ 7,016.00	$ 11,329.00	$ 25,065.00

Figure 1. *The reference to the selected range would be a lot easier to remember if it had a name like* FirstQtrSales *rather than just A4:D7.*

=SUM('Qtr 1:Qtr 4'!E4)

Figure 2.
3-D cell references make it possible to link information between worksheets or workbooks.

	A	B
1		Southwest Division
2		Total Sales
3		
4	John	$ 22,469.00
5	Jean	$ 25,777.00
6	Joe	$ 23,537.00
7	Joan	$ 27,703.00
8	Totals	$ 99,486.00

Figure 3. *Excel's consolidation feature lets you combine information from multiple source areas into one destination area—with or without live links.*

Advanced Techniques

Excel has many advanced features that you can use to tap into Excel's real power. In this chapter, I tell you about some of the advanced techniques I think you'll find most useful in your day-to-day work with Excel:

- **Names (Figure 1)** let you assign easy-to-remember names to cell references. You can then use the names in place of cell references in formulas.

- **3-D cell references (Figure 2)** let you write formulas with links to other worksheets and workbooks.

- **Consolidations (Figure 3)** let you summarize information from several source areas into one destination area, with or without live links.

- **Custom views** enable you to create predefined views of workbook contents that can include a variety of settings.

- **Macros** let you automate repetitive tasks.

✔ Tips

- The information in this chapter builds on information in previous chapters of this book. It's a good idea to have a solid understanding of the information covered up to this point in this book before exploring the features in this chapter.

- Through the use of Excel's built-in Visual Basic programming language, the macro feature also enables you to create highly customized workbook files, complete with special dialog boxes, menus, and commands. This, however, is far beyond the scope of this book.

Advanced Techniques

Names

The trouble with using cell references in formulas is that they're difficult to remember. To make matters worse, cell references can change if cells above or to the left of them are inserted or deleted.

Excel's names feature eliminates both problems by letting you assign easy-to-remember names to individual cells or ranges of cells in your workbooks. The names, which you can use in formulas, don't change, no matter how much worksheet editing you do.

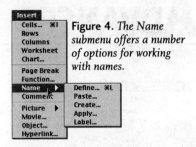

Figure 4. *The Name submenu offers a number of options for working with names.*

✔ Tips

- The Natural Language Formulas feature of Excel 98, which I discuss in **Chapter 2**, automatically recognizes cell column or row headings as cell names.
- Names can be up to 255 characters long and can include letters, numbers, periods, question marks, and underscore characters (_). The first character must be a letter. Names cannot contain spaces or "look" like cell references.

To define a name

1. Select the cell(s) you want to name (**Figure 1**).

2. Choose Define from the Name submenu under the Insert menu (**Figure 4**) or press ⌃⌘L.

3. In the Define Name dialog box that appears, Excel may suggest a name in the Names in workbook edit box. You can enter a name you prefer (**Figure 5**).

4. The cell reference in the Refers to edit box should reflect the range you selected in step 1. To enter a different range, delete the range that appears in the edit box and either type in a new range or reselect the cell(s) in the worksheet window.

5. Click OK.

Figure 5. *Use the Define Names dialog box to set a name for one or more cells. As you can see, the name of the worksheet is part of the cell reference.*

✔ Tip

- To define more than one name, follow the above steps for the first name but click the Add button in step 5. Then repeat steps 3 through 5 for each name you want to define. When you're finished, click OK.

	A	B	C	D	E
1			Southwest Division		
2			First Quarter Sales		
3		Jan	Feb	Mar	Total
4	John	$ 1,254.00	$ 1,256.00	$ 2,435.00	$ 4,945.00
5	Jean	1,865.00	1,736.00	3,495.00	7,096.00
6	Joe	1,614.00	1,284.00	2,509.00	5,407.00
7	Joan	1,987.00	2,740.00	2,890.00	7,617.00
8	Totals	$ 6,720.00	$ 7,016.00	$ 11,329.00	$ 25,065.00

Figure 6. *To use the Create Names dialog box, you must first select the cells you want to name, as well as adjoining cells with text you want to use as names.*

Figure 7.
In the Create Names dialog box, tell Excel which cells contain the text for names.

Figure 8. *Look in the Define Names dialog box to see how many names were added.*

To create names

1. Select the cells containing the ranges you want to name as well as text in adjoining cells that you want to use as names (**Figure 6**).

2. Choose Create from the Name submenu under the Insert menu (**Figure 4**).

3. In the Create Names dialog box (**Figure 7**), turn on the check box(es) for the cells that contain the text you want to use as names.

4. Click OK.

   Excel uses the text in the cells you indicated as names for the adjoining cells. You can see the results if you open the Define Names dialog box (**Figure 8**).

✔ Tip

■ This is a quick way to create a lot of names all at once.

To delete a name

1. Choose Define from the Name submenu under the Insert menu (**Figure 4**) or press ⌘L.

2. In the Define Name dialog box (**Figure 8**), click to select the name in the scrolling list that you want to delete.

3. Click the Delete button. The name is removed from the list.

4. Repeat steps 2 and 3 to delete other names as desired.

5. Click OK to dismiss the Define Names dialog box.

✔ Tip

■ Deleting a name does not delete the cells to which the name refers.

To enter a name in a formula

1. Position the cellpointer in the cell in which you want to write the formula.

2. Type in the formula, replacing any cell reference with the corresponding name **(Figure 9)**.

3. Press (Return) or (Enter) or click the Enter button on the formula bar.

   Excel performs the calculation just as if you'd typed in a cell reference.

✔ Tips

- You can use the Paste Name command to enter a name for you. Follow the steps above, but when it's time to type in the name, choose Paste from the Name submenu under the Insert menu **(Figure 4)**. Use the Paste Name dialog box that appears **(Figure 10)** to select and paste in the name you want. The Paste Name command even works when you use the Formula Palette to write formulas. I tell you about the Formula Palette in **Chapter 5**.

- When you delete a name, Excel responds with a *#NAME?* error in each cell that contains a formula referring to that name **(Figure 11)**. These formulas must be rewritten.

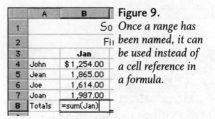

Figure 9. *Once a range has been named, it can be used instead of a cell reference in a formula.*

Figure 10. *Use the Paste Name dialog box to select and paste in a name.*

Figure 11. *If you delete a name used in a formula, a #NAME? error results.*

Figure 12. *Select the names that you want to apply to formulas in your worksheet.*

	A	B	C	D	E
1		Southwest Division			
2		First Quarter Sales			
3		Jan	Feb	Mar	Total
4	John	$1,254.00	$1,256.00	$2,435.00	$4,945.00
5	Jean	1,865.00	1,736.00	3,495.00	7,096.00
6	Joe	1,614.00	1,284.00	2,509.00	5,407.00
7	Joan	1,987.00	2,740.00	2,890.00	7,617.00
8	Totals	$6,720.00	$7,016.00	$11,329.00	$25,065.00

Figure 13. *Excel applies the names you selected to formulas that reference their ranges.*

Cell:	Before:	After:
B8	=SUM(B4:B7)	=SUM(Jan)
C8	=SUM(C4:C7)	=SUM(Feb)
D8	=SUM(D4:D7)	=SUM(Mar)
E8	=SUM(E4:E7)	=SUM(Total)

To apply names to existing formulas

1. Select the cells containing formulas for which you want to apply names. If you want to apply names throughout the worksheet, click any single cell.

2. Choose Apply from the Name submenu under the Insert menu (**Figure 4**).

3. In the Apply Names dialog box (**Figure 12**), select the names that you want to use in place of the cell reference. To select or deselect a name, click on it.

4. Click OK.

   Excel rewrites the formulas with the appropriate names from those you selected. **Figure 13** shows an example of formulas changed by selecting *Jan, Feb, Mar,* and *Total* in **Figure 12**.

✔ Tips

■ If only one cell is selected, Excel applies names based on your selection(s) in the Apply Names dialog box, not the selected cell.

■ If you turn off the Ignore Relative/Absolute check box in the Apply Names dialog box (**Figure 12**), Excel matches the type of reference. I tell you about relative and absolute references in **Chapter 3**.

Applying Names to Existing Formulas

To select named cells

Choose the name of the cell(s) you want to select from the Name pop-up menu on the far-left end of the formula bar (**Figure 14**).

or

1. Click the Name box at the far left end of the formula bar to select it.

2. Type in the name of the cells you want to select (**Figure 15**).

3. Press Return or Enter.

or

1. Choose Go To from the Edit menu (**Figure 16**).

   or

   Press F5.

2. In the Go To dialog box (**Figure 17**), click to select the name of the cell(s) you want to select in the Go to scrolling list.

3. Click OK.

✔ Tip

■ When named cells are selected, the name appears in the cell reference area at the far left end of the formula bar.

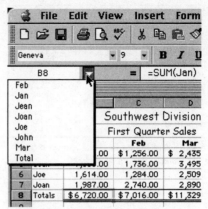

Figure 14. *The Name pop-up menu on the left end of the formula bar lets you select named ranges quickly.*

Figure 15. *If you prefer, you can type in a name and press Return to select it.*

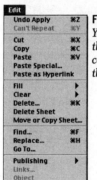

Figure 16. *You can choose the Go To command under the Edit menu...*

Figure 17. *...then select the name of the cell(s) you want to select from the Go to scrolling list.*

3-D References

3-D cell references let you write formulas that reference cells in other worksheets or workbooks. The links are live—when a cell's contents change, the results of formulas in cells that reference it change.

Excel offers several ways to write formulas with 3-D cell references:

- **Use cell names.** I tell you about cell names in the first part of this chapter. **Figure 18** shows an example.

=SUM(John,Joan,Joe,Jean)

Figure 18. *This example uses the SUM function to add the contents of the cells named* John, Joan, Joe, *and* Jean *in the same workbook.*

- **Type them in.** When you type in a 3-D cell reference, you must include the name of the sheet (in single quotes, if the name contains a space), followed by an exclamation point (!) and cell reference. If the reference is for a cell in another workbook, you must also include the workbook name, in brackets. **Figures 19, 20,** and **21** show examples.

='Results for Year'!$B$9

Figure 19. *This example refers to cell B9 in a worksheet called* Results for Year *in the same workbook.*

- **Click on them.** You'll get the same results as if you had typed the references, but Excel does all the typing for you.

- **Use the Paste Special command.** The Paste Link button in the Paste Special dialog box lets you paste a link between cells in different sheets of a workbook or different workbooks.

=SUM('Qtr 1:Qtr 4'!E9)

Figure 20. *This example uses the SUM function to add the contents of cell E9 in worksheets starting with* Qtr 1 *and ending with* Qtr 4 *in the same workbook.*

✔ Tips

- When you delete a cell, Excel displays a #REF! error in any cells that referred to it. The cells containing these errors must be revised to remove the error.

- Do not make references to an unsaved file. If you do and you close the file with the reference before saving (and naming) the file it refers to, Excel won't be able to update the link.

=[Sales]'Results for Year'!$B$9

Figure 21. *This example refers to cell B9 in a worksheet called* Results for Year *in a workbook called* Sales.

3-D References

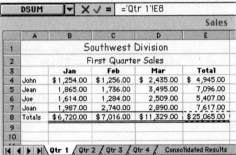

To reference a named cell or range in another worksheet

1. Select the cell in which you want to enter the reference.

2. Type an equal sign (=).

3. If the sheet containing the cells you want to reference is in another workbook, type the name of the workbook (within single quotes, if the name contains a space) followed by an exclamation point (!).

4. Type the name of the cell(s) you want to reference (**Figures 22 and 23**).

5. Press Return or Enter or click the Enter button on the formula bar.

✔ Tip

■ If the name you want to reference is in the same workbook, you can paste it in by choosing Paste from the Name submenu under the Insert menu (**Figure 4**). I tell you how to use the Paste Name dialog box earlier in this chapter.

To reference a cell or range in another worksheet by clicking

1. Select the cell in which you want to enter the reference.

2. Type an equal sign (=).

3. If the sheet containing the cells you want to reference is in another workbook, switch to that workbook.

4. Click on the sheet tab for the worksheet containing the cell you want to reference.

5. Select the cell(s) you want to reference (**Figure 24**).

6. Press Return or Enter or click the Enter button on the formula bar.

Figures 22 and 23. *Two examples of 3-D references utilizing names. The first example refers to a name in the same workbook. The second example refers to a name in a different workbook.*

DSUM		▼	X ✓ =	='Qtr 1'!E8	
					Sales
	A	B	C	D	E
1			Southwest Division		
2			First Quarter Sales		
3		Jan	Feb	Mar	Total
4	John	$1,254.00	$1,256.00	$2,435.00	$4,945.00
5	Jean	1,865.00	1,736.00	3,495.00	7,096.00
6	Joe	1,614.00	1,284.00	2,509.00	5,407.00
7	Joan	1,987.00	2,740.00	2,890.00	7,617.00
8	Totals	$6,720.00	$7,016.00	$11,329.00	$25,065.00
9					
10					

Qtr 1 / Qtr 2 / Qtr 3 / Qtr 4 / Consolidated Results

Figure 24. *After typing an equal sign in the cell in which you want the reference to go, you can select the cell(s) you want to reference.*

Figure 25. *You can click the Paste Link button in the Paste Special dialog box to paste a reference to cells you copied.*

✔ Tips

■ Do not press [Enter] after using the Paste Special command! Doing so pastes the contents of the Clipboard into the cell, overwriting the link.

■ Using the Paste Link button to paste a range of cells creates a special range called an *array*. Each cell in an array shares the same cell reference and cannot be changed unless all cells in the array are changed.

To reference a cell or range in another worksheet by typing

1. Select the cell in which you want to enter the reference.

2. Type an equal sign (=).

3. If the sheet containing the cells you want to reference is in another workbook, type the name of the workbook within brackets ([ ]).

4. Type the name of the sheet followed by an exclamation point (!).

5. Type the cell reference for the cell(s) you want to reference.

6. Press [Return] or [Enter] or click the Enter button on the formula bar.

✔ Tip

■ If the name of the sheet includes a space character, it must be enclosed within single quotes in the reference. See **Figures 19**, **20**, and **21** for examples.

To reference a cell with the Paste Special command

1. Select the cell you want to reference.

2. Choose Copy from the Edit menu (**Figure 16**), press ⌘C, or click the Copy button on the Standard toolbar.

3. Switch to the worksheet in which you want to put the reference.

4. Select the cell in which you want the reference to go.

5. Choose Paste Special from the Edit menu (**Figure 16**).

6. In the Paste Special dialog box (**Figure 25**), click the Paste Link button.

To write a formula with 3-D references

1. Select the cell in which you want to enter the formula.

2. Type an equal sign (=).

3. Use any combination of the following techniques until the formula is complete.

   ▲ To enter a function, use the Formula Palette or type in the function. I tell you how to use the Formula Palette in **Chapter 5**.

   ▲ To enter an operator, type it in. I tell you about using operators in **Chapter 2**.

   ▲ To enter a cell reference, select the cell(s) you want to reference or type the reference in. If typing the reference, be sure to include single quotes, brackets, and exclamation points as discussed on the previous page.

4. Press Return or Enter or click the Enter button on the formula bar.

To write a formula that sums the same cell on multiple, adjacent sheets

1. Select the cell in which you want to enter the formula.

2. Type =*SUM(* (**Figure 26**).

3. If the cells you want to add are in another workbook, switch to that workbook.

4. Click the sheet tab for the first worksheet containing the cell you want to sum.

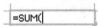

Figure 26. *Type the beginning of a formula with the SUM function...*

Figure 27. *...select all of the tabs for sheets that contain the cells you want to sum...*

=SUM('Qtr 1:Qtr 4'!

Figure 28. *...so the sheet names are appended as a range in the formula bar.*

	A	B	C	D	E
1		Southwest Division				
2		First Quarter Sales				
3		Jan	Feb	Mar	Total
4	John	$ 1,254.00	$ 1,256.00	$ 2,435.00	$ 4,945.00
5	Jean	1,865.00	1,736.00	3,495.00	7,096.00

Figure 29. *Then click on the cell you want to add...*

=SUM('Qtr 1:Qtr 4'!E4

Figure 30. *...so that its reference is appended to the formula in the formula bar.*

The workbook you opened contains automatic links to information in another workbook. Do you want to update this workbook with changes made to the other workbook?

• To update all linked information, click Yes.
• To keep the existing information, click No.

[Yes]   [No]

Figure 31. *This dialog box appears if you open a workbook that contains links to another workbook.*

5. Hold down (Shift) and click on the sheet tab for the last sheet containing the cell you want to sum. All tabs from the first to the last become selected (**Figure 27**). The formula in the formula bar should look something like the one in **Figure 28**.

6. Click the cell you want to sum (**Figure 29**). The cell reference is added to the formula (**Figure 30**).

7. Type).

8. Press (Return) or (Enter) or click the Enter button on the formula bar.

✔ Tips

■ Use this technique to link cells of identically arranged worksheets. This results in a "3-D worksheet" effect.

■ Although you can use this technique to consolidate data, the Consolidate command, which I begin discussing on the next page, automates consolidations with or without links.

Opening Worksheets with Links

When you open a worksheet that has a link to another workbook file, a dialog box like the one in **Figure 31** appears.

■ If you click Yes, Excel checks the other file and updates linked information. If Excel can't find the other workbook, it displays a standard Open dialog box so you can find it.

■ If you click No, Excel does not check the data in the other file.

Consolidations

The Consolidate command lets you combine data from multiple sources. Excel lets you do this in two ways:

- **Consolidate based on the arrangement of data.** This is useful when data occupies the same number of cells in the same arrangement in multiple locations (**Figure 3**).

- **Consolidate based on identifying labels or categories.** This is useful when the arrangement of data varies from one source to the next.

✔ Tip

- With either method, Excel can create links to the source information so the consolidation changes automatically when linked data changes.

To consolidate based on the arrangement of data

1. Select the cell(s) where you want the consolidated information to go (**Figure 32**).

2. Choose Consolidate from the Data menu (**Figure 33**).

3. In the Consolidate dialog box (**Figure 34**), choose a function from the Function pop-up menu (**Figure 35**).

4. Switch to the worksheet containing the first cell(s) to be included in the consolidation. The reference is entered into the Reference edit box.

5. Select the cell(s) you want to include in the consolidation (**Figure 36**). The reference is entered into the Reference edit box.

6. Click Add.

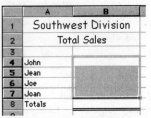

Figure 32. *Select the cells in which you want the consolidated data to go.*

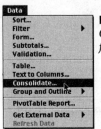

Figure 33. *Choose Consolidate from the Data menu.*

Figure 34. *Use the Consolidate dialog box to identify the cells you want to combine.*

Figure 35. *Choose a function for the consolidation from the Function pop-up menu.*

	Total
.00	$ 4,945.00
.00	7,096.00
.00	5,407.00
.00	7,617.00
.00	$25,065.00

Figure 36. *Enter references for cells in the Consolidate dialog box by selecting them.*

Consolidating Based on Data Arrangement

All references:

'Qtr 1'!$E$4:$E$7
'Qtr 2'!$E$4:$E$7
'Qtr 3'!$E$4:$E$7
'Qtr 4'!$E$4:$E$7

Figure 37. *The cells you want to consolidate are listed in the All references scrolling list in the Consolidate dialog box.*

1 2		A	B
	1	Southwest Division	
	2	Total Sales	
	3		
+	8	John	$ 22,469.00
+	13	Jean	25,777.00
+	18	Joe	23,537.00
+	23	Joan	27,703.00
	24	Totals	

Figure 38. *Excel combines the data in the cell(s) you originally selected.*

7. Repeat steps 4, 5, and 6 for all of the cells that you want to include in the consolidation. When you're finished, the All references scrolling list in the Consolidate dialog box might look something like **Figure 37**.

8. To create links between the source data and destination cell(s), turn on the Create links to source data check box.

9. Click OK.

Excel consolidates the information in the originally selected cell(s) **(Figure 38)**.

✔ Tips

- For this technique to work, each source range must have the same number of cells with data arranged in the same way.

- If the Consolidate dialog box contains references when you open it, you can clear them by selecting each one and clicking the Delete button.

- If you turn on the Create links to source data check box, Excel creates an outline with links to all source cells **(Figure 38)**. You can expand or collapse the outline by clicking the outline buttons. I tell you more about outlines in **Chapter 10**.

Consolidating Based on Data Arrangement

Consolidating Based on Labels

To consolidate based on labels

1. Select the cell(s) in which you want the consolidated information to go. As shown in **Figure 39**, you can select just a single starting cell.

2. Choose Consolidate from the Data menu (**Figure 33**).

3. In the Consolidate dialog box (**Figure 34**), choose a function from the Function pop-up menu (**Figure 35**).

4. Switch to the worksheet containing the first cell(s) to be included in the consolidation. The reference is entered into the Reference edit box.

5. Select the cell(s) you want to include in the consolidation, including any text that identifies data (**Figure 40**). The text must be in cells adjacent to the data. The reference is entered into the Reference edit box.

6. Click Add.

7. Repeat steps 4, 5, and 6 for all cells you want to include in the consolidation. **Figures 41** and **42** show the other two ranges included for the example. When you're finished, the Consolidate dialog box might look something like **Figure 43**.

8. Turn on the appropriate check box(es) in the Use labels in area to tell Excel where identifying labels for the data are.

9. Click OK.

   Excel consolidates the information in the originally selected cell(s) (**Figure 44**).

Figure 39. *Select the destination cell(s).*

Figures 40, 41, & 42. *Select the cell(s) you want to include in the consolidation.*

Figure 43. *The Consolidate dialog box records all selections and enables you to specify where the data labels are.*

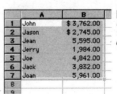

Figure 44. *The final consolidation accounts for all data.*

Figure 45. *Create a view you'd like to save.*

Custom Views

Excel's custom views feature lets you create multiple *views* of a workbook file. A view includes the window size and position, the active cell, the zoom percentage, hidden columns and rows, and print settings. Once you set up a view, you can choose it from a dialog box to see it quickly.

Figure 46.
*Choose Custom
Views from the
View menu.*

✔ Tip

■ Including print settings in views makes it possible to create and save multiple custom reports for printing.

To add a custom view

1. Create the view you want to save. **Figure 45** shows an example.

2. Choose Custom Views from the View menu (**Figure 46**).

3. In the Custom Views dialog box (**Figure 47**), click the Add button.

4. In the Add View dialog box (**Figure 48**), enter a name for the view in the Name edit box.

5. Turn on the appropriate Include in view check boxes:

   ▲ **Print settings** includes current Page Setup and other printing options in the view.

   ▲ **Hidden rows, columns and filter settings** includes current settings for hidden columns and rows, as well as filter selections.

6. Click OK.

Figure 47. *The Custom Views dialog box.*

Figure 48. *Use the Add View dialog box to name and set options for a view.*

Adding Custom Views

To switch to a view

1. Switch to the sheet containing the view you want to see.
2. Choose Custom Views from the View menu (**Figure 46**).
3. In the Custom Views dialog box (**Figure 49**), select the view you want to see from the Views scrolling list.
4. Click Show.

    Excel changes the window so it looks just like it did when you created the view.

To delete a view

1. Switch to the sheet containing the view you want to delete.
2. Choose Custom Views from the View menu (**Figure 46**).
3. In the Custom Views dialog box (**Figure 49**), select the view you want to delete from the Views scrolling list.
4. Click Delete.
5. In the confirmation dialog box that appears (**Figure 50**), click Yes.
6. Follow steps 3 through 5 to delete other views if desired.
7. Click Close to dismiss the Custom Views dialog box without changing the view.

✔ Tip

■ Deleting a view does not delete the information contained in the view. It simply removes the reference to the information from the Views scrolling list in the Custom Views dialog box (**Figure 49**).

Figure 49. *To see or delete a view, select the name of the view in the Custom Views dialog box, then click Show or Delete.*

Figure 50. *When you click the Delete button to delete a view, Excel asks you to confirm that you really do want to delete it.*

Switching to & Deleting Views

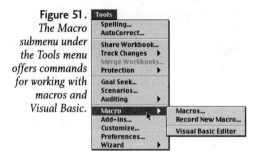

Figure 51. *The Macro submenu under the Tools menu offers commands for working with macros and Visual Basic.*

Figure 52. *Enter a name and set options for a new macro in the Record Macro dialog box.*

Figure 53. *When you're finished recording macro steps, click the Stop Recording button on the tiny Stop toolbar.*

Macros

A macro is a series of commands that Excel can perform automatically. You can create simple macros to automate repetitive tasks, like entering data or formatting cells.

Although macros are created with Excel's built-in Visual Basic programming language, you don't need to be a programmer to create them. Excel's Macro Recorder will record your keystrokes, menu choices, and dialog box settings as you make them and will write the programming code for you. This makes macros useful for all Excel users, even raw beginners.

To record a macro with the Macro Recorder

1. Choose Record New Macro from the Record Macro submenu under the Tools menu (**Figure 51**) to display the Record Macro dialog box (**Figure 52**).

2. Enter a name for the macro in the Macro name edit box.

3. If desired, enter a keystroke to use as a shortcut key in the Option+Cmd+ edit box.

4. If desired, edit the description automatically entered in the Description edit box.

5. Click OK.

6. Perform all the steps you want to include in your macro. Excel records them all—even the mistakes—so be careful!

7. When you're finished recording macro steps, click the Stop Recording button on the tiny Stop toolbar (**Figure 53**).

To run a macro

Press the keystroke you specified as a shortcut key for the macro when you created it.

or

1. Choose Macros from the Macro submenu under the Tools menu (**Figure 51**).

2. In the Macro dialog box (**Figure 54**), select the macro you want to run from the scrolling list.

3. Click Run.

Excel performs each macro step, just the way you recorded it.

✔ Tips

■ Save your workbook *before* running a macro for the first time. You may be surprised by the results and need to revert the file to the way it was before you ran the macro. Excel's Undo command cannot undo the steps of a macro, so reverting to the last saved version of the file is the only way to reverse macro steps.

■ Excel stores each macro as a *module* within the workbook. View and edit a macro by selecting it in the Macro dialog box and clicking the Edit button. **Figure 55** shows an example. I don't recommend editing macro code unless you have at least a general understanding of Visual Basic!

■ More advanced uses of macros include the creation of custom functions and applications that work within Excel.

Figure 54. *The Macro dialog box enables you to run, edit, and delete macros.*

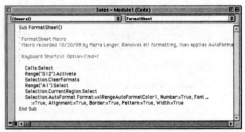

Figure 55. *Here's the code for a macro that removes cell formatting, then applies AutoFormatting.*

WEB PAGES & HYPERLINKS

Web Pages

The World Wide Web has had a bigger impact on publishing than any other communication medium introduced in the past fifty years. Web pages, which can include text, graphics, and hyperlinks, can be published on the Internet or an intranet, making them available to audiences 24 hours a day, 7 days a week. They can provide information quickly and inexpensively to anyone who needs it.

Excel 98's Internet Assistant Wizard enables you to save worksheets and charts as HTML documents, making it easy to publish Excel data on the Web.

✔ Tips

- This chapter explains how to create Web pages from Excel documents. Modifying the HTML underlying those pages is beyond the scope of this book.

- *HTML (or HyperText Markup Language)* is a system of codes for defining Web pages.

- To learn more about the World Wide Web, Web publishing, and HTML, check these Peachpit Press books:

  - ▲ *The Little Web Book* by Alfred and Emily Glossbrenner.

  - ▲ *Home Sweet Home Page* by Robin Williams.

  - ▲ *The Non-Designer's Web Book* by Robin Williams and John Tollett.

  - ▲ *HTML 4 for the World Wide Web: Visual QuickStart Guide* by Elizabeth Castro.

- Web pages are normally viewed with a special kind of software called a *Web browser.* Microsoft Internet Explorer and Netscape Navigator are two examples of Web browsers.

- To access the Internet, you need an Internet connection, either through an organizational network or dial-up connection. Setting up a connection is beyond the scope of this book; consult the documentation that came with your System or Internet access software for more information.

- To publish a Web page, you need access to a Web server. Contact your organization's Network Administrator or Internet Service Provider (ISP) for more information.

- A *hyperlink (or link)* is text or a graphic that, when clicked, displays other information from the Web.

- An *intranet* is like the Internet, but it exists only on the internal network of an organization and is usually closed to outsiders.

To use the Internet Assistant Wizard

1. Open the workbook that you want to save as a Web page (**Figure 1**).

2. Choose Save as HTML from the File menu (**Figure 2**).

3. The Internet Assistant Wizard Step 1 dialog box appears (**Figure 3**). Its Ranges and charts to convert scrolling list indicates the worksheet ranges and charts that will be converted into Web pages. You can modify the list as follows:

▲ To add a range or chart, click the Add button. A dialog box like the one in **Figure 4** appears. Select the worksheet range or chart you want to add to enter its reference in the dialog box. Then click OK.

▲ To remove a range or chart, click the range to select it, then click the Remove button.

▲ To change order of items in the list, click a range or chart you want to appear earlier or later in the list, then click the appropriate Move button to move it up or down. Repeat this process for items until they appear in the desired order.

4. Click Next.

5. The Internet Assistant Wizard Step 2 dialog box appears (**Figure 5**). Select the appropriate radio button for the way you'd like the data converted into a Web page:

▲ **Create an independent, ready-to-view HTML document that contains your formatted data** creates a complete Web page.

▲ **Insert the converted data into an existing HTML file** creates HTML code for the data. Once the code has been created, you must insert it into an existing HTML file.

Figure 1. Here's a simple workbook ready to be converted into a Web page.

Figure 2. *Choose Save as HTML from the File menu to open the Internet Assistant Wizard.*

Figure 3. *The first step of the Internet Assistant Wizard enables you to select the ranges and charts to include on the Web page.*

Figure 4. *You can use this dialog box to add ranges or charts.*

Using the Internet Assistant Wizard

Figure 5.
*In Step 2,
you tell Excel
how you want
to convert the
data.*

Figure 6.
*If you're
creating an
independent
Web page,
you can set
options to
customize it.*

Figure 7.
*If you're
inserting
data into an
existing Web
page, you
must tell
Excel where
it is.*

Figure 8.
*Finally,
specify a
name and
location for
the page.*

6. Click Next.

7. The Internet Assistant Wizard Step 3 dialog box appears next. How it appears depends on the option you selected in the previous dialog box:

▲ If are creating an independent HTML document, the dialog box looks like the one in **Figure 6**. Use it to set options to customize the appearance of the Web page.

▲ If you are inserting converted data into an existing Web page, the dialog box looks like the one in **Figure 7**. Use the Select button to locate and select the existing HTML file into which the converted data should be inserted. Then open the HTML file with a text editor or your HTML editing application and insert the following characters into the document where you want the Excel data to be inserted:
<!--##Table##-->

8. Click Next.

9. The Internet Assistant Wizard Step 4 dialog box appears next **(Figure 8)**. Use it to specify a file name and location in which to save the completed Web page.

10. Click Finish.

Excel creates a new Web page to your specifications. It converts any charts to GIF format and saves them as separate files referenced in the Web page file.

✔ Tips

■ By default, Excel includes all workbook cell ranges and charts in the Internet Assistant Wizard Step 1 dialog box (**Figure 3**). This puts the entire workbook's contents on a single Web page. You can create separate Web pages for worksheets and charts by repeating the steps on the previous two pages for individual ranges and charts you specify in the Step 1 dialog box.

■ In step 9, you must name the completed HTML document using the file naming conventions supported by your Web browser software. If you're not sure how to name an HTML document, ask your System Administrator, Webmaster, or ISP.

■ You can check the appearance of a Web page created by Excel by opening it with your Web browser software. **Figure 9** shows what the page created from the worksheet in **Figure 1** looks like.

■ You can further customize the appearance of a Web page created by Excel by modifying it with your favorite Web authoring program or HTML editor.

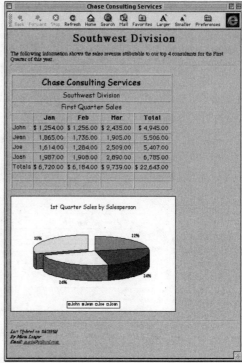

Figure 9. *Here's an independent worksheet created using settings in* **Figures 1** *through* **6** *and* **8**.

Figure 10. *A hyperlink can appear as blue, underlined text. When you point to it, the mouse pointer turns into a hand with a pointing finger.*

Hyperlinks

A hyperlink is text or a graphic that, when clicked, displays other information. Excel enables you to create two kinds of hyperlinks:

■ A link to a *URL* (*Uniform Resource Locator*), which is the address of a document or individual on the Internet. There are three main types of URLs:

   ▲ **http://** links to a Web page on a Web server.

   ▲ **ftp://** links to a downloadable file on an FTP server.

   ▲ **mailto:** links to an e-mail address.

■ A link to another document on your hard disk or network.

By default, hyperlinks appear as blue, underlined text (**Figure 10**).

✔ Tip

■ Although you can create a link to any document on your hard disk or accessible over a local area network or the Internet, clicking the link will only open the document if you have a program capable of opening it—such as the program that created it.

Hyperlinks

To insert a hyperlink

1. Select the cell or object that you want to convert to a hyperlink.

2. Choose Hyperlink from the Insert menu (**Figure 11**) .

   or

   Click the Insert Hyperlink button on the Standard toolbar.

   The Insert Hyperlink dialog box appears (**Figure 12**).

3. To link to a URL, enter the complete URL in the Link to file or URL edit box (**Figure 12**).

   or

   To link to a document on your hard disk or another computer on your network, enter the complete path name to the file or click the Select button to use the Link to File dialog box (**Figure 13**) to locate and link to the file.

4. Click OK.

   The selected cell (**Figure 10**) or object turns into a hyperlink.

✔ Tips

- If you have not saved the document in which you want to insert the link, a dialog box like the one in **Figure 14** appears in Step 2. Click the Save button to save the document.

- You can use the Link to file or URL pop-up menu (**Figure 15**) to enter the characters for the beginning of a hyperlink or select a recently inserted hyperlink.

- If desired, you can link to a specific location within a document by entering a bookmark name (for Word documents), range name (for Excel documents), or slide number (for PowerPoint documents) in the Named location in file edit box. I tell you about named ranges in **Chapter 11**.

Figure 11.
Choose Hyperlink from the Insert menu.

Figure 12. *Use the Insert Hyperlink dialog box to enter hyperlink location information.*

Figure 13. *You can use the Link to File dialog box to locate and select a file to link to on your hard disk or network.*

Figure 14. *This dialog box appears if you attempt to insert a hyperlink in an unsaved document.*

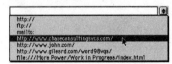

Figure 15. *The Link to file or URL pop-up menu helps you enter links.*

To follow a hyperlink

1. Position the mouse pointer on the hyperlink. The mouse pointer turns into a pointing finger and the link location appears in a yellow box above the hyperlink (**Figure 10**).

2. Click once.

If the hyperlink points to an Internet URL, Excel launches your default Web browser, connects to the Internet, and displays the URL.

or

If the hyperlink points to a file on your hard disk or another computer on the network, the file opens.

Figure 16. *The Web toolbar.*

Figure 17. *Use the Edit Hyperlink dialog box to remove or modify a link.*

✔ Tip

■ The Web toolbar appears above the Excel document window when you follow a link (**Figure 16**). You can use this toolbar to navigate linked pages on your computer, your local area network, or the Web.

To remove a hyperlink

1. Select the cell or object containing the hyperlink.

2. Choose Hyperlink from the Insert menu (**Figure 11**).

or

Click the Insert Hyperlink button on the Standard toolbar.

3. In the Edit Hyperlink dialog box that appears (**Figure 17**), click the Remove Link button.

4. Click OK.

✔ Tip

■ You can also use the Edit Hyperlink dialog box (**Figure 17**) to change the URL or pathname for a linked file.

SETTING EXCEL PREFERENCES 13

The Preferences Dialog Box

Excel's Preferences dialog box offers eight categories of options that you can set to customize the way Excel works for you:

- **View** preferences control Excel's on-screen appearance.
- **Calculation** preferences control the way Excel calculates formulas.
- **Edit** preferences control editing.
- **General** preferences control general Excel operations.
- **Transition** preferences control options for Excel users who also work with other spreadsheet programs.
- **Custom Lists** preferences enable you to create or modify series lists.
- **Chart** preferences control the active chart and chart tips.
- **Color** preferences control standard, chart fill, and chart line colors.

✔ Tips

- Excel's default preference settings are discussed and illustrated throughout this book.
- Some of the preference settings affect only the active sheet or workbook file while others affect all Excel operations. If you want a setting to affect a specific sheet or file, be sure to open and activate it before opening the Preferences dialog box.

To set preferences

1. Choose Preferences from the Tools menu (**Figure 1**) to display the Preferences dialog box (**Figure 3**).

2. Click the tab to display the category of options that you want to set.

3. Set options as desired.

4. Repeat steps 2 and 3 for other categories of options that you want to set.

5. Click OK to save your settings.

✔ **Tip**

■ I illustrate and discuss all Preferences dialog box options throughout this chapter.

To restore preferences to the default settings

1. If Excel is running, choose Quit from the File menu or press ⌘ Q to quit it.

2. In the Finder, open the Preferences folder inside the System Folder.

3. Locate the file named *Excel Settings (8)* (**Figure 2**) and drag it to the Trash.

4. Choose Empty Trash from the Special menu.

5. Launch Excel.

✔ **Tip**

■ When the Excel Settings (8) file is deleted, Excel automatically creates a new file with the same name, using default preference settings.

Figure 1.
To open the Preferences dialog box, choose Preferences from the Tools menu.

Figure 2. *Excel preferences are stored in the Excel Settings (8) file.*

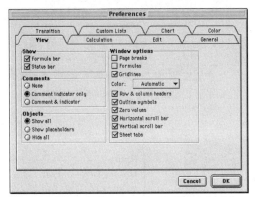

Figure 3. *The default options in the View tab of the Preferences dialog box. Some of the Window options are not available when a chart sheet is active.*

View Preferences

The View tab of the Preferences dialog box (**Figure 3**) offers options in four categories: Show, Comments, Objects, and Window options.

✔ Tip

- The available options in the View tab vary depending on the type of sheet that is active when you open the Preferences dialog box. When a chart sheet is active, many of the Window options are gray.

Show

Show options determine what Excel elements appear on screen:

- **Formula bar** displays the formula bar above the document window.
- **Status bar** displays the status bar at the bottom of the screen.

Comments

The Comments area enables you to select one of three radio buttons for displaying comments:

- **None** does not display comments or comment indicators.
- **Comment indicator only** displays a small red triangle in the upper-right corner of a cell containing a comment. When you point to the cell, the comment appears in a yellow box.
- **Comment & indicator** displays cell comments in yellow boxes as well as a small red triangle in the upper-right corner of each cell containing a comment.

continued on next page…

View Preferences

continued from previous page

Objects

The Objects area enables you to select one of three radio buttons for displaying graphic objects, buttons, text boxes, drawn objects, and pictures:

- **Show all** displays all objects.

- **Show placeholders** displays gray rectangles as placeholders for pictures and charts. This can increase performance when scrolling through a window with many graphic objects.

- **Hide all** does not display any objects. Excel will not print objects with this option selected.

Window options

Window options determine how various Excel elements are displayed in the active window.

- **Page breaks** displays horizontal and vertical page breaks.

- **Formulas** displays formulas instead of formula results (**Figure 4**). You may find this feature useful to document your worksheets.

- **Gridlines** displays the boundaries of cells as gray lines.

- **Color** offers a pop-up menu (**Figure 5**) for selecting a gridline color. Automatic (the default option) displays gridlines in gray.

- **Row & column headings** displays the numeric row headings and alphabetical column headings.

- **Outline symbols** displays outline symbols when the worksheet includes an outline.

	A	B	C	D	E
1		Jan	Feb	Mar	Total
2	John	1254	1256	2435	=SUM(John)
3	Jean	1865	1736	3495	=SUM(Jean)
4	Joe	1614	1284	2509	=SUM(Joe)
5	Joan	1987	2740	2890	=SUM(Joan)
6	Totals	=SUM(B2:B5)	=SUM(Feb)	=SUM(Mar)	=SUM(Total)

Figure 4. *If desired, you can display formulas rather than their results.*

Figure 5.
Use the Color pop-up menu to select a color for the gridlines that appear in a worksheet window.

- **Zero values** displays a 0 (zero) in cells that contain zero values. Turning off this check box instructs Excel to leave a cell blank if it contains a zero value.

- **Horizontal scroll bar** displays a scroll bar along the bottom of the window.

- **Vertical scroll bar** displays a scroll bar along the right side of the window.

- **Sheet tabs** displays tabs at the bottom of the window for each sheet in the workbook file.

Figure 6. *The default settings for the Calculation tab of the Preferences dialog box.*

Calculation Preferences

Calculation preferences (**Figure 6**) control the way formulas are calculated (or recalculated) in a worksheet. There are several groups of options: Calculation, Iteration, Calc buttons, and Workbook options.

Calculation

The Calculation area enables you to select one of three radio buttons for specifying how formulas should be calculated:

- **Automatic** tells Excel to recalculate all dependent formulas whenever you change a value, formula, or name.

- **Automatic except tables** is the same as Automatic, but does not recalculate data tables. With this option selected, you must click the Calc Now button or press ⌘= to recalculate data tables.

- **Manual** recalculates formulas only when you click the Calc Now button or press ⌘=. With this option selected, you can turn on the Recalculate before save check box to ensure that the worksheet is recalculated each time you save it.

Iteration

The Iteration check box enables you to set limits for the number of times Excel tries to resolve circular references or complete goal seeking calculations. To use this advanced option, turn on the check box, then enter values in the two edit boxes below it:

- **Maximum iterations** is the maximum number of times Excel should try to resolve circular references or solve goal seeking problems.

- **Maximum change** is the maximum amount of result change below which iteration stops.

continued on next page…

Calculation Preferences

continued from previous page

Calc buttons

The Calculation Preferences dialog box offers two buttons for calculating formulas:

- **Calc Now (Cmd+=)** recalculates all open worksheets and updates all open chart sheets. You can also access this option by pressing ⌘=.

- **Calc Sheet** recalculates the active worksheet and updates linked charts or updates the active chart sheet.

Workbook options

Workbook options control calculation in the active workbook file.

- **Update remote references** calculates formulas with references to documents created with other applications.

- **Precision as displayed** permanently changes values stored in cells from 15-digit precision to the precision of the applied formatting. This may result in rounding.

- **1904 date system** changes the starting date from which all dates are calculated to January 2, 1904. This is the date system used on Macintosh computers. Wintel computers begin dates at January 1, 1900. Turning off this option enhances compatibility with Wintel system spreadsheet programs.

- **Save external link values** saves copies of values from linked documents within the workbook file. If many values are linked, storing them can increase the file size; turning off this option can reduce the file size.

- **Accept labels in formulas** enables the Natural Language Formulas feature, which allows you to use column and row headings to identify ranges of cells.

Figure 7. *The default options in the Edit tab of the Preferences dialog box.*

Figure 8. *Use the Direction pop-up menu to select a direction in which to move the cellpointer when you press* Return.

Edit Preferences

Edit preferences (**Figure 7**) control the way certain editing tasks work:

- **Edit directly in cell** enables you to edit a cell's value or formula by double-clicking the cell. With this option turned off, you must edit a cell's contents in the formula bar.

- **Allow cell drag and drop** enables you to copy or move cells by dragging them to a new location. With this option turned on, you can also turn on the **Alert before overwriting cells** check box to have Excel warn you if a drag-and-drop operation will overwrite the contents of destination cells.

- **Move selection after Return** tells Excel to move the cellpointer when you press Return. With this option turned on, you can use the **Direction** pop-up menu (**Figure 8**) to choose a direction: Down, Right, Up, or Left.

- **Fixed decimal places** instructs Excel to automatically place a decimal point when you enter a value. Turn on the check box and enter a value in the **Places** edit box. A positive value moves the decimal to the left; a negative value moves the decimal to the right.

- **Cut, copy, and sort objects with cells** keeps objects with cells that you cut, copy, filter, or sort.

- **Ask to update automatic links** prompts you to update links when you open a workbook containing links to other files.

- **Provide feedback with animation** displays worksheet movement when you insert or delete cells. Turning on this option may slow Excel's performance on some systems.

- **Enable AutoComplete for cell values** turns on the AutoComplete feature for entering values in cells based on entries in the same column.

Edit Preferences

General Preferences

General preferences (**Figure 9**) control the general operation of Excel. There are two main categories—Settings and Command underline—and a number of other options.

Settings

The Settings options offer check boxes to set a variety of options:

- **R1C1 reference style** changes the style of cell references so both rows and columns have numbers.

- **Ignore other applications** prevents the exchange of data with other applications that use Dynamic Data Exchange (DDE).

- **Macro virus protection** displays a warning dialog box like the one in **Figure 10** when you open an Excel workbook file that contains macros or customized toolbars, menus, or shortcut keys. (These features could contain Excel macro viruses.) When this dialog box appears, you have three options:

  ▲ **Enable Macros** opens the file the normal way. The macros will function as intended. If the file contains a macro virus, your Excel files may become infected. Use this option only if you are certain that the file does not contain any viruses.

  ▲ **Do Not Open** does not open the file. Your Excel files cannot become infected if the file contains a macro virus.

  ▲ **Disable Macros** opens the file with the macros disabled. This prevents the macros from operating as intended. Your Excel files cannot become infected if the file contains a macro virus.

Figure 9. *The default options in the General tab of the Preferences dialog box.*

Figure 10. *Excel displays a warning dialog box like this when you open a workbook file that contains macros or other Visual Basic modules.*

General Preferences

Figure 11. *You can use the Summary tab of the Properties dialog box to enter information about the file the first time you save it. You can also open this dialog box by choosing Properties from the File menu.*

- **Recently used file list** enables you to specify the number of recently opened files that should appear near the bottom of the File menu. Turn on the check box and enter a value in the **Entries** edit box. This feature is handy for quickly reopening recently accessed files.

- **Prompt for workbook properties** displays the Properties dialog box **(Figure 11)** the first time you save a file. You can use this dialog box to enter summary information about a file.

- **Provide feedback with sound** plays sounds at certain events, such as opening, saving, and printing files and displaying error messages. If this option is turned on in one Microsoft Office application, it is automatically turned on in all Office applications.

Other options

The bottom half of the dialog box lets you set a variety of other workbook options:

- **Sheets in new workbook** enables you to specify the number of worksheets that should be included in each new workbook you create. Enter a value in the edit box.

- **Standard font** enables you to select the default font for worksheets and charts.

- **Default file location** allows you to specify the default location in which new workbook files should be saved. Click the Select button and use the dialog box that appears to locate and select a location on your hard disk or a network.

- **Alternate startup file location** lets you specify a secondary startup folder in which Excel should look for files when it launches.

continued on next page...

General Preferences

continued from previous page

- **User name** is the name that appears when Excel displays a user name.

Command underline

The Command underline area of the dialog box enables you to select one of three options to control "mouseless menus":

- **On** turns on the display of underlines on menus beneath keyboard shortcut keys **(Figure 12)**. This enables you to use mouseless menus any time.

- **Off** turns off the display of underlines on menus beneath keyboard shortcut keys.

- **Automatic** displays underline beneath keyboard shortcut keys on menus **(Figure 12)** only when you press the menu keystroke (/). This enables you to use mouseless menus only after pressing /.

To use mouseless menus

1. In the General tab of the preferences dialog box **(Figure 9)**, make sure the On or Automatic radio button is selected in the Command underline area. Click OK to save your setting.

2. If Automatic Command underline is selected, press /.

3. Press the letter key corresponding to the underlined letter on the menu you want to display **(Figure 12)**.

4. If necessary, press the letter key corresponding to the underlined letter for the submenu you want to display.

5. Press the letter key corresponding to the underlined letter of the command you want to use **(Figure 12)**.

Excel activates the command.

Figure 12. *Command underlines enable you to choose menu commands without reaching for your mouse.*

Figure 13. *The default settings in the Transition tab of the Preferences dialog box.*

Figure 14.
Use the Default save as type pop-up menu to select a default file format in which to save files.

Transition Preferences

Transition preferences (**Figure 13**) offer options to help you transition between Excel and other spreadsheet software packages, such as Lotus 1-2-3.

- **Default save as type** enables you to specify the default file format for every Excel file you save. Choose an option from the pop-up menu (**Figure 14**). The option you select will automatically appear in the Save As dialog box. You can override this choice if desired when you save a file. This option is useful if you often share the Excel files you create with people who use a different version of Excel or some other spreadsheet or database application.

- **Microsoft Excel menu or help key** allows you to specify the keyboard key that will activate Excel's menu bar if the Command underline option discussed on the previous page is set to Automatic.

- **Transition formula evaluation** instructs Excel to evaluate Lotus 1-2-3 formulas without changing them. This option may be extremely helpful if you often open files created with Lotus 1-2-3.

Transition Preferences

Custom Lists Preferences

The Custom Lists preferences (**Figure 15**) enable you to create, modify, and delete custom lists. Once created, you can use the AutoFill feature I discuss in **Chapter 3** to enter list contents into cells.

✔ Tip

■ You cannot modify or delete the pre-defined lists in the Custom lists scrolling list (**Figure 15**).

To create a custom list

1. In the Custom Lists tab of the Preferences dialog box, select NEW LIST in the Custom lists scrolling list (**Figure 15**).

2. Enter the list contents in the List entries area (**Figure 16**). Be sure to press [Return] after each item.

3. Click Add.

   The list appears in the Custom lists scrolling list (**Figure 17**).

To import cell contents as a custom list

1. In the Custom Lists tab of the Preferences dialog box, select NEW LIST in the Custom lists scrolling list (**Figure 15**).

2. Click in the Import list from cells edit box.

3. In the worksheet window, drag to select the cells containing the values you want to use as a custom list (**Figure 18**).

4. Click Import.

   The list appears in the Custom lists scrolling list (**Figure 17**).

Figure 15. *The default settings in the Custom Lists tab of the Preferences dialog box.*

Figure 16.
Enter the values you want to include in the list, one per line.

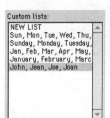

Figure 17.
The list appears in the Custom lists scrolling list.

Figure 18. *Select the cells containing the values you want to appear in the custom list.*

Figure 19. *Excel displays this dialog box when you delete a custom list.*

To modify a custom list

1. In the Custom Lists tab of the Preferences dialog box, select the list you want to modify in the Custom lists scrolling list.

2. Edit the list contents as desired in the List entries area.

3. Click Add.

    The custom list changes.

To delete a custom list

1. In the Custom Lists tab of the Preferences dialog box, select the list you want to delete in the Custom lists scrolling list.

2. Click Delete.

3. A confirmation dialog box like the one in **Figure 19** appears. Click OK.

    The list disappears from the Custom list scrolling list.

✔ Tip

■   Deleting a custom list does not delete any data from your workbook files. It simply removes the list from the Custom Lists tab of the Preferences dialog box so you can no longer use it with the AutoFill feature.

Custom List Preferences

Chart Preferences

Chart preferences (**Figure 20**) let you set options for the active chart and chart tips.

Active chart

Active chart options affect the active chart only. Be sure to activate the chart for which you want to set these options before opening the Preferences dialog box.

■ **Empty cells plotted as** enables you to select one of two or three options to specify how Excel should plot empty cells on the chart:

▲ **Not plotted (leave gaps)** tells Excel not to plot the cell values at all. This leaves gaps in the chart.

▲ **Zero** tells Excel to plot empty cells as zeros, thus including a zero data point for each empty cell.

▲ **Interpolated** tells Excel to interpolate data points for blank cells and fill in the chart gaps with connecting lines. This option is not available for all chart types.

■ **Plot visible cells only** tells Excel to plot only the cells that are displayed on the worksheet. If one or more cells are in hidden columns or rows, they are not plotted.

■ **Chart sizes with window frame** resizes the chart in a chart sheet window so it fills the window, no matter how the window is sized. This option is not available for charts embedded in worksheets.

Chart tips

Chart tips options enable you to specify what displays in chart tips.

■ **Show names** displays the names of data points.

■ **Show values** displays the values of data points.

Figure 20. *The default settings in the Chart tab of the Preferences dialog box.*

Figure 21. *The default settings in the Color tab of the Preferences dialog box.*

Figure 22. *Use the Colors dialog box to select a different color.*

Figure 23. *You can copy the color palette from another open workbook file by choosing it from the Copy colors from pop-up menu.*

Color Preferences

The Color tab of the Preferences dialog box (**Figure 21**) enables you to set the color palettes used within the Excel workbook file.

- **Standard colors** are the colors that appear in color pop-up menus throughout Excel.

- **Chart fills** are the first eight colors Excel uses as chart fills.

- **Chart lines** are the first eight colors Excel uses as chart lines.

To modify the color palette

1. Click the color that you want to change to select it.

2. Click the Modify button.

3. In the Standard (**Figure 22**) or Custom tab of the Colors dialog box, click to select a color.

4. Click OK. The selected color changes.

5. Repeat steps 1 through 4 for each color you want to change.

To copy colors from another workbook file

1. Before opening the Preferences dialog box, open the workbook file from which you want to copy colors.

2. Open the Color tab of the Preferences dialog box.

3. From the Copy colors from pop-up menu (**Figure 23**), choose the workbook file from which you want to copy colors.

   The palette changes to reflect the colors from the other workbook file.

To reset the color palette

Click the Reset button. The colors change back to the default colors.

MENUS & SHORTCUT KEYS

Menus & Shortcut Keys

This appendix illustrates all of Excel's standard menus for worksheets and charts and provides a list of shortcut keys you can use to access menu commands.

To use a shortcut key, hold down the modifier key (usually ⌘) and press the keyboard key corresponding to the command. For example, to use the Save command's shortcut key, hold down ⌘ and press S.

✔ Tip
- I tell you more about menus and short-cut keys in **Chapter 1**.

File menu (worksheets)

⌘N	New
⌘O	Open
⌘W	Close
⌘S	Save
⌘P	Print
⌘Q	Quit

File menu (charts)

⌘N	New
⌘O	Open
⌘W	Close
⌘S	Save
⌘P	Print
⌘Q	Quit

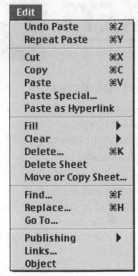

Edit menu (worksheets)

⌘Z	Undo
⌘Y	Repeat/Redo
⌘X	Cut
⌘C	Copy
⌘V	Paste
⌘D	Fill Down
⌘R	Fill Right
Del	Clear All
⌘B	Clear Contents
⌘K	Delete
⌘F	Find
⌘H	Replace

Edit menu (charts)

⌘Z	Undo
⌘Y	Repeat/Redo
⌘X	Cut
⌘C	Copy
⌘V	Paste
⌘D	Fill Down
⌘R	Fill Right
⌘B	Clear All

Edit Menu

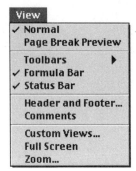

View menu (worksheets)

(no shortcut keys)

View menu (charts)

(no shortcut keys)

Insert menu (worksheets)

 Cells

Insert menu (charts)

(no shortcut keys)

Format menu (worksheets)

 Cells

Format menu (charts)

(no shortcut keys)

View, Insert, & Format Menus

Tools menu (worksheets)

(no shortcut keys)

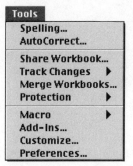

Tools menu (charts)

(no shortcut keys)

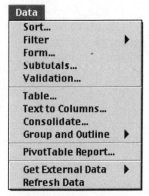

Data menu (worksheets)

(no shortcut keys)

Chart menu (charts)

(no shortcut keys)

Window menu (worksheets)

(no shortcut keys)

Window menu (charts)

(no shortcut keys)

Help
| About Balloon Help... |
| Show Balloons |
| Microsoft Excel Help |
| Contents and Index |
| Help on the Web
Online Registration |

Help menu (worksheets)

(no shortcut keys)

Help
| About Balloon Help... |
| Show Balloons |
| Microsoft Excel Help |
| Contents and Index |

Help menu (charts)

(no shortcut keys)

Help Menu

FUNCTION REFERENCE

Functions

Functions are predefined formulas for making specific kinds of calculations. Functions make it quicker and easier to write formulas. I tell you about functions in **Chapter 5**. In this appendix, I provide a complete list of every function installed as part of a standard installation of Excel 98, along with its arguments and a brief description of what it does.

Financial Functions

DB(cost,salvage,life,period,month)	Returns the depreciation of an asset for a specified period using the fixed-declining balance method.
DDB(cost,salvage,life,period,factor)	Returns the depreciation of an asset for a specified period using the double-declining balance method or some other method you specify.
FV(rate,nper,pmt,pv,type)	Returns the future value of an investment.
IPMT(rate,per,nper,pv,fv,type)	Returns the interest payment for an investment for a given period.
IRR(values,guess)	Returns the internal rate of return for a series of cash flows.
MIRR(values,finance_rate,reinvest_rate)	Returns the internal rate of return where positive and negative cash flows are financed at different rates.
NPER(rate,pmt,pv,fv,type)	Returns the number of periods for an investment.
NPV(rate,value1,value2,...)	Returns the net present value of an investment based on a series of periodic cash flows and a discount rate.
PMT(rate,nper,pv,fv,type)	Returns the period payment for an annuity.
PPMT(rate,per,nper,pv,fv,type)	Returns the payment on the principal for an investment for a given period.
PV(rate,nper,pmt,fv,type)	Returns the present value of an investment.
RATE(nper,pmt,pv,fv,type,guess)	Returns the interest rate per period of an annuity.
SLN(cost,salvage,life)	Returns the straight-line depreciation of an asset for one period.

SYD(cost,salvage,life,per)

Returns the sum-of-years'-digits depreciation of an asset for a specified period.

VDB(cost,salvage,life,start_period,end_period,factor,...)

Returns the depreciation of an asset for a specified or partial period using a declining balance method.

Date & Time Functions

DATE(year,month,day) — Returns the serial number of a particular date.

DATEVALUE(date_text) — Converts a date in the form of text to a serial number.

DAY(serial_number) — Converts a serial number to a day of the month.

DAYS360(start_date,end_date,method) — Calculates the number of days between two dates based on a 360-day year.

HOUR(serial_number) — Converts a serial number to an hour.

MINUTE(serial_number) — Converts a serial number to a minute.

MONTH(serial_number) — Converts a serial number to a month.

NOW() — Returns the serial number of the current date and time.

SECOND(serial_number) — Converts a serial number to a second.

TIME(hour,minute,second) — Returns the serial number of a particular time.

TIMEVALUE(time_text) — Converts a time in the form of text to a serial number.

TODAY() — Returns the serial number of today's date.

WEEKDAY(serial_number,return_type) — Converts a serial number to a day of the week.

YEAR(serial_number) — Converts a serial number to a year.

Math & Trig Functions

ABS(number) — Returns the absolute value of a number.

ACOS(number) — Returns the arccosine of a number.

ACOSH(number) — Returns the inverse hyperbolic cosine of a number.

ASIN(number) — Returns the arcsine of a number.

ASINH(number) — Returns the inverse hyperbolic sine of a number.

ATAN(number) — Returns the arctangent of a number.

ATAN2(x_num,y_num) — Returns the arctangent from x- and y-coordinates.

ATANH(number) — Returns the inverse hyperbolic tangent of a number.

CEILING(number,significance)	Rounds a number to the nearest whole number or to the nearest multiple of significance.
COMBIN(number,number_chosen)	Returns the number of combinations for a given number of objects.
COS(number)	Returns the cosine of a number.
COSH(number)	Returns the hyperbolic cosine of a number.
DEGREES(angle)	Converts radians to degrees.
EVEN(number)	Rounds a number up to the nearest even whole number.
EXP(number)	Returns e raised to the power of a given number.
FACT(number)	Returns the factorial of a number.
FLOOR(number, significance)	Rounds a number down, toward 0.
INT(number)	Rounds a number down to the nearest whole number.
LN(number)	Returns the natural logarithm of a number.
LOG(number,base)	Returns the logarithm of a number to a specified base.
LOG10(number)	Returns the base-10 logarithm of a number.
MDETERM(array)	Returns the matrix determinant of an array.
MINVERSE(array)	Returns the matrix inverse of an array.
MMULT(array1,array2)	Returns the matrix product of two arrays.
MOD(number,divisor)	Returns the remainder from division.
ODD(number)	Rounds a number up to the nearest odd whole number.
PI()	Returns the value of pi.
POWER(number,power)	Returns the result of a number raised to a power.
PRODUCT(number 1,number2,...)	Multiplies its arguments
RADIANS(angle)	Converts degrees to radians.
RAND()	Returns a random number between 0 and 1.
ROMAN(number,form)	Converts an Arabic numeral to a Roman numeral, as text.
ROUND(number,num_digits)	Rounds a number to a specified number of digits.
ROUNDDOWN(number,num_digits)	Rounds a number down, toward 0.
ROUNDUP(number,num_digits)	Rounds a number up, away from 0.
SIGN(number)	Returns the sign of a number.
SIN(number)	Returns the sine of a number.
SINH(number)	Returns the hyperbolic sine of a number.

Math & Trig Functions

SQRT(number)	Returns a positive square root.
SUBTOTAL(function_num,ref1,...)	Returns a subtotal in a list or database.
SUM(number1,number2,...)	Adds its arguments.
SUMIF(range,criteria, sum_range)	Adds the cells specified by a given criteria.
SUMPRODUCT(array1,array2,array3,...)	Returns the sum of the products of corresponding array components.
SUMSQ(number1,number2,...)	Returns the sum of the squares of its arguments.
SUMX2MY2(array_x,array_y)	Returns the sum of the difference of squares of corresponding values in two arrays.
SUMX2PY2(array_x,array_y)	Returns the sum of the sum of squares of corresponding values in two arrays.
SUMXMY2(array_x,array_y)	Returns the sum of squares of differences of corresponding values in two arrays.
TAN(number)	Returns the tangent of a number.
TANH(number)	Returns the hyperbolic tangent of a number.
TRUNC(number,num_digits)	Truncates a number to a whole number.

Statistical Functions

AVEDEV(number1,number2,...)	Returns the average of the absolute deviations of data points from their mean.
AVERAGE(number1,number2,...)	Returns the average of its arguments.
AVERAGEA(value1,value2,...)	Returns the average of its arguments, including text and logical values.
BETADIST(x,alpha,beta,A,B)	Returns the cumulative beta probability density function.
BETAINV(probability,alpha,beta,A,B)	Returns the inverse of the cumulative beta probability density function.
BINOMDIST(number_s,trials,probability_s,cumulative)	
	Returns the individual term binomial distribution probability.
CHIDIST(x,degrees_freedom)	Returns the one-tailed probability of the chi-squared distribution.
CHIINV(probability,degrees_freedom)	Returns the inverse of the one-tailed probability of the chi-squared distribution.
CHITEST(actual_range,expected_range)	Returns the test for independence.
CONFIDENCE(alpha,standard_dev,size)	Returns the confidence interval for a population mean.
CORREL(array1,array2)	Returns the correlation coefficient between two data sets.

COUNT(value1,value2,...)	Counts how many numbers are in the list of arguments.
COUNTA(value2,value2,...)	Counts how many values are in the list of arguments.
COUNTBLANK(range)	Counts the number of blank cells within a range.
COUNTIF(range,criteria)	Counts the number of non-blank cells within a range which meet the given criteria.
COVAR(array1,array2)	Returns covariance, the average of the products of paired deviations.
CRITBINOM(trials,probability_s,alpha)	Returns the smallest value for which the cumulative binomial distribution is greater than or equal to a criterian value.
DEVSQ(number1,number2,...)	Returns the sum of squares of deviations.
EXPONDIST(x,lambda,cumulative)	Returns the exponential distribution.
FDIST(x,degrees_freedom1,degrees_freedom2)	Returns the F probability distribution.
FINV(probability,degrees_freedom1,degrees_freedom2)	Returns the inverse of the F probability distribution.
FISHER(x)	Returns the Fisher transformation.
FISHERINV(y)	Returns the inverse of the Fisher transformation.
FORECAST(x,known_y's,known_x's)	Returns a value along a linear trend.
FREQUENCY(data_array,bins_array)	Returns a frequency distribution as a vertical array.
FTEST(array1,array2)	Returns the result of an F-test.
GAMMADIST(x,alpha,beta,cumulative)	Returns the gamma distribution.
GAMMAINV(probability,alpha,beta)	Returns the inverse of the gamma cumulative distribution.
GAMMALN(x)	Returns the natural logarithm of the gamma function.
GEOMEAN(number1,number2,...)	Returns the geometric mean.
GROWTH(knowy_y's,known_x's,new_x's,const)	Returns values along an exponential trend.
HARMEAN(number1,number2,...)	Returns the harmonic mean.
HYPGEOMDIST(sample_s,number_sample,population_s,...)	Returns the hypergeometric distribution.
INTERCEPT(known_y's,known_x's)	Returns the intercept of the linear regression line.

KURT(number1,number2,...)	Returns the kurtosis of a data set.
LARGE(array,k)	Returns the k-th largest value in a data set.
LINEST(known_y's,known_x's,const,stats)	Returns the parameters of a linear trend.
LOGEST(known_y's,known_x's,const,stats)	Returns the parameters of an exponential trend.
LOGINV(probability,mean,standard_dev)	Returns the inverse of the lognormal distribution.
LOGNORMDIST(x,mean,standard_dev)	Returns the cumulative lognormal distribution.
MAX(number1,number2,...)	Returns the maximum value in a list of arguments.
MAXA(value1,value2,...)	Returns the maximum value in a list of arguments, including text and logical values.
MEDIAN(number1,number2,...)	Returns the median of the given numbers.
MIN(number1,number2,...)	Returns the minimum value in a list of arguments.
MINA(value1,value2,...)	Returns the minimum value in a list of arguments, including text and logical values.
MODE(number1,number2,...)	Returns the most common value in a data set.
NEGBINOMDIST(number_f,number_s,probability_s)	Returns the negative binomial distribution.
NORMDIST(x,mean,standard_dev,cumulative)	Returns the normal cumulative distribution.
NORMINV(probability,mean,standard_dev)	Returns the inverse of the normal cumulative distribution.
NORMSDIST(z)	Returns the standard normal cumulative distribution.
NORSINV(probability)	Returns the inverse of the standard normal cumulative distribution.
PEARSON(array1,array2)	Returns the Pearson product moment correlation coefficient.
PERCENTILE(array,k)	Returns the k-th percentile of values in a range.
PERCENTRANK(array,x,significance)	Returns the percentage rank of a value in a data set.
PERMUT(number,number_chosen)	Returns the number of permutations for a given number of objects.
POISSON(x,mean,cumulative)	Returns the Poisson distribution.
PROB(x_range,prob_range,lower_limit,upper_limit)	Returns the probability that values in a range are between two limits.

Statistical Functions

QUARTILE(array,quart)	Returns the quartile of a data set.
RANK(number,ref,order)	Returns the rank of a number in a list of numbers.
RSQ(known_y's,known_x's)	Returns the square of the Pearson product moment correlation coefficient. If you know what that means, I hope you're making a lot of money.
SKEW(number1,number2,...)	Returns the skewness of a distribution.
SLOPE(known_y's,known_x's)	Returns the slope of the linear regression line.
SMALL(array,k)	Returns the k-th smallest value in a data set.
STANDARDIZE(x,mean,standard_dev)	Returns a normalized value.
STDEV(number1,number2,...)	Estimates standard deviation based on a sample.
STDEVA(value1,value2,...)	Estimates standard deviation based on a sample, including text and logical values.
STDEVP(number1,number2,...)	Calculates standard deviation based on the entire population.
STDEVPA(value1,value2,...)	Calculates standard deviation based on the entire population, including text and logical values.
STEYX(known_y's,known_x's)	Returns the standard error of the predicted y-value for each x in the regression.
TDIST(x,degrees_freedom,tails)	Returns the Student's t-distribution.
TINV(probability,degrees_freedom)	Returns the inverse of the Student's t-distribution.
TREND(known_y's,known_x's,new_x's,const)	
	Returns values along a linear trend.
TRIMMEAN(array,percent)	Returns the mean of the interior of a data set.
TTEST(array1,array2,tails,type)	Returns the probability associated with a Student's t-test.
VAR(number1,number2,...)	Estimates variance based on a sample.
VARA(value1,value2,...)	Estimates variance based on a sample, including text and logical values.
VARP(number1,number2,...)	Calculates variance based on the entire population.
VARPA(value1,value2,...)	Calculates variance based on the entire population, including text and logical values.
WEIBULL(x,alpha,beta,cumulative)	Returns the Weibull distribution.
ZTEST(array,x,sigma)	Returns the two-tailed P-value of a z-test. Really.

Statistical Functions

Lookup & Reference Functions

ADDRESS(row_num,column_num,abs_num,a1,sheet_text)	
	Returns a reference as text to a single cell in a worksheet.
AREAS(reference)	Returns the number of areas in a reference.
CHOOSE(index_num,value1,value2,…)	Chooses a value from a list of values.
COLUMN(reference)	Returns the column number of a reference.
COLUMNS(array)	Returns the number of columns in a reference.
HLOOKUP(lookup_value,table_array,row_index_num,…)	
	Looks in the top row of a table and returns the value of the indicated cell.
HYPERLINK(link_location,friendly_name)	Creates a shortcut that opens a document stored on a network computer or the Internet.
INDEX(…)	Uses an index to choose a value from a reference or array.
INDIRECT(ref_text,a1)	Returns a reference indicated by a text value.
LOOKUP(…)	Looks up values in a vector or array.
MATCH(lookup_value,lookup_array,match_type)	
	Looks up values in a reference or array.
OFFSET(reference,rows,cols,height,width)	Returns a reference offset from a given reference.
ROW(reference)	Returns the row number of a reference.
ROWS(array)	Returns the number of rows in a reference.
TRANSPOSE(array)	Returns the transpose of an array.
VLOOKUP(lookup_value,table_array,col_index_num,…)	
	Looks in the first column of a table and moves across the row to return the value of a cell.

Database Functions

DAVERAGE(database,field,criteria)	Returns the average of selected database entries.
DCOUNT(database,field,criteria)	Counts the cells containing numbers from a specified database and criteria.
DCOUNTA(database,field,criteria)	Counts nonblank cells from a specified database and criteria.
DGET(database,field,criteria)	Extracts from a database a single record that matches the specified criteria.
DMAX(database,field,criteria)	Returns the maximum value from selected database entries.

DMIN(database,field,criteria)	Returns the minimum value from selected database entries.
DPRODUCT(database,field,criteria)	Multiplies the values in a particular field of records that match the criteria in a database.
DSTDEV(database,field,criteria)	Estimates the standard deviation based on a sample of selected database entries.
DSTDEVP(database,field,criteria)	Calculates the standard deviation based on the entire population of selected database entries.
DSUM(database,field,criteria)	Adds the numbers in the field column of records in the database that match the criteria.
DVAR(database,field,criteria)	Estimates the variance based on a sample from selected database entries.
DVARP(database,field,criteria)	Calculates variance based on the entire population of selected database entries.

Text Functions

CHAR(number)	Returns the character specified by the code number.
CLEAN(text)	Removes all nonprintable characters from text.
CODE(text)	Returns a numeric code for the first character in a text string.
CONCATENATE(text1,text2,…)	Joins several text items into one text item.
DOLLAR(number,decimals)	Converts a number to text, using currency format.
EXACT(text1,text2)	Checks to see if two text values are identical.
FIND(find_text,within_text,start_num)	Finds one text value within another. This function is case-sensitive.
FIXED(number,decimals,no_commas)	Formats a number as text with a fixed number of decimals.
LEFT(text,num_chars)	Returns the leftmost characters from a text value.
LEN(text)	Returns the number of characters in a text string.
LOWER(text)	Converts text to lowercase.
MID(text,start_num,num_chars)	Returns a specific number of characters from a text string.
PROPER(text)	Capitalizes the first letter in each word of a text value.
REPLACE(old_text,start_num,num_chars,new_text)	Replaces characters within text.

Database, Text Functions

REPT(text,number_times)	Repeats text a given number of times.
RIGHT(text,num_chars)	Returns the rightmost characters from a text value.
SEARCH(find_text,within_text,start_num)	Finds one text value within another. This function is not case-sensitive.
SUBSTITUTE(text,old_text,new_text,instance_num)	
	Substitutes new text for old text in a text string.
T(value)	Converts its arguments to text.
TEXT(value,format_text)	Formats a number and converts it to text.
TRIM(text)	Removes spaces from text.
UPPER(text)	Converts text to uppercase.
VALUE(text)	Converts a text argument to a number.

Logical Functions

AND(logical1,logical2,...)	Returns TRUE if all of its arguments are TRUE.
FALSE()	Returns the logical value FALSE.
IF(logical_test,value_if_true,value_if_false)	Specifies a logical test to perform and the value to return based on a TRUE or FALSE result.
NOT(logical)	Reverses the logic of its argument.
OR(logical1,logical2,...)	Returns TRUE if any argument is TRUE.
TRUE()	Returns the logical value TRUE.

Information Functions

CELL(info_type,reference)	Returns information about the formatting, location, or contents of a cell.
ERROR.TYPE(error_val)	Returns a number corresponding to an error value.
INFO(type_text)	Returns information about the current operating environment.
ISBLANK(value)	Returns TRUE if the value is blank.
ISERR(value)	Returns TRUE if the value is any error value except #N/A.
ISERROR(value)	Returns TRUE if the value is any error value.
ISLOGICAL(value)	Returns TRUE if the value is a logical value.
ISNA(value)	Returns TRUE if the value is the #N/A error value.
ISNONTEXT(value)	Returns TRUE if the value is not text.
ISNUMBER(value)	Returns TRUE if the value is a number.
ISREF(value)	Returns TRUE if the value is a reference.

ISTECT(value)	Returns TRUE if the value is text.
N(value)	Returns a value converted to a number.
NA()	Returns the error value #N/A.
TYPE(value)	Returns a number indicating the data type of a value.

Information Functions

INDEX

Index

Index

Index

..8, 172, 177

..179
..white, 173
..ges, 173
..sing print quality, 168, 172, 177
..lumn and row titles, 172
to file, 180
gridlines, 172
major steps, 165
new features in Excel 98, xiv
page setup options, 167–173
selective, 178
workbooks, 178
worksheets, 165, 172
PRODUCT function, 75
PROPER function, 91
publishing, Web, xv, 211
push buttons, dialog box, 12
PV (present value) function, 85

Q

Quit command, 19

R

RADIANS function, 78
radio buttons, dialog box, 12
RAM, 18, 19, 62
RAND (random number) function, 77
Random Access Memory, 18, 19, 62
Range Finder feature, xii, 34, 144, 145
ranges, cell
defined, 22
entering in formulas and functions, 70
linking to, 216
selecting, 23, 25
using colon (:) to designate in formulas, 29
R1C1 reference style, 226
read-only options, Save command, 64
records, database
browsing, 183

defined, 181
searching, 184–187
sorting, 188–189
Redo command, xii, 49–50
#REF! error message, 37, 38, 54, 199
reference functions, 87, 248
references. See cell references.
relative cell reference, 45
Repeat command, 49–50
reports, monthly, 20
RIGHT function, 91
rotating 3-D charts, 164
rotating text, 99
ROUND function, 68, 75, 83, 94
ROUNDDOWN function, 75
ROUNDUP function, 75
row headings, 2, 3, 24, 222
row height, 111–114
rows
hiding/unhiding, 111, 113
inserting and deleting, 36–37
selecting, 24

S

Save As command, 62, 64
Save As dialog box, 62
Save command, 59, 62, 63
Save File as Type menu, 63
Save Options dialog box, 64
saving
documents, 165
print options, 179
workbook files, 62–64
Zoom command magnification settings, 60
savings goal, calculating payments required to reach, 84
scaling charts and worksheets, 161, 168
scientific notation, 94
screen, Excel, 2–3
scroll bars, 2, 3, 11, 13, 222
scrolling
contents of document window, 13
lists in dialog boxes, 11
range of cells in worksheet windows, 25
searching databases, 184
Select All button, 24
selecting
cells, 22, 23–25
rows and columns, 24
worksheets, 24
Series command, 43
SERIES function, 144
series (of cells), 43

Series (Y) axis, 153, 154, 161
server, Web, 211
Settings option, General preferences, 226–227
Share Workbook command, *xiv*
sheet names, 54
sheet tabs, 2, 3, 52, 222
sheets, 51. *See also* chart sheets; worksheets.
   changing order of (in workbook), 56
   deleting, 54
   hiding, 55
   inserting, 53
   moving or copying, 56
   renaming, 54
   switching between, 52
   working with multiple, 52, 57
Shift key, 7
shortcut keys, 7, 235–237
shortcut menus, 5, 6
Show options, View preferences, 221
Shrink to fit option, 96, 100
SIN function, 78
size box, 2, 3
SLN (straight-line depreciation) function, 81
sorting database records, 188–189
Source Data dialog box, 145, 146, 149
special effects, 101
splash screen, Excel, 18
Split command, 61
spreadsheets. *See also* worksheets.
   outlining data, 191, 205
   purpose of, *xi*, 1, 17
SQRT (square root) function, 77
Standard toolbar, 2, 8
statistical functions, 79–80, 244–247
status bar, 2, 3
STDEV/STDEVP (standard deviation) functions, 80
stock quotes, *xv*
Style feature, 108
StyleWriter 2500, 166, 168, 177
Subtotal dialog box, 190
SUBTOTAL function, 190–191
subtotal outline, 191
SUM function, 67, 68, 73–74, 202
support, technical. *See* help options.
SYD (sum-of-years' digits) function, 81
syntax errors, formula, 29

T

tabs
   dialog box, 11
   sheet, 2, 3, 52, 222
tags, HTML, *xv*

TAN (tangent) function, 78
templates
   disabling macros in, 21
   saving documents as, 63
   workbook files based on, 20–21
text
   aligning in cells, 27, 96–100
   converting case, 91
   formatting, 94
   functions, 68, 91–92, 249–250
   rotating, 99
text functions, 91–92
tick marks, chart, 162
tiled windows, 58
time, formatting, 94
time functions, 89–90, 242
time-scale formatting option, for charts, 154
title bar, 2, 3
titles
   axes, 141, 153
   chart, 141, 153
   column and row, 172
TODAY function, 90
toolbars
   docked, 8, 9, 10
   floating, 8, 9, 10
   Formatting, 2, 8, 95, 97, 98
   Standard, 2, 8
   tips for using, 8–10
Tools menus, 238
ToolTips, 8, 9
Top 10 AutoFilter, 185
Track Changes feature, *xiv*
Transition preferences, 219, 229
triangle symbol
   in edit box, 12
   in menu commands, 5
   on toolbar button, 8, 9
trigonometric functions, 73–78, 242–244
troubleshooting. *See* help options.
TRUE/FALSE values, 68, 86, 87
truncation of cell contents, 111
typeface, 93, 101–104, 159, 227

U

Underline button/shortcut, 103
underlining options, 101, 103, 104
Undo command, *xii*, 49–50, 54
Unhide command, 55, 59, 113
Unhide dialog box, 55, 59
Uniform Resource Locators, 215, 216
UPPER (uppercase) function, 91
URLs, 215, 216

Also From Maria Langer:

Word 98 for Macintosh: Visual QuickStart Guide

Maria Langer

Word 98 has been dramatically reworked to more fully utilize and integrate with the Mac OS user interface and functionality. Now more powerful and friendly than ever, Word 98 enables users to create a wide range of documents, from simple, one-page letters to complex multi-file reports with figures, table of contents, and indexes to Web pages with hyperlinks and graphics.

The *Word 98 for Macintosh: Visual QuickStart Guide* will introduce new and experienced Word users alike to the host of new features and improved Web integration and functionality. Using concise steps and numerous illustrations, the book covers everything from word processing basics and formatting fundamentals to desktop and Webtop publishing techniques. This is a comprehensive introduction to the powerful capabilities of Word 98.

272 pages • ISBN 0-201-35354-7 • $17.95

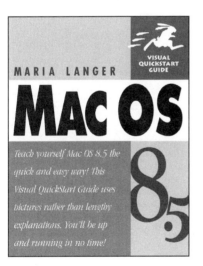

Mac OS 8.5: Visual QuickStart Guide

Maria Langer

This is the right book at the right time for the dedicated community of Macintosh users. Both new and longtime Mac users will need this clear, visual guide to Mac OS 8.5 with its significantly overhauled graphical interface. *Mac OS 8.5: Visual QuickStart Guide* covers all new and existing features, including the System Software Installer, Extensions Manager, Text-to-Speech, File Translation Utilities (working with PC files), as well as Internet connection features. Seasoned Mac author Maria Langer describes and illustrates the new Mac OS 8.5 features, including new file finding and navigation techniques and the new user interface "Themes."

336 pages • ISBN 0-201-35357-1 • $17.95
Available October 1998

To order these and other Peachpit Press books, visit our Web site at www.peachpit.com
or call toll-free 1-800-283-9444